THE REMARKABLE MR MORRISON
THE VIRTUOSITY AND VERSATILITY OF AUSTRALIA'S MASTER MUSICIAN

Published by Melbourne Books
Level 9, 100 Collins Street,
Melbourne, VIC 3000
Australia
www.melbournebooks.com.au
info@melbournebooks.com.au

Copyright © Mervyn E. Collins 2014

All rights reserved. No part of this publication may be reproduced, stored in a retrieval system, or transmitted in any form or any means electronic, mechanical, photocopying, recording or otherwise without the prior permission of the publisher.

Title: The Remarkable Mr Morrison: The Virtuosity and Versatility of Australia's Master Musician
Author: Mervyn E. Collins
ISBN: 9781922129444 (paperback)

A catalogue record for this book is available from the National Library of Australia

Front cover photo: Mr Remarkable, James Morrison 2014, Image courtesy: Morrison Management

Back cover photo: James poses for publicity shots prior to the BMW Celebrity Challenge at the Australian Grand Prix in Adelaide in 1987. Image courtesy: Eric Myers

THE REMARKABLE MR MORRISON
THE VIRTUOSITY AND VERSATILITY OF AUSTRALIA'S MASTER MUSICIAN

Mervyn E. Collins

M
MELBOURNE BOOKS

'Jazz is music made by and for people who have chosen to feel good in spite of the conditions.'

— Johnny Hodges, tenor saxophone player

Contents

Prelude Introduction to a Talent   9

1   Making a Start   15
2   The Coming of Jazz   21
3   No Practise Makes Perfect!   30
4   High School Dropout   34
5   It Happened in Monterey   39
6   Don Burrows   48
7   'It comes from my side, the Seller side'   55
8   From Boorowa to Bayview   59
9   Playtime in Paradise   63
10 The Prof and the Protégé   74
11 The Michelin Man in Asia!   81
12 Big Bad Band   89
13 New York, New York   101
14 The Boy in Ipanema   108
15 Another Bite of the 'Apple'   119
16 A Romantic Interlude   126
17 A Year to Celebrate   131
18 Back to Rio   141
19 Superband Tours   147
20 Snappy Doo   156
21 Careering On   164
22 Fun and Games   171

23	Cars and Cameras	181
24	'Flash Harry' and the Jazz Police	187
25	Mission Made Possible	196
26	More Jazz at the Symphony	205
27	James and Brass Bands: From Dizzy to 'the Dyke'	214
28	Back to High School	222
29	Generations in Jazz	231
30	'Oh what a circus! Oh what a show!'	238
31	'Then who's the real James Morrison?'	246
32	Hot Horn Happenings	255
33	Living on the Edge	263
34	The Others	273
35	'Very lazy …'	280
36	'… and very lucky!'	287
	Coda	295
	Acknowledgements	299
	Bibliography	301
	James Morrison's Honours and Awards	306
	Discography	307
	Index	308

Prelude

Introduction to a Talent

James Morrison first dumbfounded me back in the late 1980s, when I sat in a high school theatre in Kew in suburban Melbourne, half listening to a visiting brass band from Adelaide. I understand that brass bands aren't everyone's musical genre of choice, but I'd been brought up on them and in them. I'd heard the great bands of the North of England, the 'Corp' (Manchester CWS Band) and the 'Dyke' (the Black Dyke Band, formerly the Black Dyke Mills Band), in summer tents on Plymouth Hoe, near my home town, Tavistock, in the South of England. This was at about the same time I played Brahms' 'Lullaby' on my cornet as Little Boy Blue in the annual primary school play.

I loved the sound of a good band — the agility of the cornets, the grandeur of the trombone, the warmth of the euphonium — and I knew what good playing was. I thought Derek Garside, Corp's Principal Cornet, was the prince of players and still remember his shapeless uniform pants from weeks on the road as clearly as his rippling air variations and slow melodies. When he played his obligatory encore, the Irish ballad 'Killarney', I almost wept. An old bandie, seeing the excitement in my eyes, tousled my hair and whispered, 'He's great, isn't he?' and I was too choked to reply.

Years later, I found myself in Australia, more world-wise, less impressionable. I served my time in a Forces band and was introduced to recordings of players who, I grudgingly admitted, shaded even Garside. I admired Rafael Méndez, the freakish Mexican virtuoso playing five-minute moto perpetuos without coming up for air, Doc Severinsen on the Johnny Carson Show with his fat sound and garish dinner jackets, and the late Maynard Ferguson, who played screech trumpet *and* an instrument created for him — the Superbone.

I played in a military band for a living, in a Salvation Army brass band by conviction, in jazz and rock bands for fun, and thought I knew, and had heard, it all. My world-weariness and complacency was articulated by a military band colleague who once asked, 'Does nothing impress you?'

Certainly, as I sat in that small theatre that night, nothing did. The first half was over and I was underwhelmed. I suspect, in retrospect, South Australia's leading band, sponsored then by a chemical company, had been at least competent in their performance of traditional marches, test pieces and instrumental solos.

I don't remember — I may have slept.

But I was wide awake four bars into the second half. A short, slightly rotund young man with receding hair had taken possession of the stage with his talent and presence. James Morrison had arrived, a man for whom 'virtuoso' seemed too small a word.

He opened on the trombone, with a gorgeous sound ranging from the cellar to the stratosphere. Then, as if that wasn't enough, he deposited the trombone like a cue in the rack, picked up his trumpet and hit, I swear, super G as his first note.

I don't remember that he wiped his 'chops' between instruments. He didn't flex the corners of his mouth to prepare a new set of muscles; he just planted the note dead centre, with a sound that reverberated round the hall.

Long ago I'd been disabused of the childish belief that 'high C', as we called it, was the apex of the trumpet range; 'Cat' Anderson had been hitting screech notes at the end of Duke Ellington Orchestra numbers for years, but I still thought you had to sit back for four bars and suck in deep before blasting off. You certainly didn't belt out super G from cold after playing energetic trombone solos on its much larger mouthpiece.

Morrison sailed on, unaware of my astonishment. His first note was just that — a starting point and a launch-pad for jazz improvisations of imagination and technical brilliance.

He talked a bit and easily made the crowd laugh. His brother John, a drummer with showbiz flair of his own, played a percussion solo all over the hall, tattooing patterns on any available surface, and then James borrowed a tuba from a player up the back of the band and played a florid jazz solo on that. Not a prepared instrument, as far as I could tell, no special mouthpiece, just, 'Lend me your tuba, mate,' and, 'Thanks very much!'

To compound my astonishment, he played 'Misty' on the alto sax and then a rumbustious 'stride' piano solo, sitting side-saddle on the stool so he could share his enjoyment with the audience. In the middle of all this, to my shame, I remember thinking, *Yeah, but you can't improvise on the tenor horn because it's in a different pitch.* Perhaps he's a mind-reader, too — the next moment he 'borrowed' an E-flat horn and blew my pathetic theory right out of the building.

It was time to finish. As the band provided a mellow chord structure underneath, James' trumpet softly crooned 'The Old Rugged Cross' with all the tenderness of a black gospel singer. The arrangement intensified, became punchier, and Morrison soared to 'cling to the old rugged cross' in the chorus, then came back to earth for the final line 'and exchange it some day for a crown'. It was almost a religious experience; a beautiful old hymn beautifully played — a prayer and a benediction.

At the conclusion, I sat in silence. I was in the presence of greatness. Maybe if I'd worked hard enough I could have played like Derek Garside long ago, maybe even Rafael Méndez. It's possible, with effort and determination, I could have conquered two related instruments like Ferguson, but I realised that no matter what I did and however long I worked at it, I could never come near to Morrison's musical achievements. The man was born with gifts beyond exceptional.

He was on a different plane to the rest of us — I felt I was in the presence of musical genius.

Later, I learned just how multifaceted Morrison's freakish abilities are. Virtually without formal training, he has conquered most musical instruments: brass (his strongest suit), saxophones, piano and double bass. He is comfortable in all the streams of jazz, from trio to big band and from trad to bebop. He is equally at home in modern orchestral concert halls, performing works specially written for him by contemporary composers, and in brass band auditoriums, as well as in not-so-smoky-anymore jazz venues around the world.

Every brass instrument I've ever heard Morrison play, he plays to the standard of the best performers who specialise in that instrument. He changes like a chameleon. His trumpet sound is brilliantly bright, his trombone ranges from Dixieland brassy to balladic lushness. His euphonium, while eschewing the quick vibrato of the English brass band exponents, is equal to the world-renowned Childs Brothers, with whom I've heard him play amazing trios.

Of course, there have always been performers who claim to be multi-instrumentalists. In Australia in the mid-nineteenth century, the theatres advertised performers like 'Mr Barton' and Richard Wildblood Kohler, who played an array of obscure instruments, like the flageolet, the now-extinct bones and the rock harmonium, as well as flutes, violins, horns and keyboards. In the early 1930s, a versatile Melbourne jazz musician, Benny Featherstone, had a spectacular floor show act in which he played twelve instruments in the one tune. He was easily outdone by Roy Castle, the English comedian and compere of *Record Breakers*, who in a segment on his own show claimed a world record by playing the same tune on forty-three instruments in four minutes — just enough time to squeeze the entire act between commercial breaks, perhaps. It is difficult to discover what the forty-three instruments were and, though Castle was a competent trumpet player, the tune is more likely to have been 'Merrily We Roll Along' than 'I Can't Get Started'.

These were all music hall entertainers, almost circus acts, playing for effect and sensation, or merely to get into the record books. Morrison plays multiple instruments not because he simply can, but to enhance the music. He's interested in the sounds he makes and selects the appropriate tool for a song. He creates a 'wow' factor incidentally, not necessarily intentionally. It's the music that counts; he's a musician, not a freak show. He just happens to be phenomenally gifted.

Maynard Ferguson, the Canadian-born big band leader, was undoubtedly a marvellous performer on two bona-fide instruments: the trumpet and his own valve trombone, the Superbone. Glyn Williams, currently the principal euphonium of the celebrated Foden's Band in England, has a party piece where he plays variations on the old tune 'Rule Britannia'. Williams plays each variation on a different instrument, six in all: the euphonium, cornet, trombone, flugelhorn, E-flat tenor horn, soprano cornet in E-flat, before finishing, for comedic effect, with four notes on the xylophone.

These achievements are not to be sneezed at, but they pale almost into insignificance alongside Morrison's jazz CD, *Snappy Doo,* recorded when he was still in his twenties, in 1989. In that, he accomplished a feat never before attempted in the history of big band music. He overdubbed all the trumpet, trombone *and* saxophone parts, after having composed or arranged all the charts himself, bar one. To make sure the rhythm section was up to scratch he also played piano himself, and engaged Ray Brown on bass, Herb Ellis on guitar and Jeff Hamilton on drums, players who would lend their names to nothing but music of the highest quality.

This was no novelty recording, except in the sense that reviewer Bill Swanson wrote on the respected *All About Jazz* website:

> After fifty years of playing jazz detective, nothing new fazed these old jaded ears — not until I met up with James Morrison. James is phenomenal. He is, in my view, the ninth wonder of the jazz

universe. What he can't do on his instruments isn't worth doing. And he does it all with wit, polish and humour.

But Morrison topped even that achievement in 2012, when he played all the parts except drums on the follow-up recording *Snappy Too*.

In 1989, James was invited to play with the Philip Morris Superband, directed by pianist Gene Harris. James led a trombone line-up, which included the legendary Urbie Green. A year later, he played with the same band with many of the same American jazz luminaries — players like Ray Brown, Kenny Burrell, and Green again. This time, James was the featured trumpet soloist in a section, alongside Harry 'Sweets' Edison from the Count Basie Big Band, a man with a CV second to none.

Think about it for a moment — Morrison is capable of playing all the parts, except drums, on exceptional big band CDs for which he's written virtually all the music. As well as that, he is good enough to be recognised by the American jazz world as fit to lead an all-star band, first on trombone and then on trumpet!

How could all this have happened to a nervous little boy from Pittwater, a beautiful stretch of water north of Sydney, who until grade 4 cried every day when his mother left him at the primary school gate?

Chapter 1

Making a Start

At the Montreux Jazz Festival in 1989, James Morrison, young Australian multi-instrumentalist, found himself 'trading fours' — exchanging four-bar ad-lib solos — with his hero, Dizzy Gillespie, one of the greatest jazz trumpeters the world has ever seen. It wasn't a moment for the fainthearted; a less confident man would have shrivelled. But 26-year-old James Morrison was in no way overawed. He felt very honoured and very privileged, but not undeserving. He knew he could do it — his musical experience had led to this moment. There wasn't a flicker of doubt. He admits you had to be a good player to be there — you don't step onstage with Gillespie if you can't play — but, said James, 'I'd figured I was a good enough player since I was seven years old!'

He's exaggerating, but the tongue-in-cheek claim does indicate the early age at which he realised what he was and what he would be. He told Peter Thompson on ABC's *Talking Heads* that he 'never did decide to be a musician. I discovered that I was one. If I drove a tractor, I'd be a musician who's not playing. It's not defined by what you do, it's the thing that's in you.' James started to realise at primary school that 'the thing' was in him.

At seven, though, he'd barely held a trumpet, only surreptitiously blown a few raspberries on the cornet big brother John had brought home from Mona Vale Primary School, the school closest to the family home in Bayview, Sydney. Neither of the two Morrison boys thought much of the 'reading, writing and 'rithmetic' at the string of primary schools they attended as a result of their Pastor-father's ecclesiastical appointments, or later at Pittwater High in outer Sydney. The only subject that caught their interest was music. James enjoyed playing castanets and tambourines to accompany the 'Toreador Song' on the gramophone in infants' classes, but when he heard the school brass band live, he was intrigued and inspired: 'There's no record! They're doing it all themselves. This is for real, they're not playing along. I'm going to do that!'

He had to wait; band was for 5th and 6th graders, not tiny 3rd graders. John, two years older, qualified and got his opportunity when Jack Akhurst, Mona Vale Primary School's vice-principal, strode into his classroom one day. Jack was tall and bluff, with the military bearing that befitted an indomitable returned World War II soldier who spent almost four years in a Japanese prisoner of war camp.

He wore, as always, his long grey pants, short-sleeved white shirt and maroon tie. His manner with students was gruff and 'no nonsense', though another student at the time valued him as highly for his pastoral care as much as for his professional skills. Ruth Cunningham, self-confessed teacher's pet in Jack's grade 6 class, said, 'He taught the three Rs better than any other teacher, and restored me from the C Class, to which I slumped after the death of my father, to his A Class. I never forgot his support and kindness.'

But Jack's demeanour could be a bit fearsome on first acquaintance.

'Now,' he announced to young John's class, 'I'm the deputy head and I'm also the band master, and I'm recruiting people for the band.'

He wrote a complicated multiplication sum on the board.

'Can any one of you answer this?' he boomed as he sneaked 'times zero' at the end of the digits. There was silence, a roomful of students cowed by his presence and the immensity of the problem.

'None of you are smart enough to be musicians. If there's times zero in there, the answer's zero. Because you're all hopeless, I'll have to try you all out!'

He may have winked at the classroom teacher as he swept out with his first auditioners.

John Morrison passed with flying colours — in fact, he was too proficient to be granted his own preference. He wanted to play drums, but because his embouchure and note production was so good, he quickly found himself at the top end of the trumpet section. He continued to hassle Mr Akhurst for two years for an opportunity to change to the percussion section, without success. 'You're much too good to play drums,' roared Jack, foreshadowing the innumerable drummer jokes James would tell at the expense of his percussive brother in the years to come. He was offered the trombone and the tuba instead and was annoyingly successful on both, thus obviating any slight chance he might have had of becoming the school's principal drummer. It didn't diminish John's interest in the band, though. He loved the music and the social life. He was the 'golden boy' in those days, Ruth says, not his younger brother who was just a 'scrawny little kid.' It was John and Ruth who formed a quartet with two other friends, to feature Tijuana Brass numbers. And it was John, now taking private lessons, who starred in drum solos at end-of-year concerts.

It was all great fun for the older brother. He would run to practice to prepare for the band trips and excursions, especially the big trip to the Sydney Eisteddfod. Jack, for all his superficial gruffness, loved the band kids and made them feel special. Through music, John said, 'school lost its horrible face.' Ruth 'never wanted to leave primary school and band; it had such a warm fuzzy feeling.'

No wonder young James was busting to join in. He experimented on all the instruments John brought home. By the time his audition came, he could comfortably negotiate the C major scale on the trumpet, more than enough to impress Jack Akhurst. Jack's further instruction to the young brass players was pretty rudimentary. Kenny Ball, the English trumpeter who had worldwide trad jazz hits like 'Midnight in Moscow' and 'Sukiyaki', relates that his bugle band instructor told him, 'to make a sound come out of a trumpet, my son, you've got to spit into it'. 'So I did!' Ball says, 'Over the next twenty years, so much saliva went down the tube, I could've launched a battleship on it!'

Ten years later, this writer's own country town bandmaster — my mother's brother — told me to inject air into the mouthpiece by pretending to spit a hair off my lips with the tip of my tongue. It works, but it isn't the best method. Nowadays, brass players are taught to place their tongue behind their top teeth before taking it away sharply, to release air into the instrument. The trumpet, contrary to popular belief, doesn't have to be blown hard to make a sound; it's just a case of setting the column of air inside in motion. Increased air velocity merely increases volume.

Jack Akhurst's instruction was of the old school. He told James to spit tea leaves off his lip. James could have been in trouble — he didn't even drink tea — but he'd already taught himself to produce a note. 'Righto, boy, [everyone was 'boy' to Akhurst, regardless of sex] you're in!' Less well-prepared applicants, those who failed to make a sound, were 'relegated' to the drums.

Kenny Ball's teacher taught him to 'read music' by writing fingerings under the notes, another no-no these days. The trumpet, unlike a woodwind instrument, uses the same fingering for several notes — it has to, it only has three valves so there are only eight possible combinations on which to achieve usually a three, but in James' case a five, octave range. Unfortunately, writing the figure '1' under a note indicates the fingering, but gives no indication of the pitch to a young player.

Jack Akhurst had his own answer to the difficulties of learning to read music. 'Not necessary,' he'd say, tersely. Jack would buy a full set of band parts printed on paper and Clag them onto a roll of cardboard to make them lyre-usable and primary-school-kid-durable. He'd then hang the roll out of his second-floor classroom window to dry in the sun. A festoon of march cards, fluttering in the breeze, forewarned band members of a new addition to the repertoire. And they generally were 'march cards'; the repertoire was largely martial music, old traditional British Army favourites, like 'Colonel Bogey'. Jack Akhurst had no truck with America's 'Stars and Stripes Forever', and the other Sousa favourites. During class time, Jack marked the fingerings under each note with a red pen before handing a card, cut to a suitable size for marching band lyres, to each player at the next rehearsal.

Since none of the students could really read music, and the red numerals on the parts only indicated which valve to press down and not which pitch to aim for, Jack would play the band a recording of the new piece. Each child learned his part by ear, a relatively easy task for cornet and euphonium players, playing the melodic lines and counter melodies. But it was a greater challenge for the offbeat horns and oompahing basses, whose parts were less easy to isolate.

Somehow it worked. Jack Akhurst, a clarinettist himself, constructed, with patience and determination, a very acceptable junior brass band able to play a march-a-day on school assembly, the National Anthem 'God Save the Queen' and accompany the Mona Vale School song — 'the school we love the best' — which the non-playing students bellowed out to the tune of 'The Battle Hymn of the Republic'.

Rehearsal was held during sport time on Tuesday afternoons, which suited James perfectly. 'Sport,' he recalled, 'was all about football and things. I didn't want any of that, running around chasing a ball in the heat. It looked a bit rough and I was about as athletic as …' He wearied of looking for the metaphor. Perhaps if it had been boating, or skydiving, or abseiling, or motor racing, it might have been different. They were all in the future, not part of the Mona Vale Primary School curriculum in 1971!

But at least there was a store full of instruments in the music room. James tried them all; trumpet first, tuba, euphonium. James could say,

'Can I take a tenor horn home for a couple of days?'

'Righto, boy,' Akhurst would harrumph. 'Don't break it!'

Formal musical tuition was very limited. James had no individual lessons or even a learn-to-play manual. The *Arban Cornet Method* — the trumpet player's Bible — was, literally, a closed book to him. This lack of curriculum could have been an advantage. No-one mentioned the difficulties of double and triple tonguing, no-one informed him of the limitations of any instrument, and no-one told him that you can't play all the brass instruments equally well. Consequently, James single tongues at a phenomenal speed, and soon played 'screamers' — the very high notes — on the trumpet (that ability 'came in fairly early' he says modestly, as if anyone could do it), and quickly conquered the valved brasses regardless of their varying mouthpiece sizes. He started to play the slide trombone as soon as his arm was long enough to reach distant seventh position.

It was on that instrument that he made his solo debut, playing the old folk tune 'Lucy Long'. Unfortunately, at one point in the performance he lost control of the ungainly instrument. His modern concert stage story, increasing in colour and imagery every time he tells it, involves the slide flying out of his right hand and injuring little old ladies several rows back in the auditorium.

The truth, while more mundane, brought him the realisation that the concert stage was a good place to be; the audience applauded his less-than-perfect performance warmly. It was a moment of inspiration and enlightenment. *Even when it's a complete mess,* he thought, *everyone still loves you. This is where I'm going to spend the rest of my life!*

The boy was a natural; whatever he wanted to do musically, he found he could. It was Jack Akhurst and the brass band at primary school that got him off the ground, but it was at the family church around the corner where he heard the music that would allow him to fly.

Chapter 2

The Coming of Jazz

It was natural that James would spend a lot of his early years in church. His father was the minister, his mother played the organ, and the minister's children were expected, by their parents and the congregation, to be in attendance more regularly than most. But mere attendance is no guarantee of saintliness, particularly among energetic boys, and John admits they often played up in the pews. 'We were just going to Father's work, after all,' he explains.

But the children, three by now with the addition of young sister, Kathryn, found the environment ultimately beneficial, both spiritually and musically. John appreciates that he 'learned all those values early in life', and James did a bit of lay-preaching and even considered becoming a minister himself in his late teens.

Early on, at Father's appointments in country New South Wales, the music in church was traditional and predictable, the organ or piano accompanying the communal hymn-singing and the choir was nothing exceptional to pin a youngster's ears back. It was when a sea change came and the family started attending the Mona Vale Methodist Church, part of the Pittwater Regional Mission, that James heard a style of music attuned to his innate musical inclinations. It was the first of many serendipitous occasions when Morrison found himself in exactly the right place at the right moment. Mona Vale Methodists had a band, not merely a keyboard accompaniment. When Morrison heard the banjo player he was mightily impressed. But when he heard the pastor, Neil Gough, on the trombone, he was transfixed.

The Reverend Neil had recently returned from America, and had realised the impact good modern music in church could make to his ministry. By the time the Morrisons arrived at Mona Vale Methodists, there was an eight-piece band playing for the services — three or four trumpets and saxophones, an electric bass, piano and drums, fronted by Neil himself doing very acceptable vocals and good trombone improvisations.

The group played for the traditional hymns on Sunday mornings, but once a month in the evenings the church would take over the Memorial Hall and the band would swing into 'When The Saints Go Marching In', and other Dixieland standards, for the general public. There was no hymn-singing, but Neil would give a brief homily. It became a popular and effective outreach for the church members in their community, but didn't sit particularly well with the church authorities.

Even in the 1970s, many churches saw dancing as sinful — 'a perpendicular expression of a horizontal wish', they muttered — and pop music as the Devil's music. Neil had other convictions: he saw music as a bridge between those who attended church and those who didn't. James remembers that when the very talented musician Chris Marshall, a concert pianist and flautist who married Neil's daughter, was appointed as musical director, the standard improved dramatically. Neil realised the band was ready to accept professional bookings.

Sadly, this is the same Chris Marshall who, years later and alienated from the Goughs, gained some TV celebrity for his piano and organ ads chirping, 'As Donna [his new partner] and I say: have a musical day,' and went into receivership in the early 1990s, owing creditors about $5 million.

Long before his fall from grace, though, he and Neil Gough put together a club show, with Neil singing and playing, and got gigs at the local RSL Club. They covered Sinatra songs, themes from musicals, and Ray Charles gospel numbers. People who enquired into their background were told of the church connection. It was a way of encouraging Saturday nightclub patrons to become Sunday morning churchgoers.

Not surprisingly, the Methodist Church establishment couldn't countenance their Mona Vale minister and his band performing among the beer tables and poker machines, and when things reached an impasse, Reverend Neil broke away to form his own church. He called it the Kerugma Fellowship, named from the Greek word *kerugma*, meaning 'the core of the Gospel'. Several families, including the Morrisons, went with him to support his 'performing arts' church.

The ecclesiastical disputes and manoeuvrings were of little concern to young James Morrison. Mona Vale Meths or Kerugma Fellowship, it made little difference — he just knew he was in a place where the music was galvanising. Playing the cornet in the school marching band was enjoyable, but this new style of music grabbed him like nothing before. The exhilaration of the syncopated up-tempo melodies, the pathos of the gently swung prayer choruses and the freedom of the improvisations of Neil's trombone struck chords inside him and fired his imagination.

'That's what I want to do, Mum,' he said, 'I'm going to be a famous musician.'

'Of course you will, of course you will, my son,' crooned his mother, as mothers do, but with, as yet, precious little evidence of the creative and instrumental genius wrapped up inside her eight-year-old son.

Morrison went back to primary school with a new sense of mission — musical, not evangelical. He wanted to play gospel and jazz with Neil Gough's sanctified swingers. If he wasn't good enough to do that yet, the obvious alternative was to form his own band. He quickly recruited some of the best of Mona Vale Primary's musicians: Robert Dancer on trumpet, Russell Carter to play bass on his tuba, and brother John on drums. Fortuitously, another student, Matthew Young, learned clarinet outside of school, so he was in. With James himself now on trombone, the line-up of his first band was complete. James' career was off and running; he had the personnel, he had the rehearsal space at school, and they all had the time to practise before lessons started and during lunchtime.

It wasn't as straightforward as it sounds. Not all the members were as dedicated or single-minded about music as James; some preferred a little primary school sporting activity at lunchtime. James moaned:

> I'd have to go out into the playground to find them. There'd be Matthew playing handball.
>
> I'd say, 'Come on, we're rehearsing!'
>
> He'd say, 'No, I just want …'
>
> 'Now!'
>
> I'd drag him up there, make him get his clarinet out.
>
> I'd go, 'Come on! We've got a gig on Saturday and I've got some new songs.'
>
> Handball was nearly the death of my band!

And the other lads were so slow in James' estimation; not thick-witted, just dilatory in getting their instruments out and unhurried in setting up. For the young band leader with no time to waste, there was too much *andante* and not enough of his own *appassionato* about their attitude. They practised songs James had heard in church concerts. 'Maple Leaf Rag' was probably the first, then 'Tiger Rag' and 'The Saints' to feature John at the drum kit. The group found some printed Dixieland charts, which James distributed to the band members. Meanwhile, he played his own parts by ear and, he said, 'mucked around with them'. Already, he was improvising.

The group was invited to play unpaid gigs at the local fete, at school concerts and the church, and they performed outside the local shopping centre. The Coles New World Supermarket at Mona Vale turned James and John Morrison and their friends into professionals one day by offering them a dollar each to play on Saturday mornings. It was a good rate when weekly pocket money for household chores only brought in sixty cents. 'We'd always save the big drum solo for a quarter to twelve, so all the people rushing to get their last-minute milk or bread would have to stop and watch. It was great mischief,' James said.

And, as soon as he thought James was good enough, Neil Gough invited the new 'pro' to play in the Kerugma ensembles. 'Occasionally Neil would say, "Let's put all the kids in a group and let them do a number." This was all really big, and eventually I became a soloist with the various groups that developed there,' James said. In fact, the Fellowship provided James with a whole lot of new musical opportunities. In the concert band he started on the cornet, his original primary school instrument, but was asked to play the mellophone with his slightly older friend and church organist, David Pudney. Pudney himself was a good all-round musician who came to play an important part in James' development. The pair played the mellophones — virtually tenor horns facing backwards, like French horns, but easier to pitch — to replicate the gorgeous F horn parts in concert band music.

James was content for a while, but he still really wanted the trombone, the instrument he fell in love with when the Reverend had played it from the pulpit. He eventually got his wish and became a trombonist at both church and school, but quickly realised there were

> some spots going on trumpet in other groups like the big band, so I thought, *I'll do that too*. I became a multi-instrumentalist because there were all these different groups going and many different opportunities to play. I was looking for holes where I could get a blow; I didn't care what it was on — trombone, trumpet, mellophone. It didn't make any difference, I just looked for any opportunities to play.

Chris Marshall, the musical director at Kerugma, provided one such opening. The seasoned Sydney gig player decided James and John were ready for work outside the Kerugma ensembles. 'He could see we could play. "I'm going to get you boys into the clubs as a professional floor show act," he said — and he did!' said John. It was a tough introduction to the real entertainment world. It wasn't their own show that was the problem — they'd been polishing that outside Coles and in church concerts for some time. The difficulty was the weekly turnover of special guest artists with their bags full of charts of varying quality expecting instant performance. There was no rehearsal. Guests would arrive, talk through their arrangements — 'This is what I do here,' 'Don't forget the drum roll and change of tempo there,' — and on with the show!

John said:

> We had no choice but to learn to read — fast! We were fifteen and thirteen years old, playing pro backings for some of Sydney's best-known acts. We thought we were pretty good at it, until Chris Marshall started to talk about 'Gus Mercy'.
>
> 'Just watch out when Gus Mercy comes, he's got the hardest charts of all!' he'd say one week. Then next week he'd say, 'One day he's going to come and you guys are going to fall flat on your faces.' Perhaps Chris was just trying to keep our feet on the ground.

The boys didn't know what to expect once Marshall had put the fear of Gus into them. Maybe Mercy the Merciless would have horns on his head.

He turned out to be Gus Merzi, a lovely guy and probably Australia's leading jazz accordionist since the 1950s. Only his charts were wicked; devilishly hard up-tempos for 'Tico Tico' and the standard flying-fingered solos of a virtuoso.

But the reading experience was as invaluable as working in an authentic showbiz setting. The Morrison brothers got an insight into what was required to capture and hold an audience. 'We were jazz musicians,' said John, 'but we were learning how to entertain.'

This was all happening in James' second year at Pittwater High School. When he arrived there a year earlier he was hoping for a good standard big band to play in, but found only a concert band, which Ruth Cunningham described as 'crummy.' James literally wasn't having a bar of it! If there was no big band in the school, he'd start his own. He'd been running a band for three years at primary school so, notwithstanding the tardiness of handball players, he could do it again.

Somewhat impudently, and certainly quite boldly, in his first week as a year 7 student at high school, he got permission to front morning assembly. 'I'm starting a big band,' he announced, 'I need trumpets, trombones, saxophones, everyone who plays instruments. Turn up in the hall at lunchtime.'

'A bunch of people came along,' he remembers. 'I think I had thirteen trumpets, two trombones, eight saxophones, and a rhythm section. That was the big band.'

Brother John was less charitable; he described them as 'a large group of misfits'. 'We had no access to real music,' he added, 'so it was a very important part of James' development to arrange for them, but it wasn't really a traditional American big band.'

James told his misfits, on the first day, 'Now we're going to play a blues. Trumpets, you play this; trombones, you've got that,' and so on, and he'd count them in.

For the second rehearsal, he notated what he'd been telling them — the riffs and figures — and the band gradually got better, to the extent that a couple of teachers wanted to join. 'Bob Hamilton, my science teacher, volunteered to play,' laughed the student bandleader. 'He wasn't very good, but I put him on third trumpet and he loved it!' This generosity paid dividends when later the same teacher was prepared to turn a blind eye when James wrote musical arrangements during science lessons.

The Pittwater High School Big Band even entered the annual City of Sydney Eisteddfod, in which there was no 'big band' category. All the other groups were concert bands. James tells the story with his usual quota of hyperbole:

> The bands would come on with white gloves, blazers and ties, with shiny shoes and all the instruments looking perfect, and they would play a very tight classical piece and all walk off together.

> Then the announcer said, 'And now the Pittwater High School Big Band,' and he said it with distaste. I wandered on in a denim jacket, and we were all very scraggy. We dragged on an amp for the bass; all our horns were dirty. I started clicking my fingers, whereas the other bands had started without a count-in. The whole place went into a hushed silence, and the adjudicator's face went slightly red ... We came second — but it was a lot of fun.

Pittwater didn't play a 'very tight classical piece'; it played an arrangement by its junior student band leader, James Morrison, an achievement in itself. But, surprisingly, this wasn't James' first attempt at scoring for bands. He cut his teeth in grade 5 at Mona Vale, when he was asked to form a pit orchestra and write the parts for the school's original musical production. James was aware, even at his young age, that the producer put Jack Akhurst's nose out of joint by sidestepping the school band for the event. But Jack, to his credit, swallowed his pride for the sake of his school and the advancement of his precocious young musician.

Typically, James can't see anything unusual in the fact that, at the age of ten and without any theoretical background, he was capable of writing music for an entire children's musical. Similarly, when confronted with the suggestion that most people can't just 'start writing big band charts', as he did in high school, he says,

> If you don't put a qualifier on how good the charts have to be, then yes we can. We can all write a big band chart, just how good would it be? The first ones were probably awful, but over time I learned to write for big band. I learned by trial and error. I'd try writing a big shout chorus, and I'd hand it out and we'd play it.

Then James would figure out what worked and what didn't and why.

Importantly, for his musical development, James began listening to great jazz music. Not at home, though — there was no Glenn Miller, let alone Miles Davis, in the family collection. Neil Gough and other Kerugma musicians lent both James and John albums they thought might interest them. John once found one for himself in a record store. He went home with a copy of Sandy Nelson's *Drums, Drums, Drums*. The album was instantly confiscated and returned to him in a brown paper bag when Mum saw the bikini-clad girls all over the cover. He got the sleeve back on his thirty-fifth birthday, when his parents finally decided he was old enough to cope with it. In the meantime, he played the record so often there were virtually no grooves left on it, and decided to become a showman drummer himself. Who knows, it might attract ladies like it did for Sandy!

When James was twelve or so, a church friend, Dennis, an older man in perhaps his early thirties, gave him the Modern Jazz Quartet's *Under the Jasmine Tree*. 'The music was kind of nice,' he thought, 'but there was nothing really happening in it for me at the time. It was too sophisticated; it didn't even have a trumpet!'

But when he heard Louis Armstrong for the first time, his mouth opened in astonishment. When he discovered Dizzy Gillespie, his chin hit the floor! *So the trumpet can do that?* he thought to himself in amazement. 'I immediately wanted to play like him, phrase like him, the same sort of lines, the same sort of speed, range and effects.' He started to work on it, but for a musician he took a road less travelled.

Chapter 3

No Practise Makes Perfect!

It would be reasonable to assume that any ambitious young trumpet player anxious to follow in Gillespie's huge footsteps would knuckle down to serious hard work behind his mouthpiece, to achieve that stratospheric range and technique. James denies that he ever did this. His parents confirm it.

'The neighbours complained about me when I was trying to teach myself the saxophone to play at Kerugma,' his mother Jessie laughed, 'but they never complained about James because he didn't play!'

'We did get a complaint about John on the drums, too,' chimed in George, his father, 'but never about James because he didn't seem to practise.'

The pattern hasn't changed. Nowadays, just occasionally, a contemporary orchestral or brass band composer might write a line or figure that James describes as 'outside of the technique I've got now and which is not going to come naturally in the time I've got available. I'm actually going to have to sit here and play this over a few times.' James calls that 'work', and tries hard to avoid it.

He also points out that these days,

> I've got enough ability on the instrument that generally I only need to sit with the music when I'm on a plane somewhere and read through it a few times. I can work it out and rehearse it in my head without actually playing the instrument.
>
> That's another thing about work. If you can sit down to do something that's normally done standing up, sit down; if

there's practice you can do without the instrument in your hand, then do it empty-handed. The less work the better. I really am quite lazy.

It's a dangerous philosophy to broadcast now that he has teenage boys of his own: 'My wife wants them to do their homework and study — all the things I just wouldn't and didn't do when I was their age. I find myself saying, "Make sure you do your study," while inside I'm going, *There's no way I'd do it!*'

He has worked, of course, but in James' lexicon, if it's enjoyable because it's something he wants to do, it's not 'work'. 'Work' is having to do something he dislikes or finds tedious. He practised hard and regularly by incessantly playing, but only to be able to do the things he wanted to do, to play the music he wanted to play:

> Some players spend a lot of time developing the tools or the ability to play the instrument, without it having anything actually to do with the music. I was the other way around. I started hearing Louis Armstrong on a record or Neil Gough in front of me on the trombone, and I said, 'What do I need to do to be able to do that?'

He's never sat facing a music stand for hours on end battling with the technical exercises, the major and minor scales, or even the thirteen Grand Studies in *Arban's*, the classic etude book and sine qua non of most trumpet students. James asked what point there was in practising those things if no-one would ever want to hear him play them in public. The answer was generally, 'If you learn that technique, then you'll be able to play all the great solos.' James had a ready answer: 'How about I just learn the solos, then I'll be able to play all the exercises!'

He adds:

> I've seen guys with a lot of technique who, whenever they go to play, play something simpler. I think, *What have they got all this technique for?* I've always approached it the other way around. My

> technique has only ever been just enough to manage what I've heard and wanted to play. Now, because I'd heard Dizzy Gillespie, I needed a lot of technique; for Maynard Ferguson, I needed a lot of range. So I developed those. I've never had one note higher or one beat more per minute than I absolutely needed to play what I'd heard. Technique was always subservient to that. I'm not interested in having one iota more than I absolutely need.

Interestingly, he had no early heroes to imitate on the trombone; once he'd overtaken Neil Gough, he had no-one to look up to. He heard J. J. Johnson and thought, *That's lovely, but it doesn't get me the way Dizzy does*. So while he tried to make his trumpet sound like Gillespie, he modelled his trombone playing on the piano stylings of Oscar Peterson.

> I listened to his articulation and his lines. I'd say, 'I want to play like that and I want to do it on the trombone.' I didn't have a trombone hero and I think that was, by chance, a great thing. I was trying to be a pianist on the trombone. That gave me much more agility on the trombone than I would otherwise have had. And also being a trumpet player, range on the trombone was open-ended to me. If I just went with what I heard other trombonists do, I'd have an octave less than I've got. But I know what it feels like to play up there — I do it all the time — so playing very high register on the trombone never fazed me. Like a lot of things, it never occurred to me not to do it. I was just doing what I did. Later on, you have a look and you think, *Why isn't anyone else doing that?* I ended up where I am because I was listening to sounds and going, 'Whoa, I like that, I want to do that!'

Nowadays, if a student wants to play the Gillespie solos, James recommends they transcribe them note for note to play along. He never actually did this himself — 'much too lazy', he claims. He wanted to play like Gillespie, not be Gillespie, so he never jotted down the solos he was practising.

It would be lovely to be able to say it was to do with this free creative spirit, but it was pure laziness. I couldn't be bothered listening to it that many times. It's quite laborious learning a solo note for note. Too much work! It wasn't fun; it was fun to play like him, not to actually play his solos.

'There's a great thread of laziness through all of this,' he confesses. 'No *Arban's*, no exercises — too hard, couldn't be bothered.'

He compares his form of laziness to a water-skier who'll hang onto a bar behind a high-speed boat, nearly ripping his arms off because it's his relaxation. If you ordered him to do it, he'd probably refuse. So Morrison only ever practised to conquer what he wanted to play — first to sound like the great players he heard on record, then to develop his own style and sound. He was driven to do that by his love of it, not because he was told to. He didn't practise as a means to an end — he went directly for the end itself.

Whether you put it down to laziness, good fortune or innate ability, he went straight for his goal — to play like the virtuosos he heard. He didn't have time for mundane exercises that might slow him down. There was too much to be done — he had gigs to do, instruments to learn (he was adding piano and sax to his stable) — charts to write and a big band to run. By the time he was thirteen, there wasn't even room in his schedule for a typical secondary school education.

Chapter 4

High School Dropout

James was once told by a physical education teacher at Pittwater High that he held the record at the school for the most days absent without being expelled. It was evident from his demeanour that the jock was intending to do something about it.

The teacher was only partially right. James was at school most days, he just didn't attend classes. In fact, he got there early, probably before the physical education teacher, to run band before the first bell. Then, when everyone else went to class, he'd hide out in the School Hall, the large concert and assembly building set apart from the rest of the school across the sports field. Teachers and other students rarely came within earshot, so he could practise the piano for hours on end. He and John had discovered Erroll Garner's work in a box of records they'd been given by the Sydney jazz entrepreneur and record producer, Horst Liepolt, who was giving away some of his large collection of jazz records in preparation for a move to the States. Liepolt, with his familiar greeting, 'Hey, you guys have really got it together; swinging and grooving, baby!' was well-known in both Melbourne and Sydney. After migrating from Germany in 1951, he opened the Jazz Centre 44 club in Melbourne. Ten years later, when he moved to Sydney, he booked bands for the city's best-known club, The Basement. He founded the Manly Jazz Festival, introduced jazz to the Sydney Festival and organised his own series, *Music is an Open Sky*, at the Sydney Opera House, the Sydney Town Hall and other prestigious venues. In Australia, he produced over thirty jazz albums before moving to the

US in the early 1980s, to open more jazz clubs (Sweet Basil and Lush Life), run more festivals, like the Greenwich Village Jazz Festival, and produce fifty more recordings, including Gil Evans' Grammy Award-winning *Bud and Bird*. His knowledge of the scene was as extensive as his record collection was comprehensive. He certainly had too many LPs to cart to America, so he gave many of them away to two tyros he thought deserving. 'It was an incredible gift,' said John, 'just that simple gesture of giving two young guys those records; all the things you needed to hear when you had no formal training. It was pure gold.'

In the collection, James found the Dudley Moore Trio and assumed Moore was African American. This brought about two surprises: firstly, when James heard Oscar Peterson, he claimed he sounded like Moore — a bad case of carts and horses — and, secondly, when Dudley appeared onscreen in a Hollywood film, James cried, 'Look at this guy, he's got the same name as the old jazz player!' Erroll Garner's playing was a revelation, and James spent many surreptitious hours in the school hall trying to work out his keyboard secrets. 'That was a big job. It took a couple of years. He had three hands!' James said. 'If he's playing this with one hand, and this with the other, who's playing that?' he wondered. James had had some formal piano tuition using the familiar starter book, the *John Thompson Piano Method*, in primary school, but had been bored by the banal tunes and quickly given it up. When he discovered jazz piano, his interest was ignited fully and, as always, once engaged he burned with enthusiasm. Morrison never pursues anything with less than total commitment.

Figuring out Garner and writing scores for the band practices took up a lot of James' time. 'I was probably working harder than anyone else in the school,' he claims. He just wasn't doing it according to any Education Department curriculum or timetable. On occasions when there was no way of avoiding the classroom, he'd take his score paper and his one exercise book with him. The exercise book was dual purpose

— English, geography, history and essay material at the front, and mathematical figures at the back. His system for avoiding class work was to have the appropriate end of the book open when the teacher, doing his rounds, walked past, only to return to his compositions under the desk when the emergency was over. The scheme seemed to work well, perhaps due in part to the fact that teachers were happy for James to be inattentive as long as he wasn't disruptive.

He had little interest in any subjects, and chose woodwork, art and music as his electives. Even music, as an academic study, had scant appeal, but he did come to a compromise with the music teachers who saw his practical playing potential. In fact, his mother remembers them as being supportive of him when other teachers were trying to remove him from the school for not doing any work. 'Sometimes,' she said, 'they'd run him home to our place in Bayview to pick up his instruments or jazz books when he'd forgotten them. They recognised the talent he had and nurtured it.'

They were prepared to overlook the absence of written assignments as long as he passed the end-of-semester exams. The test would consist of music history and theory, at which James would perform poorly, and aural tests and practical assessments, for which his scores would be nigh on perfect. The strong suits dragged up the low scores to a pass mark and all parties were happy, especially James, who did well in the portions of the exam he saw as having any relevance to his musical career.

Several times he was called before the school counsellor to explain the lack of written work submitted to other areas. Generally, young James would agree to toe the line and then blithely continue as before. Threats of being unable to find a job in the future held little terror for him, as he was already earning good money gigging in a trio with his brother John, and David Pudney.

On the last counselling encounter, James was confronted by a steely-eyed woman determined not to be outpointed by a cocky and uncooperative year 9 student.

'You've got to start doing some work,' she demanded.

'But I'm very busy,' replied young James, quite reasonably.

The counsellor was not deterred.

'I understand you're hoping to go to the Conservatorium of Music when you leave here. You realise you need good grades here to get in?'

'But it's a music school!'

'Yes, but if you go there for years 11 and 12, you do ordinary subjects, too. If you haven't got good enough grades here, you won't get into the Con.'

James was stunned.

'Well,' he retorted, 'If they don't want me to go there even though I can play well, I wouldn't want to go anyway!'

'I suggest,' said the counsellor, 'you just leave and look for work. All this talk about your music is fine, but you're going to need a real job.'

James had heard that expression before and it needled him.

'It is a real job. I'm fourteen years old and I'm already making as much as you!'

James was right. He was working regularly in a trio with David Pudney (on piano with bass pedals underneath) and John on drums. Three or four nights a week, at about $40 a night, brought him in as much as a teacher's stipend in the 1970s. They were good gigs, too, at respectable venues like the Royal Motor Yacht Club and the Palm Beach Golf Club. The Morrison boys were underage to attend licensed venues, but David Pudney, several years older, got them in and their music ensured return bookings.

The counsellor never spoke to James again and he was never again called to the office. He left high school as soon as he was old enough, just before the end of year 10. Since he hadn't completed the year, he was awarded no certificate. His mother Jessie, herself a teacher, was disappointed enough to call at the school to try to rectify this situation. The school remained adamant — no completion, no certificate — even when Jessie wept a little. It was only when she threatened to send James back to school that they relented.

James got his Leaving Certificate, but Jessie still doesn't value it as highly as the Order of Australia and the Doctorate at the University of Sydney he was given in more recent years. She thought they gave a little respectability to a bloke who wouldn't get a real job!

James looks back on Pittwater High with more affection than you might expect. He wanted to go to the Conservatorium Secondary School straight from Mona Vale Primary School, but his parents decided it was too far for a young lad to travel every day. Instead, he went to Pittwater. 'It was good that I did. There's no way I'd have got the same opportunities at the Con. I wouldn't have got the same freedom there to learn to write, arrange by trial and error, and run my own big band in my own way.'

James, having done his 'porridge' at high school — he sometimes describes it as 'like being in prison' — and despite the warnings of his counsellors, was still determined to enrol in the tertiary jazz course at the Con. That was easier said than done — the Con took in high-scoring secondary school graduates from year 12, not year 10 dropouts without folio. The incorrigible Morrison found a way, but took a brief detour to Monterey before arriving at the august portals of the Sydney Conservatorium of Music.

Chapter 5

It Happened in Monterey

The Monterey Jazz Festival in California, founded in 1958, can claim to be the longest continuously running jazz festival in the world. The line-up in its first year included Louis Armstrong and his All-Stars, Dizzy Gillespie, the Harry James Orchestra, the Dave Brubeck Quartet and the inimitable Billie Holiday, among many illustrious others. It's reported that the ailing 'Lady Day', battling her drug addictions, 'bone weary and soul-sore', as Studs Terkel put it, was unsteady on her feet and had to be supported physically by Buddy DeFranco, Benny Carter and Gerry Mulligan. She sang eleven of the classic songs of her repertoire, including 'What a Little Moonlight Can Do', 'Billie's Blues' and 'God Bless the Child'. It was her only performance at a Monterey Jazz Festival; a year later, she was dead.

Twenty-one years later, in 1979, the program again boasted the biggest names in the jazz world. Dizzy Gillespie was back, and so were the Buddy Rich and the Woody Herman Big Bands, and the Stan Getz Quartet. Also appearing, as an unheralded surprise packet, was the Young Northside Big Band from, of all places, Sydney, Australia. The band was directed by Johnny Speight, an indefatigable educator and jazz promoter.

Speight was enthusiastic about many things; he was a grade cricketer, a golfer, photographer, artist and joiner who wrote a jazz column for the *Manly Daily* for many years. This latter indicates his greatest passion. He was a primary school teacher; he taught at Harbord Public for more than thirty years where, when most schools were singing folk tunes and childish ditties, he introduced a jazz curriculum and produced musicals like *My Fair Lady* at the school. He ran the highly successful Manly Jazz Festival, started the Northside Jazz Club and formed the Young Northside Big Band, and later the Warringah Stage Band as a feeder group for it.

Sydney's best-known jazz writer, John Shand, wrote, 'Speight pursued everything with boundless enthusiasm and set high standards.' The Young Northside Big Band was a case in point. It originated through a sixteen-year-old student, Cary Bennett from Manly Boys High School, who, inspired by a Daly-Wilson Big Band concert, was eager to start a big band at the school. His own music master was supportive, but unable to lead a band of that style. Cary sought out his old primary school teacher and invited him to rehearsal. Speight told Mike Williams of *Jazz* magazine:

> I was a little bit stunned because there were about 25 to 30 players, girls and boys, all shapes and sizes, ranging from about 15 to 17, with no idea how to perform what they were playing in the jazz sense. I was so impressed that I went home and talked it over with my wife. She said I should get in and get things going. To be honest, I was only a part-time musician with no experience of big bands. I was sort of blazing a trail without any real knowledge — very dangerous.

Johnny, realising how dangerous it was, encouraged others to help. 'But every Saturday afternoon the band would rehearse, wet or fine. And the kids kept on coming.' Two of those kids were Dale Barlow and James Morrison.

Dale Barlow, a leading Australian saxophonist for many years, and a onetime member of Art Blakey's Jazz Messengers, says, 'These days, there are jazz bands in all the high schools, but back then Northside was the only one.' He added,

I've always played. My father, Bill, was a well-known Sydney musician and it was natural I should play. We lived over the other side of town at Concord, but I had to join the Northside Big Band. It was the first of its kind and the only way to learn the ropes. We learned to breathe and articulate together, to obey dynamics, match tones and play as a section — all important stuff a young developing player needs to know.

Johnny Speight was, Shand wrote, 'a competent, economical and elegant pianist', and even when chronic arthritis destroyed his playing career, his enthusiasm for jazz remained indestructible. Barlow described him as 'a powerhouse. He gave the kids the best he possibly could and wanted to develop the whole jazz scene. He did a brilliant job.'

The band became a professional-quality student band and cut its first album, *Quiet Breaker*, a copy of which was given to Count Basie, who was playing at the Sydney Opera House. Speight said, 'Basie liked it and rang me at the school, saying he'd like to meet the band and asked if they would be coming to the show.' Tim Rollinson, who played sax, remembers the Northside players lining up to shake hands with Basie — just like meeting the Queen after a Royal Variety performance, except the young musicians much preferred to be face to face with this legendary member of jazz aristocracy.

Basie was equally impressed by the young band. He paid them the ultimate compliment: he told them they really swung, and proved his sincerity by talking to his friend, Jimmy Lyons, who ran the Monterey Festival. 'The next thing was,' said Speight, 'we got a letter of invitation to the Festival, through Horst Liepolt, who produced the record.' The enthusiastic bandleader, realising the opportunity was important not just for the Northside Young Big Band, but for the future of Australian jazz, accepted and set about raising $25,000 to take twenty young Australian men and women across to California.

Local, State and Federal grants provided just under half. Speight, who had long worked in the public school system, knew something about fundraising and organised carwashes, raffles and dances, to find the rest. The band played gigs for cash, irritating the Musicians' Union, and eventually raised enough money to cover the cheap fare arranged through a Qantas employee, father of band member Peter Neesby.

Some of the Californian accommodation booked was pretty basic. Johnny Speight took one look at the lobby of the YMCA in San Francisco, full of hippies with flowers in their hair and weed on their breath, and deemed it unsuitable for his young charges. Ever resourceful, he found national park cabins within spitting distance of the Golden Gate Bridge.

'We were accommodated three or four to a room, like backpackers,' Barlow recalls. 'But at least it was secure, and anyway, we were a bunch of young guys who didn't mind roughing it a bit.'

Another time, they arrived at a prearranged camp after dark and out of season, to find that the electricity and water had been turned off. Everyone was starving so Horst Liepolt, who was helping Johnny Speight, arranged a McDonald's supper. 'One hamburger each,' laughs Barlow, 'that's all we got!'

It certainly wasn't all plain sailing for the indomitable Speight. Apart from the accommodation hiccups, some gigs were cancelled and one group of young men, led by Barlow, absconded to New York at the end of the tour. Barlow explained,

> We jumped on a plane and went to hear the biggest jazz names in the country: Phil Woods, Art Blakey, Dizzy Gillespie, everybody. We thought, *This is a once-in-a-lifetime opportunity. We've come from Australia and we won't get a chance like this again for years and years.* We had no money; we all stayed in one room for about two weeks. It must have been a nightmare for John. He was our official guardian, even though most of us were over eighteen.

But the Monterey Jazz Festival, the reason for the tour, was an undisputed triumph. Even the accommodation — billets with local families — was excellent, though two young men, Morrison and Rollinson, arrived at the home of their host with an 'only-in-America' name, Ross Ross, to be greeted by a startled Mrs Ross Ross, who was expecting girls. Tim had to sweep a menagerie of soft toys off a pink eiderdown before pulling the bedclothes back for a good night's rest.

The Monterey Jazz Festival ran all weekend, from Friday night to Sunday. The Northside Big Band had one performance on Sunday afternoon in the Youth Band section, which included the frighteningly good California All-Star Youth Band. 'We got to hear bands from all around the country. Some were really amazing; we were just stunned,' said Barlow. The Australian contingent had backstage passes. They were able to wander around the site, almost tripping over Stan Getz or Buddy Rich just as they went onstage. It was a priceless experience, which Barlow said 'upped the ante' — raised the bar and showed him and the other aspiring professionals from Australia the musical possibilities and the standards they had to meet.

Speight said,

> On the day, our band arrived and the California band was playing onstage. I could see the hearts of our fellows go down. I knew there was only one way to succeed; we had to start well. I went to Andrew Gander, our drummer, and said, 'It's up to you. Are you nervous?' He said he had no nerves, which I believed. I said, 'Fire it up from the word go, because if you don't, nothing will happen.' We were rushed onstage and the curtain went up. There were 7000 people in front of us — and the band really fired. The first number got mild applause. The second was 'Queen Bee', and we got good applause for that, and the third was James Morrison's feature.

James walked front stage without a note of music and, despite being warned to tread carefully in front of all the Monterey jazz buffs, opened, in the two-bar break leading into his solo, with an audacious *glissando* in a gut-bucket style. 'All caution was thrown to the wind,' said James, 'but that's how I felt — like having a good time.' The audience loved it and warmed to the courage and audacity of the sixteen-year-old soloist. 'The upshot of the concert,' Speight remembered, 'was that the wild applause went on for several minutes.'

James claims he played trumpet solos, too. He says he sat in the trombone section, playing second chair to Scott Kardash, but kept his trumpet under his seat, 'much to the annoyance of the trumpet section'. This probably didn't happen on the one-set gig in Monterey; neither Dale Barlow nor Tim Rollinson remembers it, though Barlow admits James was 'probably a better trumpet player than anybody else in the section, even at that stage'.

Ralph Pyl, a younger Northside player who still regrets missing the cut for Monterey because of his tender years, confirms that it did happen on other occasions and that the trumpet section was often more than a little miffed by his cheek and insouciance. Pyl attended practices before and after the trip. He recalls Morrison sitting, at both Northside Big Band and later when he played a few gigs with the celebrated Daly-Wilson Big Band, in the trombone section with his trumpet available.

Pyl said,

> If there was a solo, he'd sometimes pick it up and play it. It could be quite humiliating for the other trumpet players; here was this young trombone player who could get the trumpet out and play all over the instrument. One time, John Hoffman, a well-known Sydney trumpeter, was taking a Northside rehearsal. He was getting quite frustrated with the trumpet section not being able to play a certain passage. I remember James saying, 'I can play that.' John replied, 'I don't care who plays it, I just want to hear it.' It made the other trumpet players feel quite inadequate that a trombone player could pull his trumpet out and nail the line. James was utterly unabashed, though.

The triumphant Young Northside Big Band returned to Sydney to make a second album, *Manly to Monterey*. Morrison featured on three tracks. Reviewer Joya Jenson wrote of the 'exhilaration and incredibly powerful excitement generated by the group', and how Morrison's 'raunchy trombone' on 'My Favourite Things' and 'Tall Cotton' contrasted with his solo on the Jimmy Van Heusen ballad 'Here's That Rainy Day', which 'typifies the beauty and sadness of the theme and the Johnny Burke lyric "funny how love becomes a cold, rainy day."'

The Young Northside Big Band continued for a few more years. Johnny Speight gradually moved aside and immersed himself in running the Manly Jazz Festival, which he took over from his own old friend, Horst Liepolt. He ran it for twenty-eight years, and in 1999 was awarded an OAM for his services to music.

Barlow and Morrison moved on. Barlow was soon back in the States forging a great career of his own, but remembers Monterey as an inspiration and a turning point. The sixteen-year-old Morrison returned to Sydney, eager to enrol in the jazz course at the Conservatorium. On paper, he had Buckley's chance, despite his outstanding performances at one of the world's foremost jazz festivals and his regular employment at some of the best clubs around town. To the Con he was a mere high school leaver with a dismal academic record, hoping to be admitted to a tertiary course for eighteen-year-olds who had passed year 12, particularly in music, with flying colours. That didn't stop him completing an application form aimed at mature age entrants, which he found in the newspaper. There may have been questions about age and academic qualifications; James can't recall. 'I just ticked the form,' he says, 'I've never been very good at filling out forms. I just tick the piece of paper and reckon if there's something they really want to know, they'll come and ask me. Nobody asked me how old I was; no-one asked for a certificate.'

James was lucky. Roger Frampton was running the jazz course at the time. He was a wonderful pianist and a great musician but, as James put it, 'he couldn't administrate his way out of a paper bag.'

But Frampton, who was more than happy to hand back the administrative reins to jazz department founder Don Burrows a year later, was overseeing all the auditions that year. He may have been clerically inefficient, overlooking James' date of birth on the enrolment, or he may just have heard a young man whose remarkable talent demanded admission to the course. Whichever it was, James passed his audition and, at sixteen, was admitted to the tertiary institution of his choice. James was the youngest student by at least two years and in most cases, since many of the course entrants were in their mid-twenties or early thirties, considerably younger.

James was scheduled for trumpet lessons with Dick Montz, an American trumpet player who had migrated to Australia in the mid-seventies and progressed through session, commercial and teaching work to a post at the university. His singing sound and piercing top register is still familiar to millions of Australians through his recordings of the ABC's news and sports themes.

His obituary in the *Sydney Morning Herald* in early 2006 notes that his success as an educator arose 'from an unlikely style: a no-nonsense, almost military demeanour, a strict respect (unusual among musicians) for academic protocols and, most importantly, a passion to help each student find his or her voice as an artist.'

Montz' ethos, as described by the writer reflecting on his academic career, didn't augur too well for the latest recruit to his stable, James Morrison, for whom 'military demeanour' and 'a strict respect for academic protocols' were unlikely bedfellows. James acknowledges that

> on the first lesson I knew this was going to be a disaster. I thought I was going to fail the class and get thrown out. He was very correct, and I was a little screwed up and wanted to stay that way because it sounded good. So I appealed to Dick, 'I'm not going to

play the trumpet the way you did, but you have a lot of knowledge of trumpet styles and how the instrument is used in bands, so can you just talk to me about that? Play me records and tell me what's going on.'

The quality in the final clause of Dick's eulogy kicked in. He was happy to let James 'find his own voice as a student' — exactly what James wanted. 'At no stage in my life,' he says, 'have I ever wanted to do it "the way it's done". I wanted to find out how I was going to do it.'

The fact that the course was mainly concerned with the practical side of music suited James and his fellow undergraduates. There were some music history classes, but a minimum of written work and formal examinations. 'We were all jazz players and didn't fit in to university,' explains James. There was also a feeling in the young jazz department that if too many failed the course it might be cancelled. So in its early days, while playing standards were extremely high, writing assignments was less critical.

When Burrows eventually returned to head up the department, he discovered, or had it pointed out to him, that 'Morrison, J. L.' was very young to be a university student. It was a bit late now, though — if it was decided to throw him out, how could the faculty explain his admission in the first place? James thinks the embarrassing enrolment form was probably lost. At the age he should have been entering university he was graduating, with an offer to come back and teach improvisation. As well as this, he was given the opportunity of gigging with the Head of Jazz Studies at the institution, and face of jazz in Australia, Don Burrows himself.

Chapter 6

Don Burrows

The kids in the Paynesville Brass Band were gobsmacked when they first heard eighty-year-old Don Burrows play his woodwind instruments in a charity fundraiser the band put on. They only knew him as an old guy who struggled to keep up in trainer band. Don had joined the band in his late seventies, after leaving the bustle of Sydney for the seaside tranquillity of the Victorian town. He had always hankered to add brass to his list of musical achievements and now had the time to do it. He started beginner lessons on the bass trumpet, which his increasingly arthritic hands found difficult to hold. He moved on to trombone — his preferred option anyway — but got cramp in the elbow joint and finished up on baritone, which he could cuddle and play comfortably.

His impatience to conquer his new field was noted by his fellow learners, who saw him hunched over the music, straining to read the dots. One said, 'You take it too seriously; you should learn to relax!' This from a twelve-year-old who, Don said in amusement, played everything in C major, ignoring any flats and sharps of the key signature.

It's a wonder none of the seniors told the kids who Don was. Perhaps they didn't know either; they didn't appear to recognise James Morrison when he turned up for practice one night while holidaying with his old mentor — even after he played every instrument in the band cupboard to cover missing parts in the scores.

Don Burrows loved Paynesville from the moment he saw it. He could buy a property on the water; noodle his refurbished Queenscliff tugboat *Shanghai* up and down the river, fish, take photographs and play golf to his heart's content. It was a far cry from Burrows' former Sydney lifestyle as the leading light in what has become known as the Australian jazz explosion of the 1970s. Back then, jazz was filling clubs like never before. Every leading hotel either had a group or wanted one. Burrows fronted bands at El Rocco and the Sky Lounge, and his group was resident at the Wentworth Hotel for many years. Later, the Regent Hotel capitalised on his popularity by advertising its jazz venue as the Don Burrows Supper Club. He formed the Australian Jazz Quartet, an original awesome foursome, with George Golla on guitar, Ed Gaston on bass and Alan Turnbull on drums. They toured Australia and beyond, playing everything from twenties trad, swing and bossa nova, to modern jazz.

Don had his own popular ABC TV shows and produced numerous recordings. He travelled the world, representing Australia, visiting Europe and the Montreux Jazz Festival in Switzerland, the States and the Newport Jazz Festival at Carnegie Hall, as well as Japan and China. He worked with Stéphane Grappelli, Frank Sinatra and Dizzy Gillespie, among hundreds of others, and was awarded an MBE in 1972 (the first jazz musician so honoured) and an Order of Australia in 1987. Don climbed to the top of the tree from its very lowest branches. He certainly wasn't born with a silver flute in his mouth; his first instrument was a tin whistle, before he quickly moved on to his beloved clarinet.

At fourteen, he was playing in nightclubs and dance halls around Sydney, paying his dues, learning the tunes and ducking out the back door when the authorities turned up to check birth certificates. He never finished school and did no formal musical study. He said modestly, 'I've never had a piece of paper in a frame to prove I'm any good at anything.' He didn't need it but did realise that a more formal approach, such as that of classical music, would be more than useful to most young jazz musicians. 'There was a need for courses for performers and writers of jazz,' Don claimed, 'They needed to study Ellington just as classicists needed to study the Masters.'

One night in 1972, late in a gig with a quintet at the Wentworth, Di, the wife of bass player Ed Gaston, came in from a classical concert. Burrows picked up her program and started to read the introduction to the new director at the New South Wales Conservatorium of Music, Rex Hobcroft. Hobcroft was a classical pianist who came to academia after studying music part-time while working as a commercial airline pilot. Perhaps this unconventional background had led him to more catholic tastes than might have been expected. He expressed readiness to embrace new ideas and avenues of music-making, mentioning particularly electronic music and jazz. Burrows' heart leapt. He immediately wrote Hobcroft a letter, congratulating him on his appointment, his vision and on his open-minded approach to music. 'If you want to start a jazz course and you have facilities,' Don wrote, 'I'm happy to supply ideas I've gained from Europe and the United States.' Hobcroft proved the sincerity of his printed words by inviting Burrows firstly to lunch, and consequently to submit his ideas on the jazz course in writing.

Burrows discussed the project with his peers George Golla, Roger Frampton and Mike Nock, who were all full-time professional musicians — 'not a part-time cabdriver amongst them,' as Don put it. They were men who knew the business and how it worked as thoroughly as they understood the music itself.

He was also able to do some research while on tour in America for the Newport Jazz Festival of 1972. After consultation with vibes virtuoso Gary Burton, he recommended to Hobcroft a dynamic young American, Howie Smith, who was musically and academically qualified to become Head of Jazz Studies — a position that Don, who saw himself as a performer and not a pedagogue, did not want at that time. The Department of Jazz Studies at the New South Wales Conservatorium, now the Sydney Conservatorium and part of the University of Sydney, was the first of its kind in Australia. It opened in 1973 and to make it financially viable — there was no funding from the university itself — had to take on paying customers. There was an audition process but, Don said,

> We were open to all; we had to take some one-legged Tarzans to make ends meet. The university said it couldn't be a degree course, there was no payroll for the staff and we had a mixed bag of recruits. We had to sort out at the audition those of a professional standard; we had some naturally gifted improvisers who couldn't read and vice versa, so we balanced it out. There was a good roll-up of people of all standards.

Howie Smith took charge of the students, able-bodied strongmen or not; Burrows — mission accomplished — soon went back on the road. In 1979, after Smith had returned to the US, Don was invited to become Head of Jazz Studies, a post he was still somewhat reluctant to accept. He took it, though, and mostly gave up the relentless touring, which he generally enjoyed, for the next ten years.

It was early in this second tenure that Judy Bailey, the fine New Zealand-born pianist, composer and foundation member of the Jazz Faculty Don had recruited back in 1973, invited the boss to attend one of her lectures. The class, about a dozen in number, was made up of very promising musicians. 'We had the cream of the crop,' Don remembers, 'really top young people. They had to be good or they wouldn't have gotten into one of Judy's advanced classes.' But Judy particularly wanted Don to hear James Morrison. Don paraphrased her invitation with his typical vivid use of language. 'Come and hear this kid play,' he reckons she said. 'He plays trumpet and trombone, and would play the drainpipe if you asked him.'

Burrows was punctual, as he invariably is; James was late, as he frequently was, often sleeping on the train the morning after a late-night gig and finishing up on the far side of the city. Judy's room, next door to Don's office, had a double set of green felt-lined doors for soundproofing, not easy to manipulate with armfuls of trumpets, trombones and flugelhorns. The late master Morrison pushed them heavily and lurched into the presence of Australia's foremost jazz musician. James says he was mortified. If he really was, Burrows doesn't remember, and James soon recovered.

He played only trombone on the day — no trumpet, no flugelhorn, no extreme registers — but the older man was mightily impressed. Judy had been right; the boy really had it.

> You know, when he put the trombone up to his lips and played, there was quite an exceptional response inside me. I hadn't heard anybody that good, that young, in a long time. It was quite extraordinary; it was the most mature playing from a teenager I've ever heard. He played in a home-grown style, but you'd have to say that he was punching above his weight. He had an assurance and an accuracy — no bum notes anywhere. Normally, that sort of control would come a decade later. At sixteen or seventeen, he was playing like a bloke in his late twenties.

There was an immediate rapport between the two; perhaps Burrows saw a bit of himself in the young man's precociousness and talent. Just as old pros had pushed him into the principal clarinet chair with the ABC Studio Orchestra when he was only sixteen, so Don felt constrained to take the young trumpeter under his wing and present him to the world.

They played together for a while in Bailey's teaching studio. Burrows called the tunes. Morrison knew most of the repertoire, and could hear the chord changes in tunes he didn't know, as all exceptional players can.

Eventually, Don said, 'Well, listen mate, how's your reading? Do you read well?' James asserted that he did, and told Don he'd played with Johnny Speight and the Young Northside Big Band. Burrows was almost convinced. He'd heard that band, knew their high standard and the demanding charts they played.

'Did you have to have a good look at them, or could you handle them reasonably at sight?' Don asked.

James said, 'I could play most of them at sight; I've been taught to read.'

'Righto,' said Don, just like that. 'Give me your number. If anything comes up, I'll call you. Come and do some gigs with us. It'll be good experience for you because it's never the same twice.'

James was elated. He was young, but old enough to recognise what had just transpired. He was being offered an apprenticeship with the master craftsman; indentures with the ideal. 'It was just amazing,' he said. 'Up till that point, lots of great things had happened. I'd played in lots of bands but this was where it suddenly was different — this was the real thing.' At sixteen years old, he'd been invited by a jazz legend to play with the best and most famous jazz group in the country. To Burrows, Golla, Gaston, Turnbull and John Sangster (vibraphonist and composer), Morrison was added, his brass completing a perfect line-up.

Over the next six years, Burrows took Morrison with him on innumerable gigs, tours and festivals. The maestro mentored the boy, showed him musicianship, punctuality, deportment, stagecraft, programming and even fashion sense. Back then in his student days, Don recalled, the young man

> looked like Ginger Meggs; he was the boy from Boorowa. He used to shop exclusively in those days at the St Vincent de Paul second-hand shop out at Mona Vale. He'd turn up in a bargain he'd bought: a pair of trousers that would have been the right size for Oliver Hardy, and he was about the size of a jockey.

Burrows tried to introduce James to better tailoring and Morrison introduced the maestro to some of his young jazz friends: brother John the drummer, and old schoolmate Dave Pudney on bass. Their work together as a band brought Burrows much delight. He laughed,

I was older than their fathers, older than their grandfathers, but we got on so well. Their energy level was enormous and their playing skills … man, could they play! They played with a naturalness I just loved and they were good living young guys. I knew even then they had great futures. They came from good settled families, you'd be lucky to have 'em living next door. I was happy to take those young blokes everywhere, and for the next five or six years I did.

Chapter 7

'It comes from my side, the Seller side'

In one sense, Don Burrows was right to claim young James came from a 'good, settled family'; his parents, George and Jessie, have been together for over fifty years and their offspring, John, James and Kathryn, maintain a close relationship and live in easy distance from each other. But in the 1950s and 1960s, life was anything but 'settled' due to father George's calling as a Methodist minister, which required him to move to a new appointment at the behest of the church every few years.

George's own father, James (after whom young James was named) was the son of a Scottish migrant, Andrew, who met and married Mary French and set up the family home on a farm, Granchester, near Mendooran, a little town of about 500 people situated between Dubbo and Coonabarabran in country New South Wales. Their son, James, naturally became a farmer. In due course, he met and wooed Eva Jones, the daughter of the farmer on the adjoining property. When they married, the newlyweds lived at Granchester with James' parents and continued to work the farm after the older couple retired to Mendooran itself.

When Mary died, James and Eva, with new son Ray in tow, moved into Andrew's simple one-bedroom cottage in town. Accommodation there was strained to the limit, especially with the arrival of two more sons, Fred and George. George to this day can't fathom where they all slept, though he remembers clearly that he and his brothers had bedrooms on the verandah, with mere roll-down canvas blinds to keep out the heat by day and protect a young man's modesty by night.

Church was a large part of country life and the family life of the Morrisons of Mendooran. Their denomination, the Methodists, had services only once a month, but regular visits from the Presbyterians and their minister from Coonabarabran meant there were frequent united congregations and joint Sunday schools. Since Mother was the Sunday school superintendent, young George and his brothers attended everything. It obviously had an impact. George left school and served an apprenticeship in the RAAF, but within a few years, like his older brother Fred before him, felt a calling to the ministry. He was appointed as a probationer to Mona Vale Methodists, where he first set eyes on Jessie Williams, a vivacious newcomer to the church. They commenced a courtship as George served his probationary period and, as soon as he completed the obligatory three-year course at Leigh Theological College at Enfield, they were married.

Unlike the Morrisons, Jessie's family, the Williams, were not lifelong pillars of their local church community. But, curiously, it's their family tree that has a distinguished but ill-fated evangelist lodged in its branches. One of her forefathers, Reverend John Williams — 'I don't know how many "greats" back he is,' Jessie said — has been dubbed 'The Apostle of Polynesia'. The Reverend John was born in London in 1796, and in his very early twenties was sent by the London Missionary Society to the Society Islands in the South Pacific. His initial posting was to Raiatea; his missionary family was the first to visit Samoa and he was the discoverer of the beautiful tropical island of Rarotonga. John later translated the New Testament into the language of the native people.

He became famous in England for his exploits and his anthropological insights through his book *Narrative of Missionary Enterprises in the South Sea Islands* (1837), and throughout Polynesia for his humanity and Christian fervour. There was one tragic exception to his renown. He was unknown in the New Hebrides, and during a missionary visit to the island of Erromango he and his fellow missionary, James Harris, were set upon and eaten by cannibals. There are memorial stones to John Williams in both Rarotonga and London's Abney Cemetery, and his name is revered in Congregationalist church circles.

Two hundred years later, however, perhaps as a consequence of the apparent ingratitude visited upon their faithful forebear, the Australian Williamses were no longer churchgoers. Jessie's father Jack was in a successful boatshed partnership in Bayview, Sydney, and the family was more likely to spend the Sabbath mucking about in boats than making a joyful noise in church. Jack Williams, the boat engineer, married singer and dancer Doris Seller, and this is where the Morrison musical talent makes its entrance.

Doris and her siblings were all performers; they sang, they danced, they played instruments. Doris played the violin and piano and ran a dance school with her sister 'for many, many years'. Jessie, daughter of Jack and Doris, says, 'When people ask me, "Where does James' talent come from?" I say, "From my mother, Doris; from the Seller side."'

Jessie, named after her aunt Jess, inherited the gene first. She studied serious piano at the Conservatorium to the higher grades, and was able to pick up the saxophone when in her forties and play in the church Big Band. 'The Reverend Gough wanted some saxophones, and a friend and I volunteered. I'm not very good,' she claimed modestly, 'I'm a pianist, really.' And, like her mother, a dancer. She and her three sisters started classical ballet 'as soon as we could walk'. They learned tap, jazz and Scottish dancing. One of Jessie's sisters taught ballet and Highland, and Jessie herself taught 'the tap and the jazz' at Doris Porter School of Dancing, the largest dance academy north of the Harbour Bridge.

Jessie's father, Jack, would have been more than a little surprised when his light-footed and musical fourteen-year-old daughter, up to then completely unchurched, announced that she had 'met someone, a girlfriend, who was in church' and that she didn't want to go on the boats on Sundays anymore. To his credit, Jessie remembers, 'My dad said, "Okay, if that's what you want, that's fine," and I've built the rest of my life around the church.'

Call it what you like — God's plan, coincidence, serendipity — but as Jessie took up a place in the pews, the young new probationary pastor mounted the pulpit. The couple married in December 1958 and set off for George's first appointment after theological college as assistant minister at the Taree Methodist Church. The posting lasted two years, during the second of which their first son, John Andrew, was born.

John and his younger brother James caused their parents endless anxiety with their apparent fearlessness and sense of adventure, verging on the foolhardy and downright dangerous. John showed this propensity early. One morning he threw himself headfirst from his bassinet onto the dining room floor. He was concussed a little, but not deterred. He persisted in banging his head against the wall anytime he couldn't get his own way. It was harrowing for the young married couple, but only a foretaste of many hair-raising escapades to come in the Morrison family.

Not many of them were destined to happen in Taree, though. Following ordination late in 1960, a letter from the Methodist Church Conference Stationing Committee arrived in the mail. It carried the news that George had been appointed as minister in charge of the church at Boorowa. The young pastor was thrilled, even if he had to get a map of New South Wales to find out where on earth Boorowa was.

Chapter 8

From Boorowa to Bayview

Along the 500-mile tarmac ribbon that stretches from Sydney to Melbourne, nowadays there are more McDonald's outlets than towns. One of the most popular is near Yass, about 300 miles south-west of the harbour city. It provides what people want: fast food, fast travel — fill up, move on. There's no time to drive the extra five miles on one side of the road to Yass itself, or to meander fifty miles along the Lachlan Valley Way towards Boorowa and Cowra on the other. The latter route travels through the agricultural country on the edge of the fertile Southern Tablelands and passes, as it enters Boorowa, a sanctuary for the iridescent-green Superb Parrot, which thrives in the wattle trees, old red gums and nearby grasslands.

The township's main street is a step back into the past, with impressive and stately buildings on both sides, and a red 'Lego-brick' war memorial at the end. It has a handsome and cared-for courthouse built to deal with the ex-convicts and bushrangers who once infested the area, dignified Victorian mansions with lacework verandahs, and an old dynamite storehouse robbed by the bushranger Ben Hall in 1863. The area was settled by squatters and Irish convicts. The influence of the latter can be felt in the annual October Irish Woolfest.

Wool and wheat were the foundation stones the area was built on, the guidebooks say. It seems the Methodist Stationing Committee knew its man. Boorowa suited the new young Methodist minister brought up in Mendooran. He could talk the language of the locals. 'I'd had relatives that owned farms around there,' George Morrison said. 'I knew all about wheat and sheep.'

St Patrick's Catholic Church in Boorowa is a splendid little miniature of a city church, complete with stained glass windows. The Wesleyan church, built for the 'chapel brethren' among the late nineteenth-century migrants, is much less prepossessing — a small rectangular building with a porch and corrugated roofing — but is very significant in the lives of the Morrisons.

Don Burrows first called James the 'Boy from Boorowa'. In some ways, he could as easily have been described as the 'Boy from Blayney' or even the 'Boy from Orange', though the latter lacks the glib alliteration. But George insisted the 'Boy from Boorowa' was more appropriate, even though James spent parts of his childhood in those other places as his father's appointments changed: 'It was the fact of us going to our first appointment together, the first where I was in charge of a circuit. When we were there, the church was very alive. It was a real learning experience for me and I gained a lot. We stayed there for five very happy years.'

During that time, James was born. The event happened on Sunday night, 11 November 1962. George dropped Jessie off at the hospital and drove on to conduct evening service at the church. It was a different era then; fathers were persona non grata in birthing rooms. They were sent away to pace floors or smoke nervously in waiting rooms or, in George's case, to lead hymns and preach sermons.

He was, in fact, halfway through the homily that night when the news came through that 'James Lloyd' Morrison had made his first ever prestissimo entry. Like his brother before him, James inherited one Christian name from each of his grandfathers. George remembers a vociferous child; Jessie thinks of him as a little restive. Whereas John quickly mastered the ability to sleep through services and noisy situations, James 'didn't seem to have the same understanding, or consideration for, his parents' needs. He may have been exercising his lungs in preparation for his future, but he kept us aware of the presence,' George said. 'Perhaps he was getting his own back for the early disturbances he suffered before his birth.' His mother, the minister's busy and energetic wife, had continued to dance and pedal the ancient church organ for services throughout her pregnancy. James had received his first music and performance lessons in utero!

James often recalls that his earliest memories are sitting with John on the organ stool, one either side of Jessie, to keep the pair relatively quiet and under control during Dad's sermons. This subdued hour in church was just a brief respite from the welter of worry the growing boys inflicted on their parents in Boorowa and the later appointments in Blayney and Orange.

There was, for example, the Disprin overdose episode — the Morrisons still haven't worked out how young John got up to the 'safe' shelf and unselfishly shared the tablets with his little brother. The country doctor said, 'Let 'em sleep it off!'

There was the pedal car incident when the boys were supposedly taking turns pushing each other. When James realised he was doing more pushing than riding, he shoved the car and its contents off the end of the verandah, breaking John's arm.

Neither of these, alarming as they were, matched John's first lunar landing attempt. Aided by his assistant, James Lloyd, he built a space capsule from wooden crates and boxes, then packed the 'fuel tank' with enough large skyrockets to blow the astronaut into the stratosphere. Fortunately, the deathtrap failed to ignite. John was unconcerned when father pointed out the dangers. He'd felt quite secure, as he'd been wearing a plastic bag over his head as a safety helmet.

John was generally the ringleader, George recalls, in those preschool and primary school days. James was much more timid and tended to cling to the maternal apron strings.

Nevertheless, George's recorded recollections of those times, in a piece he wrote called *Being a Father*, are replete with numerous resigned and long-suffering references to his own 'anxiety', 'worry' and 'emotional distress'. The Morrisons found raising their two 'adventurous boys' to be a 'constant challenge', and this was long before the family moved back from New South Wales country towns to Sydney and the perils of Pittwater, a whole new sea world for the boys to adventure in.

Chapter 9

Playtime in Paradise

For James, the road to 'Paradise', his name for Pittwater, was via Blayney and Orange, two more postings for his reverend father. Blayney, another farming community and slightly larger than Boorowa, was where his sister Kathyrn was born, and where James encountered school for the first time. He didn't like it then, and never learned to. Despite the many escapades John coaxed him into, James' lack of confidence was a real concern for his parents. 'When I left him to go to school,' Jessie said, 'it was trauma, trauma, trauma. He cried nearly every day, till eventually we took him for psychological tests.'

The experts said, 'There's nothing wrong with him at all; this child can do anything he wants to in life.' They told the worried mother that his IQ was very high. 'I can't remember exactly what it was — it was off the board.' (James later found out that it was a formidable 152. He doesn't set much store by it: 'They don't measure creativity,' he told a reporter.)

The doctors advised Jessie to 'find something he wants to do, and the world will be his oyster.' They were right. 'Once he found music, that was it,' George added. 'He lost all that was bottled up in him when he was little. It just dissipated overnight.'

The family had to wait a further two years, the duration of the posting to Orange, before the family returned to Sydney and James 'found music' — and boats — and the confidence to take on the world.

By April 1970, when Jack Williams died, the Morrisons had already moved back to Bayview to support Jessie's mother Doris. They stayed longer than they expected and George, though he never resigned his commission, became a minister 'without pastoral charge' for the next twenty years. He worked for the ABC, eventually becoming a technical producer. Jessie was able to resume primary teaching by day and dance instruction at night at her sister's School of Dancing. James and John had fallen in love with Bayview long before on the frequent family holidays with Nan and Pop. It's tucked into a southern corner of Pittwater, a bay fifty minutes drive north of the Sydney CBD, a skeletal finger of a peninsula on its east side and the huge Ku-ring-gai Chase National Park to the west. Its beaches, rugged headland, sandstone sea cliffs and sheltered water formed a perfect playground for George's 'extremely adventurous boys'.

John reminisced one day about his idyllic childhood, as he looked out over the water he'd crossed in a tinnie just a few minutes before from his houseboat moored in the middle. His sea-soaked shorts clung to his legs; it didn't bother him at all.

John said,

> It's interesting looking over Pittwater now. There wasn't a time it was just music, and there wasn't a time it was just boats and planes. It all runs together — we'd have Christmas with Nan over the other side, just the two weeks, that was enough for her — but I remember it vividly. I remember the first time I lowered a line and watched a fish swim up to it. I was completely knocked out. They got me a fishing rod, and I'd get up at dawn every day of the holidays. They'd have to drag me back to the country kicking and screaming. This was where we first got into a boat. We couldn't even swim; I couldn't swim, James couldn't swim. We just learned by falling in the water enough times and not drowning. We never developed any real boating skills in a trained or formal way either. We just learned to survive being in the water.

The boys took to boating as naturally as they took to music; it was in their genes. Grandfather Williams had built boats right there on

Pittwater, and mother Jessie still loves to be on the water. They were never discouraged from sailing, though their madcap adventures and no-fear attitudes caused their parents untold consternation.

'One night they sailed up Pittwater and landed on Lion Island, which is Crown property,' said Jessie. 'You can't do that; it's illegal.'

'And what about the time James and another friend — it wasn't John, he may have been off preparing a spaceship for a mission to Mars — built a raft,' said George. 'The Water Police picked him up when he started to sink in the middle of Pittwater. They brought him home and ticked us off for letting him go out there.'

'Oh,' said Jessie, 'the police were always knocking on the door, saying, "We've got your kids again!" It was awful.'

One favourite family story involves the time the boys decided it made sense to combine their love of boats and music by sailing to a gig with Don Burrows and the Sydney Con Big Band at The Entrance, a seaside town on the New South Wales Central Coast, only two hours drive by road from Sydney. The Morrison boys — drummer and trumpeter/trombonist — arranged for their gear to go on the band bus and prepared their craft, a thirteen-foot Tasman Tiger dinghy, for an overnight trip out of sheltered Pittwater, through the treacherous Sydney Heads and up the coast to The Entrance.

'Prepared' is probably too charitable a word. They took, according to John, a bar compass, a torch, a bucket of KFC and the street directory. 'I didn't know what a chart was in those early days,' he said. 'I remember the first time I saw one. I thought, *It's got depths on it, and markers and navigation! We need never run aground again!*'

Jessie was worried enough about the venture to ring her brother-in-law, Uncle Henry, the family's blue water sailor. She still remembers his anger.

'You can't sail to The Entrance — there's no "entrance" there,' he said. 'It's just a sand spit. What have they sailed in?'

'Don't know,' said Jessie, 'but the Tiger's gone.'

'Don't worry then,' said Uncle Henry, obviously relieved, 'they'll still be in Pittwater somewhere. Nobody'd be silly enough to sail a two-man dinghy outside the Heads at night to go to The Entrance.'

But Uncle Henry overestimated the prudence of his nephews and underestimated their foolhardiness, overconfidence and sailing ability. They beached at dawn and, soon after, John rang his mum triumphantly. 'We've arrived,' he cried. She listened to him in some relief and asked to speak to James, too.

'He can't talk yet,' said big brother, 'he'll be able to talk soon.'

'I assumed he was exhausted,' said Jessie, 'but at least they had sense enough to ring and tell us they were alive and well.' Well enough for a gig, no doubt, but totally drenched from a night on the water. Their gig gear was on the bus, so they rang Don.

'Can you send our clothes down to the beach?'

'It's pretty informal,' said Don, 'come as you are.'

'No, we need our clothes, Don, because …'

'I don't want to know,' said the immaculate and thoroughly organised Mr Burrows. 'I'll send them down.'

'Turned out to be a good gig,' said John, 'not as much fun as the trip up, though!'

One boating adventure followed another, and the boys became so comfortable on the water. When Australia won the America's Cup yacht race in 1983, the boys celebrated by jamming on their own boat in the middle of Sydney Harbour. On board or onstage, they were equally at home. Like John said, 'There was never a time it was just boats and planes, or just music.' The two streams ran in parallel, sometimes overlapping, throughout their childhood and adolescence.

After leaving high school, John, whose dislike of formal education matched his younger brother's, took the 'Boy's Own Paper' career path — boats and planes — and studied for a commercial pilot's license. 'I never thought I'd be a muso,' he said. 'I was keen on flying and was going to be a pilot. I work in bands professionally to keep me flying. It's never been my ambition to be an international drummer.'

James, on the other hand, took the other stream for a profession; he had to be a musician. 'It's not something you do,' he's said, 'it's something you are.' And since that's what he was, he played all over town while completing his Associate Diploma of Jazz Studies at the Conservatorium. Michael Foster from the *Canberra Times* reported that James' progression through the Sydney Con 'crackled and popped but never snapped under the pressures which it and his pursuit of everything enjoyable imposed on it.' It's nicely put, and captures the energy with which the reluctant high school student attacked his college work and extracurricular activities in the clubs around the Sydney area. Sometimes, he reduced the travel time between the two by sleeping in his beat-up purple 1972 Valiant outside the campus grounds after a gig.

With his mate Dave Pudney from church and brother John, his trio played the best RSL clubs, the yacht club and the golf club. Originally it was Dave's band, but there was, James said, a

> shift of ownership. I didn't take over his band — I started a new group and invited him to be in it on bass, which he learned to play for church, instead of keyboard. Later, I got a guitarist in to give it some chordal structure, and it freed me up to wander over to play piano a bit just as I do now.

He was playing the alto saxophone 'a bit' by then, too. He claims it took him less than a week to learn it — there's no reason to doubt it, given his multi-instrumental gifts.

'I got it on Wednesday and could play it by Saturday night. You already know how to breathe, you know how to tongue, you know how to phrase. Really, all you've got to learn is where to put your fingers. It's not very hard — all the keys are in a straight line.' He explains it simply and matter-of-factly, as if anyone could play to a professional standard in three days, ignoring the difficulties of forming an embouchure completely alien to a brass player — inside the mouth instead of on the lips — an often uncooperative reed and a two-handed fingering system. 'I knew how it should sound; that's the main thing.'

Like his trumpet, trombone, tuba, euphonium and piano playing, it must have sounded alright, because after a Northside rehearsal he was invited by Dave Martin, who was scouting for new talent, to play regularly with him at one of Sydney's leading jazz clubs, the Paradise Jazz Cellar, nestled right in the heart of the bustling Kings Cross area. The Paradise Club was originally owned by Abe Saffron, an unsavoury character whose invariable press tag 'the colourful Sydney identity' covered a multitude of sins. The club manager one day phoned ubiquitous Horst Liepolt, who popped up like a fairy godmother in Morrison's developing years, and told him of the venue's change of character.

'When do we start?' Peter Boothman, in his online *Story of Jazz in Sydney* quoted Horst as saying.

'Today!' said the manager. Horst said he laughed and replied, 'Okay,' then sat down and made a program for the next few weeks. Horst says, 'Believe it or not, inside a couple of hours Sydney had a new seven-days-a-week jazz club — fully licensed, newly decorated. Very fancy!'

The club, through the well-informed and well-connected Horst, hired the best performers from Australia and overseas. The local contingent included the Dave Martin Quintet, made up of three established jazz stars — Alan Turnbull on drums, Darcy Wright on bass and Martin himself on piano — and two prodigiously talented new recruits: Dale Barlow on reeds and Morrison on brass.

It was, as Barlow put it, 'an astonishingly good rhythm section; you couldn't get a better one.' Wright was once voted, by *Rolling Stone* magazine no less, one of the top ten upright bassists in the world. Turnbull had few peers on percussion anywhere in Australia. Dave

Martin, after cutting his keyboard teeth in Melbourne, took time out to become an aeronautical engineer, go overseas to help design the Concorde and the Lockheed C5A, before returning to Sydney and forming the band, which also featured his singing wife, Norma.

Barlow said:

> Martin was an incredible guy. He was head of Qantas for a long time. I don't think he practised for the last thirty or forty years, but he loved the music and introduced us to Horace Silver, Art Blakey, and all the great quintets. We played fast, sizzling tempos that Dave could barely keep up with, but he allowed us to play them wickedly fast because we could! Turnbull could handle them great, Darcy was unbelievably good, and me and James were just hot to go. We were young guns tearing up every night. James would bring his trumpet and his trombone; I'd double on flute. Dave was a great bandleader, organiser and documenter of the music. He would get the arrangements together; they'd be absolutely perfect and beautifully written. Those Monday night gigs were crucial to James and I at that developmental stage. We were allowed to exercise our free will, in terms of our choice of instruments. James was playing trumpet, trombone, euphonium, all the different horns — he played them all great. He'd grab one of them and solo, just off-the-cuff, whichever tune, whichever key. It would always work.

Musically, the Paradise Jazz Cellar was a great place to be, with jazz artists of the stature of Freddie Hubbard, Sonny Stitt, Mal Waldron and Art Pepper dropping in. Socially, the environment around Kings Cross — a magnet for criminals and addicts, girls on the game and blokes on the make — was far from ideal for a relatively unworldly teenager. Paul Pax Andrews, a saxophone player who had been on the Northside Big Band trip to Monterey with James in 1979, was active on both sides of the club curtain. He remembers standing next to Pepper onstage:

> Art Pepper, the sublime and, still for me, timeless genius. The room was packed and we had him for ourselves for two sets. It was really something. James and I did the first set but I just wanted to get off and listen to Art. We played 'Groovin' High', 'Cool Blues', 'Tunisia', and James, who was seventeen, was screaming on trombone.

Andrews recalls vividly in his book *Without a Song* — which recounts his remarkable journey through jazz, heroin addiction and rehabilitation to redemption through Buddhism — that he witnessed and was involved in activities altogether more nefarious backstage between sets.

> The Paradise was madness at times but we loved it, a unique freedom to express our creativity amongst very talented friends and play to passionate audiences who wanted to be involved. James and Tom Baker would cook between sets, pizza mostly, or ham and beans, meanwhile drugs and money deals and other shit are all goin' down. Girls doin' deals with guys in booths and I saw Terry, one of the bosses who often had a minder next to him and a gun in his brown leather pouch on the table, take a worried looking fellow into the kitchen for some kind of persuasive therapy! I saw a bass case full of hash one night, in the back room where the beer was stored.

James saw it all too, but remained immune to the temptations. One night, Andrews relates,

> a mate and I are leaning over the kitchen sink at the Club between sets — a lot of business went down in the kitchen. We had our arms around each other, vomiting after our shot. James came in, saw the scenario and quipped, 'We're on, guys!' then walked casually out. We did the gig, playing like men repossessed!

George and Jessie Morrison, God-fearing parents in conservative Pittwater, were, unsurprisingly, concerned about it at first. 'We were worried when the boys, James and John, got into the music scene; the drink, the drugs and all that. They might have tried it, but found that they couldn't do it and be professional.'

James had done it; in fact, he'd overdone it, drunk too much through his own inexperience during a gig and finished up vomiting and making a fool of himself. It may have been aversion therapy; Morrison has remained virtually teetotal ever since. 'A counter,' as drummer friend, Len Barnard, put it, 'to those of us older musicians who have grown old disgracefully.'

'We used to get the criticism when we were bringing up our kids that we let them go too much,' says Jessie. 'We didn't put any restraints on them. We let both James and John play in nightclubs when they were well underage. Then we'd wait outside in the car, holding our breath.'

George added:

> But it was only the music they were interested in. They weren't attracted to the other stuff. We had confidence in the people they were involved with early on, too: Dave Martin up at the Paradise, and later Don Burrows. Dave kept an eye on them around the Cross. The boys used to tell us what went on there. They were aware, but never involved. Sometimes, they'd come home at two in the morning and need to talk about something. We'd get up and listen.

The laissez-faire child-raising method worked for the Morrisons. They can point proudly to three children who became well-adjusted, confident, accomplished people. Younger sister Kathyrn is also a talented jazz musician, who was previously a dancer in the Sydney professional theatre.

'We let our children go,' repeated Jessie. 'If they had their dreams and it wasn't going to kill them, we let them do it.'

If those dreams took them to the clubs and bars in some of Sydney's more unsavoury settings sometimes, well, so be it. They trusted the upbringing and values they'd taught them and believed in their capacity to keep out of trouble. Both boys were still involved at the Kerugma Church at this stage anyway. James had virtually inherited the music director's mantle there, and remained in the role until the demands of touring and interstate gigs made it impossible.

Morrison's appearances at the Paradise Jazz Cellar grew more frequent. He took the opportunity to introduce his own groups, to the extent that at one stage in August 1981 he was doing no less than five gigs a week over four nights. He played with the Dave Martin Quintet on Monday nights, the Morrison-Pudney Duo on Fridays and Saturdays (9pm to 11pm) and his eponymous Quintet on Wednesdays (11pm to 2am), and Fridays again, this time for four hours (11pm to 3am) following the duo set. To form a quintet, Morrison and Pudney were joined onstage by brother John on drums, with Paul Andrews on alto and vocals, and Steve Brien on guitar. Steve was another of James' bandleaders who later became a sideman. Three years previously, Steve had run The Black Slacks Band using the fourteen-year-old Morrison as his frontman. That group's membership included the O'Doherty brothers: Chris on bass and Peter, who played some elegant Wes Montgomery-style guitar. Their musical careers kicked off noticeably when in 1976, with some friends from art school, they formed Mental as Anything. They switched instruments; Chris became 'Reg Mombassa' and The Mentals became one of Australia's favourite and enduring New Wave rock bands.

Tim Rollinson, the sax player who later shared a billet with Morrison at the Ross Rosses' in Monterey, recalls being impressed by this early Morrison incarnation at a university gig. 'He was more mellow back then; he never played a bum note and knew all the changes. His style was always right; he never played anything inappropriate.' It was a very similar summation to that of Don Burrows after his first encounter with James at the Con. Tim Rollinson may well have heard James on a mellow night with his 'black slacked mental as anything' mates, but in June 1981 Eric Myers in the *Sydney Morning Herald* was talking about 'fiery swing, heat and vitality'. He wrote:

> As if to introduce the view that some schools of modern jazz have reached creative dead ends a new generation of young musicians in Sydney is taking jazz back to fundamental principles.
>
> In the forefront of this movement is the James Morrison Quintet at the Paradise Jazz Cellar. They are playing a rare brand of fiery, honest and committed jazz — the kind of music which reminds the listener not so much of what jazz is today, but what it once was before it became troubled and introspective ... James Morrison, like the bebop veteran Dizzy Gillespie, uses a trumpet with the bell bent upwards. This would be a pretentious gesture were it not for the fact that Morrison's fiery trumpet style has many of the hallmarks of a true Gillespie disciple: heat, vitality, brilliant technique and beautiful jazz ideas.
>
> Morrison is not only an extraordinary brass multi-instrumentalist but an excellent pianist as well. In terms of natural ability, he is one of the outstanding figures to have emerged in Australian jazz in recent years.
>
> Expressing an unfettered joy in the music, Morrison's Quintet puts on a jazz show for the people with little of the traditional concerns for what is considered 'hip'. What other band could play 'Caravan' with a straight face?
>
> It appears certain that James Morrison will become something of a jazz star. Lovers of good music are advised to turn out and listen to this young man and his quintet before people are queuing for the pleasure.

Chapter 10

The Prof and the Protégé

While all this nocturnal activity was going on, at the Paradise and in other venues around town, James was spending his days as a student at the Conservatorium. Sheila Tracy, writing for the British Trombone Society, reported in 2002 that 'when he was thirteen years of age, Morrison entered the New South Wales Conservatorium of Music'. This, while being literally true, implies he started a tertiary course extremely early. Morrison at least waited till he was sixteen, but three years before that he had been pedalling his bike twice a week from Pittwater High with the bass trombone strapped to his back to 'enter the Con' and play in the faculty big band after school. The road trip took about an hour and a half, and was the sort of physical activity his secondary school physical education teacher could never get him involved in during his secondary school years. But for music, anything was possible.

As always, his performance was notable. The visiting British virtuoso, Don Lusher, holding a master class once, was so impressed by the boy bass trombonist that he recalls asking him if he'd like to play lead.

Later, as a bona fide student at the Con, getting to class first thing in the morning was not his strong point. He'd catch a bus to Wynyard and then the train, just one stop, to Circular Quay. In that five-minute trip, though, he'd often fall asleep, overshoot the stop and finish up way out at Emu Plains. Sometimes, he tried to overcome the problem by sleeping in the Valiant after gigs rather than go home. 'When a gig finished at 4am, a nine o'clock start was always going to be tricky,' he explained. Once he did make it through the front door, his academic progress was pretty satisfactory for a bloke who'd worked around, rather than through, high school.

Mostly it was a practical course, and the emphasis on performance suited James. The intention of Howie Smith, the first Head of Jazz Studies, had been, according to Peter Boothman,

> to set up a course where people had to do things rather than study them and present their results at a sufficient level to pass an exam. The improvisation class learned to play music, not scales; students in arranging classes had their pieces performed, not just graded. Ensembles played a variety of styles, not just Basie or Kenton.

Like Sydney pianist Bob Egger, who said, 'You know, it's cementing in place all the things that we thought we knew,' James shored up his self-taught skills in arranging and improvising, underpinning his natural aptitude with a thorough theoretical basis and understanding.

At the end of 1980, just as he turned eighteen, the age at which most students were enrolling in university, James graduated from the Sydney Conservatorium with an Associate Diploma of Jazz Studies. More surprisingly, particularly to his old high school counsellor presumably, and for such a young man, he was invited to return to the Con to work part-time as a lecturer in improvisation the following year. 'In those days, you got a job if the Head of Department wanted to employ you. Don put me up for the job and the Con employed me. There's no way you'd get a job now at any New South Wales university without a degree and teacher training.'

Morrison, university lecturer, was younger than every one of his students. Some were twenty-five, some even more 'mature age'. It didn't faze him one bit. He'd always worked with older people, run school bands for older students, and employed men several years his senior in his pro bands. 'I was used to running things and being in control. It was just another one of those.'

Neither was he aware of any resentment to his youthfulness — probably because his students, irrespective of age, quickly realised he knew his stuff and, playing-wise, could certainly 'do the thing'. He took the job seriously enough to buy a suit. Don was delighted. 'Now you look like what you are: a professional,' he said. It may have gone to James' head; for a while he grew a beard and affected a pipe. He smoked it rarely — didn't enjoy it — but liked the idea of a pipe. Perhaps he felt it gave him a little gravitas, to carry it around like an Oxford don. Early morning starts were still a problem, which was not surprising considering his heavy Paradise Jazz Cellar schedule, but at least now he could timetable his classes for later in the day: 'Nothing before two, if I could help it!'

James spent six years as a part-time lecturer, working alongside his mentor Don Burrows by day and, after farewelling the Paradise Club, in his quintet by night. It is difficult to overestimate Burrows' professional standing at that time and his influence on James. As James put it, 'He wasn't just a musician — he was Australian jazz.' The Burrows quintet toured the country, playing outback towns and remote Indigenous communities, as well as capital cities. They played every style, from trad to modern, with a fair dollop of Burrows' beloved Latin rhythms in the mix.

Don can list over forty albums, including *Just the Beginning*, which scored the first gold award in Australia for a jazz recording. He has been inducted into the Australian Jazz Bell Awards' Graeme Bell Hall of Fame and twice been named a 'living treasure.' His citation for an honorary doctorate at the University of Sydney makes particular mention of his professionalism, warmth and energy, all qualities which young Morrison emulated to the enhancement of his own performances. It was an unlikely partnership in some ways: the old veteran professional who'd conquered the world and the young man barely known outside the Sydney jazz scene. The generation gap was a chasm; the year Morrison had turned ten, Burrows was being awarded the MBE for his services to music.

'Maybe I was born too late, or he was born too early,' Morrison has said, 'but we seem to have come from the same era.' Burrows agreed. 'It's quite remarkable; such a wide gap in our ages, but we have an uncanny musical empathy.'

Greg Wilesmith, in *The National Times*, wrote:

> Watching them play, the empathy is obvious. Burrows is short, chunky, knees bent in a skier's crouch, back rigid at forty-five degrees, forearms rippling, eyes closed, blowing up a storm. The face has the character lines and bags and crags earned from forty years of playing jazz and loving it. Morrison, taller, more upright and angular, blows his trumpet with a confidence and style far ahead of his years, his blond hair flopping around a chubby face framed with a sketchy beard.

The differences were visual and superficial; the similarities were aural and deep-seated and lay in their approach to music and their onstage personalities. They could both, on a variety of instruments (Burrows has mastered a whole range of woodwinds), play fluent, prolific and melodic improvisations, often of old favourite standards, easily understood by the average audience member.

They both loved to perform and to involve the audience in the performance. James has said:

> We both like to have a good time when we're up there. It takes more than simply being a good player. There are a lot of good players who don't make a living playing jazz. You have to be able to communicate with an audience and that's why Don is so successful. It's not that he doesn't play well; he plays great, but there are people who play as well as Don who aren't anywhere

near his position. It's purely because they can't entertain and communicate with an audience while they're playing their jazz.

Morrison drank it all in. Apart from learning about music itself, he discovered how to work with people and how to run a band. He learned sometimes merely by observing Burrows — watching how he conducted himself and how he communicated with an audience. He even learned how to handle a 'jevver' — the bane of a performer's life — a fan who stands in line after a gig to greet the artist. They start a sentence by saying, 'Jevver remember when …' or 'Jevver go to …' as a lead in to a long, boring story all about themselves, choosing to ignore the twenty others lined up behind them, waiting to briefly shake hands or claim an autograph. James and Don developed a shorthand to warn each other in time to take evasive action: 'Jevver at three o'clock,' and 'Jevver approaching on the left.'

James was a great pupil in most aspects of the profession. Only his punctuality and his dress sense occasionally let him down. Don worked on the former and on one occasion, after a late arrival, called James aside. 'The chart doesn't play itself; it doesn't matter if you're the best musician in the world, you don't sound very good when you're not there!'

Of his playing, by February 1983, Eric Myers could write that hearing Don and James 'side-by-side, it is difficult to decide who is the more impressive player.' The first Morrison/Burrows outings were with Don's Australian Jazz Quartet, though its performances by the early 1980s had become quite infrequent. Don was working and touring primarily as a duo with George Golla. When the gig budget permitted, he would add a bass player, then a drummer and perhaps another horn player. 'You would go with what the moment was offering. When you select people to take on tour, it depends on what the gig requires. Is it semi-classical or trad or bebop?'

Sometimes Don's band was just himself and the James Morrison trio — James, John and Dave Pudney. Don, something of a father figure to the three lads, delighted in their energy, enthusiasm and ability. They got on well as musicians and people. None of them were 'tempted by the grog', as Don put it. 'They were real; it was like discovering gold.'

If Don was blessed to unearth some unpolished nuggets, in return, James' position as a protégé of Don brought him a musical recognition and the public recognisability around Australia that might otherwise have taken years to achieve. The two men crisscrossed each other's bands and engagements: Burrows introduced Morrison on his popular ABC TV series; The Morrison Brothers Big Bad Band, formed in 1983, invited Don to be its guest artist; James appeared at Don's eponymous supper clubs; and Don hired the trio as his backing group on numerous tours.

James played on several Don Burrows records in the eighties, including *A Night in Tunisia* and *Jazz at the Opera House*, a spin-off from the TV series *The Don Burrows Collection*, which ran for six seasons. Early in 1984, Morrison was the 'featured soloist' on the *Burrows at the Winery* album, the 'odd couple' fronting a typical Burrows rhythm section of Golla, Turnbull, Craig Scott on acoustic bass and Tony Ansell on keyboards. 'Burrows,' reviewer Michael Foster said, 'plays with the controlled power, the constraint, of a fabled old bull, proceeding at his own pace to the pastures, determined to enjoy all it offers. And in the determination he offers yet again an exposition of his own fabled skills for his audience.' Morrison is 'bursting with talent and energy. He doesn't take any prisoners when he plays, he just goes straight ahead.' When Burrows 'subtly changes the direction' Morrison comes back 'a little less arrogant, caught up in what he has just heard, playing just as hard, but with skills which make his offering nicely understated. He thus invites Ansell in, flowing, almost rippling back with another imaginative directional change and so to a wailing, soaring all-in climax to the tune and to the album.'

The review captures some of the musical qualities Morrison was learning from the elder statesman: the value of light and shade, the importance of the lull before the storm, the balance between technique and tenderness. He was an apt pupil, and only three years later *The Canberra Times*, often quite generous in its admiration for James, made a significant announcement:

Burrows Upstaged by Ex-pupil

A 22-year-old Sydney musician has taken out New South Wales' top award for jazz players — and has beaten his former tutor, Don Burrows.

James Morrison, of Bayview, was named on Sunday as Jazz Musician of the Year at a presentation in the Regent Hotel, during the opening of NSW Music Week.

Morrison, who has mastered eight instruments, including piano, tuba, trumpet and trombone, was the youngest lecturer to be appointed to the NSW Conservatorium.

Burrows received the award for the most outstanding reed instrumentalist.

Chapter 11

The Michelin Man in Asia!

The newspaper headline, announcing Morrison's award as Jazz Musician of the Year in 1986, infers some sort of competition between Morrison and Burrows — Morrison had apparently 'beaten' or, as another report put it, 'eclipsed' Burrows. Morrison would have been the last to claim either, but he, often spoken of as the heir apparent to Burrows' mantle, was now undoubtedly the equal in jazz standing of the older man. There was, and is, no animosity and no envy. Their skills complement each other, and Morrison acknowledges the debt he owes the old friend with whom he still takes summer holidays. In the first five years of the eighties they did so much together — playing concerts, touring, recording and TV appearances — that it was inevitable that James' first overseas trip since Monterey in 1979 would be at Don's invitation.

One day, Don got a phone call from Geoff Brash, the owner of Brashs Music in Melbourne. Geoff had positioned his family company at the forefront of the Australian retail music industry, stocking musical instruments, in particular keyboards, as well as sound equipment and sheet music. He was a pioneer of multi-country trade and marketing, and cultivated contacts and brokered deals with and between China and Japan. In 1976, he entered into a joint venture with Taro Kakehashi, the founder and chairman of the Roland Corporation of Japan, which was developing electronic keyboards and synthesisers. The two became firm friends and trusted business partners, who brought the now-famous Roland brand to Australia.

Geoff records that 'dealings with China, too, became a major part of my life.' He helped develop the main piano factory in Peking, as it was then, and sold innumerable instruments under the 'Lisner' label. Taro Kakehashi thought that was a cute name; 'Every musician wants a good Lisner,' he said. The brand, initially because of its low prices, was popular among hard-up beginners and disadvantaged schools for a time, until teachers began to advise against them for their poor quality and finish.

In 1982, Geoff was about to undertake one of his frequent trips to the Chinese capital to check out his instrument makers and, perhaps more importantly, introduce jazz for the first time since it was outlawed during the Cultural Revolution. Geoff, a lifelong jazz lover who made a lot of money from selling rock'n'roll music and instruments, rang Don Burrows, a jazzman he'd gotten to know as a friend.

> Geoff wanted me to go to Beijing to look over some instrument factories and play some concerts. We'd spend our time in factories, different factories making different instruments, and mingle with interpreters and staff, right from the bloke making little screws to the tester at the end of the line. I'd have to check out the finished product. 'Oh, yeah,' I said, 'I'd love that but look, I can't try trumpets, I can't try trombones; I'll need to take someone with me who is very, very good on anything brass.' I told them about James. 'He's very young, but he's a good pianist, too.'

So James was in, as were — according to Geoff Brash in his book *Brash Business: Ten Business Commandments* — 'Peter Pudney and Lance Barnard'. The two recruits were actually Morrison's old friend David Pudney and, through some unique Burrows reasoning, percussionist Len Barnard. This was not just because Barnard was, as he colourfully describes himself in his own *Jottings of a Jazzman*, a 'Gentleman, Lover of Fine Things, Loather of Teenage Idols, World's Greatest Drummer — but really just a bug on the windscreen of life!' but because he was, Don claimed, 'the best exponent of washboard playing in Sydney.' Burrows said he always associated China with laundries. 'I saw it in movies and things. I assumed that they may have invented the washboard and they might like to see it used as a musical instrument.'

Don did his research on Chinese audiences. He found through inquiry at various government agencies that television had just arrived in China and, while nobody owned their own set, people gathered around shop windows to watch the new phenomenon. 'It was like what happened in Sydney. There would be demonstration sets in the electrical retailers' windows and you couldn't move for the people. They'd stand three deep and watch the test pattern!' Burrows asked what they were viewing in Beijing. 'Excerpts from *My Fair Lady* and Hollywood musicals,' he was told. *Great,* thought Don, *I'll feature the washboard in 'Singing in the Rain' and 'I'm Getting Married in the Morning'.* He sang a few bars and clickety-clacked an energetic washboard solo with his fingers in an up-tempo coda. 'That was Len,' he said. 'He'd go flat out and we'd join in for a big finish.'

The washboard inspiration turned out to be a rattling good idea. The interpreter told him at the end of one concert that the chief conductor of the Republic of China Symphony Orchestra, plus his six associate conductors and the Mayor of Beijing, would like to come onstage for a photograph. 'Oh, that's wonderful,' said Don. 'Guys! Smarten up, wipe the sweat off quick, the dignitaries are coming up for a photograph.' He continued,

> We were introduced. They were bowing and we were bowing back, and I lined the boys up for the picture. I realised the conductor and the Mayor were looking past us. They spotted the washboard against the wall, and went over and held it up between them — one on one side and one on the other. They called the photographer and that was it! No pictures of the players, just the washboard. We didn't get a look-in!

The trip was an education for the Australians. 'We stayed in a terrible hotel, the Bei-Wei, where nobody spoke English and even the baths leaked,' said Brash. They were advised not to eat there, but one day found themselves without an alternative. A party of eleven sat down for lunch. Geoff said,

> When it came to relating to the Chinese, James had the best personality so we got him to order for us. As no-one could speak English, he pointed to eleven dishes on the menu. We waited and waited, and after a long time a line of attendants in dirty white coats brought us 121 dishes. They built a pyramid on our table, with eleven dishes for each of us! To this day, I don't know whether they were very stupid or very, very smart!

The group also experienced the regimentation and organisation of the post-Mao Chinese regime just opening itself to the Western world, economically and musically. 'Every day, a different factory,' said Don, 'but every day the same tunics on the workers and the same routine: a welcome speech and an item from the factory choir.' Inevitably, it would be 'Waltzing Matilda' or, more often, 'Click Go the Shears', the latter creating pronunciation difficulties for the Chinese artisans and process workers. That, in turn, created problems for the visiting band when they were invited to join in. 'We tried not to offend them by singing "click" against their "crick",' said Don, 'so we were singing, "Crick go the shears, boys, crick, crick, crick," and I could feel the trembling bodies beside me trying not to laugh.'

The tunics worn by the workers fascinated Don. At first they seemed identical, till he worked out that the higher up the hierarchy you went, the better weave of material you got. A little higher and you got shoulder pads, and the boss would wear tailor-made.

The simplicity and uniformity might have appealed to Don, considering the difficulties he continued to have with James and his choice of formal stagewear. James would still turn up for gigs in a second-hand dinner suit. 'He'd look like an apprentice jockey ready for a ride, with his trousers pulled in with a huge belt.' Don wheezed a bit and chuckled as he continued his tale. 'I'd say, "Where in the hell did you buy that? Jesus, what you got on? You look like you're standing in a rain barrel!"'

Things reached a head when the group was invited to the Eighth Festival of Asian Arts in Hong Kong in 1983. Don saw it as an important engagement. He told James:

> Look, you've got to have a dinner suit. We're representing Australia. Britain's going to have the London Symphony Orchestra there and members of the Royal Shakespeare Company, including the distinguished actors Timothy West and his wife Prunella Scales. There will be receptions for the Australian consul, and you'll need a dinner suit — and I mean a real one! Don't make your own!

James denies he bought his wardrobe from St Vincent de Paul's Op Shops. His tastes were much further upmarket! James said:

> I bought them from Interlace, an old costume place. I found this suit I rather liked that had belonged to someone's grandfather for sure. It was a bit big. I wore braces to keep the pants up, but I could actually turn around and the pants would stay still! They were quite bunchy around the waist and way too long, so I thought I'd fix them on the plane. I had a stapler and it seemed like a good idea.

It may have seemed logical to James, but Don was aghast.

> I could see him a couple of rows in front of me on the aisle. His arms and elbows were going, material and trouser legs flying. I undid the seatbelt and stood behind him, watching him staple in more metal than in a munitions factory. 'Mate,' I said, 'we're not

going to get through the bloody metal detector with that dinner suit. We'll all be arrested!'

Don's wife, an able seamstress, volunteered her skills, but it was too late. James remembers with no small degree of satisfaction, 'I'd already stapled them and it looked good!'

It didn't feel so good, though, when a couple of days later Hong Kong was steaming hot and the humidity typically high. As the A-list, in their short-sleeved shirts and light dresses, drank cocktails at the High Commissioner's residence on the Colonnade, the trumpeter sweltered but kept his dinner suit jacket buttoned up. 'Don was perspiring more than I was, though,' laughs James. 'He was sweating on me taking that jacket off and revealing my handiwork underneath!'

'That's it!' Don decided, 'we're going to the shop and we'll buy one. I'll pay for the thing if I have to, but I'm not working with you looking like the Michelin man anymore!'

On their return to Australia, James and Don continued to work together. They were not a duo; each had a partnership with other players. Don, after his quintet of fifteen years standing had broken up, played mostly with guitarist George Golla, while James worked alongside keyboardist Dave Pudney. But the two pairs played as a double duo. The instrumentation sat neatly together; it gave them flexibility and informality, and the music suited them all. 'Maybe Dave and I would play first,' explained James, ' and then Don would join us as a trio. Then George would come on and play with Don, or we'd make up a quartet together. We could mix it around a bit.'

It worked well and sometimes took the audience by surprise. A gig in Melbourne's Beaconsfield Hotel in July 1982 was billed as 'Don Burrows and Friends'. Don's Victorian fans probably expected Golla, and perhaps some local luminaries, but witnessed Morrison's debut in the southern state. The night was constructed of two halves, each featuring a duo followed by a climactic finale for all four players. Reviewer Adrian

Jackson, now Wangaratta Festival of Jazz's artistic director, said of the Morrison-Pudney set that it 'provided brilliance that was unexpected and rather brash into the bargain.' It contrasted and complemented the 'tasteful finesse' of the older musicians' earlier offering. Morrison played flugelhorn and trumpet before commandeering the keyboard, while Pudney played bass. 'He "Garnered" a lot of applause with "Deep Purple",' Jackson added, proving that those long hours back in the Pittwater High School hall had not been wasted.

The highlight of the night was the interplay in the closing set between Don and James. 'Honeysuckle Rose' set Don's clarinet against James' trombone; 'Satin Doll', flute and trumpet; 'My Funny Valentine', Burrows' 'too-rarely-heard' baritone sax and Morrison's trumpet, while 'Basin Street Blues', the old faithful James never tires of, 'brought the house down, Morrison tearing things up when he borrowed a glass for some exciting plunger effects, and Burrows keeping up the spirit with some rousing bugged clarinet.' Adrian Jackson added:

> James Morrison is undoubtedly a young man with remarkable talents. His instrumental prowess and versatility are two qualities he has in common with his mentor. An even more important one is his ability to improvise in a way that people can understand. And most important of all is the fact that he takes great pleasure in playing and communicates that enjoyment to the audience.

It's a recurring theme; time and again commentators remarked on Morrison's ability to make his music enjoyable and accessible. It's not accidental; James has made a conscious effort to make it so:

> Presentation is the key to whether people accept the music or not. Jazz used to be the popular music of the day and, back then, there was a lot more presentation involved. It's a pity that jazz musicians are often so serious and humourless onstage. Like rock musicians, they should allow their personalities to come through.

After thoroughly ingesting the lessons of communication and showmanship from the maestro Burrows, James determined that his next venture, The Morrison Brothers Big Bad Band, would be 'stacked with players who had not only musical excellence, but personality, and could translate these attitudes into action onstage.'

Chapter 12

Big Bad Band

James finds it hard to specify which genre or style is his preferred form of jazz: duo, trio, quintet or small ensemble. He would say that his favourite is the one he's doing at the time, but there's no doubt he and his brother John have an affection for the big band. James experienced one at church and started his own during high school. He featured in the triumphant Young Northside Big Band, and played in and led one at the Con.

It was John's first love to the extent that, though he continued to perform frequently with James, he formed and fronted Swing City, with his wife and vocalist Jacki, in the late 1990s. The band has been successful at Sydney and Australian jazz festivals, after John shrewdly started it to coincide with the festivities to celebrate the Sydney Olympics in 2000. It has since become a training ground for many young musicians straight out of the Con.

Back in 1983, though there was plenty of work for James and his smaller combinations to occupy his non-Con teaching time, there was precious little big band playing. The Morrison brothers' remedy was predictable enough: if you want a band to play your music in the style you want, with the character you want, start it yourself!

The boys hand-picked their personnel using unusual criteria. Prospects must not only be among the best young players around, but also have big personalities and the ability to have a good time onstage, to the enhancement, not the detriment, of the music. Patrons could expect exciting performances, which included large dollops of humour laced with cheeky showmanship. It seemed like, and was, a group after the boys' own hearts.

The brothers were determined to prove James' statement to Adrian Jackson that 'presentation was the key'. They felt that jazz had been left behind by rock'n'roll in terms of staging, lighting and production values. Jazz had been number one, but was being swamped by the cult of pop personalities. That didn't suit the persona of either Morrison brother. Any big band they ran would try to match the razzmatazz of pop shows.

There was to be no sacrificing of musical standards in the search for entertainment, though. The band offered first-rate jazz from some of the most exciting and adventurous players around. The twelve-piece set-up used Peter Cross and Warwick Alder on trumpet, Bob Johnson and Peter Trotta on trombone, Paul Andrews, Jason Morphett and Tom Baker on sax, Steve Elphick on bass, and familiar faces Steve Brien on guitar, Dave Pudney on vibes, and John on drums. James himself played 'everything that moved', as Eric Myers put it. The critic acknowledged James as 'an extraordinary multi-instrumentalist, able to play a great range of instruments (many of them considered mutually exclusive) at a high professional standard. They include trumpet, valve and slide trombone, alto and tenor saxophones, flugelhorn, piano, bass euphonium, tenor horn, E-flat tuba, flute and guitar.' He neglected to mention string bass, another of Morrison's conquests!

The Morrison brothers promoted the venture themselves. The band made its debut at the Brisbane Warana Festival in September 1983, played the Manly Jazz Festival and the Seymour Centre in Sydney in October, and Melbourne's huge Dallas Brooks Hall in November. They booked the Sydney Opera House in March 1984 with — surprise, surprise! — Don Burrows as guest artist.

Myers, in his *Jazz* magazine, said that they provided 'an evening of marvellous and heart-warming jazz' and that 'despite Morrison's desire to make the band entertaining, there was no skimping on solos. All the soloists were free to stretch out and express themselves at length.'

It was what James had wanted when he and David Basden had done the arrangements, mostly jazz standards of the swing and bebop eras. They were done with the players in mind, and since all the players were very good soloists they were all featured, sometimes duelling among themselves, sometimes between sections. 'Yet they get on so well together,' James said, musing on the 'twisted' personalities of the members of the 'big, bad' ensemble.

> They're all crazy in different ways. Jason Morphett is just quite insane and different. Paul Andrews is the classic 'whingeing Pom' stand-up comedian. In the 'bone section, Bob Johnson's a lunatic. Peter Trotta is Bob's protégé, learning how to be ridiculous. Peter Cross and Warwick Alder are the real 'Australian musician' section, always coming out with gags. Steve Brien on guitar is a little vague. Kevin Hunt on piano is behaving according to whole different set of rules. As for John, I wouldn't call him insane just … [and perhaps he flashed quickly back to their childhood escapades] just dangerous; surpassed only by myself.

It sounded like a recipe for trouble — Jack Nicholson in *One Flew over the Cuckoo's Nest* taking the asylum residents out for a spin — but the band capitalised on the immense talent, musical and comedic, of the members. They played great music. It was, Eric Myers wrote, 'a repertoire that suggested the band was orienting itself towards the mass audience unfamiliar with jazz standards.' 'Anthropology', 'A Night in Tunisia', 'Cherokee', 'Stompin' at the Savoy', 'Take the "A" Train' and 'Caravan', as well as two of James' originals, were all on the live recording the ABC released. Those who only purchased the recording, though, missed the other element of the concerts: the band clowning around.

Paul Andrews, the 'whingeing Pom' himself, still remembers the Halloween gig in 1984 as one of the maddest shows we ever did. Three thousand people and twenty musicians. I was Master of Ceremonies and opened proceedings from inside a coffin, centre stage, complete with dry ice, make-up and dressed like Dracula. [Vocalist] Joe Lane was wheeled onstage laying on a hospital gurney covered in a white sheet. Dr John [Morrison] did an incision, pouring in a quart of Bessie Smith, a pint of Louis Armstrong and a gallon of Charlie Parker!

Joe has that genius to make ordinary people feel alive, larger than alive; feel that they had consent to be in the moment and cry and laugh. Joe gave them permission to love and to live. Right now! The audience was stunned, smiling. Big grins.

I announced his arrival: 'Ladies and gentlemen, the City of Sydney presents: JOE LANE!'

Joe sat up and announced, 'Things are getting better. A-one, a-two, a-you-know-what-to-do!' counting the big band into the opener. Suddenly, James appears, abseiling from the ceiling high above the audience, playing a screaming trumpet solo over 'Peter Gunn', while the big band is laying it down. *Dundun, dundun, dundun, dundun.* As he hit the stage, there was a series of explosions; fireworks and smoke bombs [James had a mate who was into pyrotechnics].

Unfortunately no-one had informed the Fire Department, Commonwealth Police or the National Trust about our little party, so by interval the heavies had all turned up to close the joint down and send home early a couple of thousand happy people. Apparently, it's not cool to light fires in the Sydney Town Hall. Somehow, they let us do the second set (closely supervised).

James abseiled into concerts at several venues, including the Concert Hall of the Sydney Opera House, the Seymour Centre in Sydney and the Concert Hall in Melbourne.

They wouldn't allow it now, but there were no Health and Safety regulations back then. The Opera House people just said, 'Where do you want to come in? We'll show you how to get up there.' They left me there on my own. I tied my own knots and slid down my own rope. Can you imagine that happening now?

During one tune, smoke billowed alarmingly from underneath John's drum kit; Baker, Andrews and the Morrisons sang a barbershop quartet-style 'By the Light of the Silvery Moon' (something of a collector's item for those who were there — Morrison doesn't sing much on gigs) and at the beginning of the second half, the brothers abseiled onto the stage.

Later, nine of the group had trumpet chops enough to somehow manage a hilarious 'Bugler's Holiday', conducted by Paul Andrews. Myers appended,

Of course, Morrison confirmed his reputation as the most exciting young musician in Australian jazz. Principally, he played trumpet and trombone throughout the evening — an unlikely combination of instruments, considering that both require a completely different embouchure, or lip position. But Morrison reinforced his extraordinary multi-instrumental talent by playing the tune 'Out of Nowhere' on the piano in a pumping individual style. He received a great ovation.

Onstage receptions weren't matched by box office receipts, though. Bluntly, not enough people turned up. 'We didn't fill the halls,' James said. The Morrison brothers had done hundreds of gigs, but never been the promoters before. 'We had little idea what we were doing. We had all sorts of problems with ticket sales and ticketing companies. People were calling and being told the concerts were sold out when they weren't.'

It was a financial disaster. They hired the halls, put on the concerts, paid the players, and lost everything. *Tiki*, their floating home on

Pittwater which they were paying off, was repossessed. It was their first entrepreneurial venture, and their last. They learned a valuable lesson: James reckoned 'if that's what it's like to be a concert promoter, I'm better off to just turn up, do a gig and get paid irrespective of how many people turn up.'

The Morrisons had looked forward to the band's future; somehow, but not surprisingly, it was mixed up with boats. They had often rehearsed, eaten (Tom Baker was an excellent cook) and drunk on board the old trawler in Pittwater. Morrison mused about a larger boat, one big enough to accommodate the band and their better halves — a kind of floating rehearsal room. 'Then we could do the festival circuit by boat, and a world tour for a year!'

Obviously, the 'world tour by boat' was never going to happen, but the Big Bad Band continued, and still continues intermittently, to do some great gigs for other promoters. They toured nationally, filmed a TV special for the ABC in 1983, played in front of a huge crowd at the Sydney Midsummer Jazz Festival in January 1985, released the album *A Night in Tunisia*, which was reviewed enthusiastically and, later the same year, went to Tsukuba, a town sixty miles north of Tokyo, to represent Australia at the World Expo.

During the six months at the Expo, each of the 111 participating countries had three special days in which to celebrate its culture before the massive audiences that passed through the turnstiles. Australia displayed its various facets, with performances by Australian Indigenous actor David Gulpilil and the Arnhem Land Dancers, and the wobbleboard-accompanied 'Tie Me Kangaroo Down, Sport' of the unique Rolf Harris. There was also The Four Kinsmen, a contemporary boy band of the time, and singer Barry Crocker, often more readily recognised as Barry Humphries' uncouth, lantern-jawed comic book character Barry from the very successful, if essentially lowbrow, 1972 Australian film *The Adventures of Barry McKenzie*.

If the beer-sodden 'yobbo' Barry McKenzie was something of an Australian stereotype at the time, the appointed musical director of the country's entertainment team didn't fit it. James Morrison didn't even drink, but it was he and his big band that backed all the guest artists, played their own spots and captivated the thousands who sought out the iconic offerings in the Australian Pavilion.

In their downtime, the band sat in with the locals at the Tokyo Bluenote. They were instant celebrities, regaled with delicacies and sake. Warwick Alder set the tone, literally, with his singing trumpet ballad 'I Loves You, Porgy', and Paul Andrews played 'Midnight Sun' on, he noted, 'a night that didn't seem to end.' The saxophonist went on,

> The club was getting excited and had a feeling of anticipation. James played the trombone to a room that had come alive. The Japanese went ballistic, as if they couldn't believe it, presenting us with more sake and best scotch now, plus even more noodles and soup. Such warmth and hospitality, and James was in form. We'd been playing in a stadium to a hundred thousand people, so a small club was a thrill; we could hear every note. The Japanese were so polite and listening, yeah, they were listening, wicked. When James played the 'bone, man, everyone listened.

The Expo gig had been arranged by Ken Laing, who was playing an increasing role in James' career. As James' profile snowballed through his nightclub gigs, his tours with Don Burrows and his TV appearances, his need for a business manager became increasingly apparent. In 1981, when James approached him, Ken Laing had influence and contacts beyond the limited jazz pool where James was now a fish of some considerable size.

Laing had started his company, Media Music, which offered 'event management and artistic direction', only two years earlier in 1979. He wasn't yet the entrepreneur who would direct several Royal Command performances at the Opera House, produce seventeen annual New South

Wales Premier's Gala Concerts at the Entertainment Centre, and bring Liberace, Shirley MacLaine, Dionne Warwick and other household names to Australia. But his experience as a 'legit' percussionist with the Sydney Symphony and Australian Opera Orchestras gave him firsthand knowledge of the sort of management and career advice young performers needed.

He was a perfectionist with, as the late Tommy Tycho described it, 'a brilliant, vital brain'. James said he needed 'a classy, showbiz manager, not a "Joe Skiver"', and Laing, a dapper man with a Van Gogh beard, filled that bill precisely. He transformed James from jazz instrumentalist into celebrity performer; from 'smart casual' to 'formal', literally and metaphorically. He told James, 'We're going to have to buy proper clothes.' He meant tailored dinner suits and bow ties — suits tailored for James, not someone else who had later given them to an op-shop. Neither would he allow James to play clubs like the Paradise anymore. 'You can't work in a place where people can come and see you for nothing, when I'm going to be charging $300 for a 15-minute solo spot.' James was disappointed; he still wanted to play with his old friends occasionally. 'You can go and sit in if they don't know you're coming, but it can't be advertised,' said Laing.

James was moving into a whole new milieu. He became a cabaret act with a star on the dressing room door. Laing booked him into the brightest and most expensive nightspots, those inhabited by the well-to-do enjoying the biggest artists of the time. He worked with Tommy Tycho, bandleader of the best-known orchestra in Sydney, and featured on the very popular *Ray Martin Show* on commercial television, with a far bigger audience than the ABC commanded, and jetted off to several overseas bookings.

Laing had plans for John Morrison, too. 'I don't want you to drum anymore,' he told him. 'I want you to be a musical director. You can run bands; that's what you do well. You guys can be a great team; I'll manage you both.' John wasn't particularly interested in the proposal. He thought Laing saw James as another Liberace, a huge entertainer, not merely a jazz musician. 'He had a lot of insight and he could have been right,' reflects the older brother, 'but in the end, James is a jazz player and I'm a drummer, not a manager.'

Ken Laing managed James from 1981 to 1985, helping to mould him into the entertainer and stage personality he is today. He was looking after James' affairs in 1984, when Musica Viva was looking for a jazz player to represent Australia at the Olympic Jazz Festival, running in parallel with the Los Angeles Olympic Games. They had Don Burrows in mind and contacted the National Jazz Coordinator, Eric Myers, for a phone number. Myers recalls:

> My ears pricked up immediately. 'Why do you want to send Don?' I said.
>
> 'Well, who else is there?' they said. 'We don't know anyone else. Don Burrows is the only jazz musician we know.'
>
> That's pretty much the way it was back then, so I said, 'Look, this is something we should handle through our office.'
>
> I ended up recommending James to go because at that stage he was our outstanding young talent. Don would have done a great job, but if I had any influence, I was going to give the opportunity to someone else.

When James got his invitation, he reasoned, 'I'd better go; it's the only way I'm ever going to represent my country in the Olympic Games!'

The festival ran for four days in the outdoor amphitheatre at LA's Ford Theatre. James was scheduled to appear on the Sunday afternoon — the final day — accompanied by an American all-star band. Tommy Vig, the Festival producer and big band leader, heard James at rehearsal on the Saturday and immediately slotted him into the Saturday night show as well. The audience response was incredible. Leonard Feather, the world's most respected jazz critic, summed James up in one word:

'Brilliant!' But another, more compelling story completes the picture. Much of the festival seemed to be celebrating modern and avant-garde jazz, and some of the experienced old hands, like drummer Shelly Manne, were wearying of it. James played what he knew and loved: standards, bebop and swing. The relief was palpable; James was a breath of familiar air to the older musos. Manne's face glowed with excitement as he fell in behind him. 'At f---ing last!' he shouted in relief and excitement. Myers remembers,

> I got terrific testimonials about James' participation in the Festival. No better person could have been selected. He was a sensation there. James fitted in beautifully with the expectations of those West Coast jazz musicians. The other thing was it showed James that, as young as he was, as green as he was, he could do it with the best of players. It was his first trip to the US since Monterey. It must have boosted his confidence; he must have thought, *I can make it. I can do this; I can play with the best.*

James was on the crest of the wave at home and overseas. He could stand in the spotlight on the world stage or exhibit his multi-instrumental skills in Australia. Earlier in 1984, just before the Olympic Games trip with Ken Laing, he'd starred in the *Tribute to the Giants of Jazz* season at the Don Burrows Supper Club in the Regent Hotel. Some punters quibbled at the 'exorbitant' $9.50 entrance fee, but for their money they got a galaxy of local stars paying their musical respects to the greatest players. This was on the whole range of jazz solo instruments: Monday night was trumpets, Tuesday trombones, Wednesday saxophones, then piano, bass and drums at the end of the week.

Morrison was the only instrumentalist who got two guernseys. On Monday he was on trumpet, alongside Sydney legends Bob Barnard and Keith Stirling, honouring Beiderbecke, Armstrong, Gillespie and Miles Davis. And the next night he was setting the place alight as a trombonist, recalling Teagarden, Dorsey, Green and Watrous.

James displayed his easy but impeccable high register playing in 'Getting Sentimental Over You', and a perfect Rosolino bebop style in 'Autumn Leaves'. He even made an admirable attempt to evoke iconoclastic German free trombonist Albert Mangelsdorff, who he'd recently heard at the LA Olympic Jazz Festival, with multiphonics and experimental sounds.

Morrison, unlike the other performers, used no music; he'd been copying the master trombonists since his teenage years and was perfectly at home with all his material. His confident, positive approach broke through the somewhat reverential atmosphere in the room, and it was his sparkling, dynamic playing that brought the other players out of themselves and the audience to its feet.

James could always conquer a room; it was one of his many strengths. He was a superb player and a very fine entertainer, with a winning personality. Things were looking good. He'd been very successful on short trips overseas, he commanded high fees in all the best venues and clubs around Sydney and had impressed the rest of Australia on tours with Don Burrows, he was at the top of the Australian scene, was known to a very wide TV audience and had played on numerous recordings. He was even a part-time university lecturer. It seemed a very odd time to be called to Ken Laing's office, along with brother John, for a gentle bollocking. John recalls,

> Ken wasn't upset. He just said, 'Here's a letter that says I'm sacking you. You're out on the boats all the time; you're not serious about this.' He was right, to a point. We were living on a boat; out there on the water without a mobile phone, having jam sessions with our friends, hanging out and fishing. Ken had decided James could become a Liberace, but didn't think we were tuned in.

James' recollection was that,

> there was some kind of letter like that. There was a time when he was going, 'Where are you? What are you doing? Why can't I get

hold of you?' At the end when we parted company, it was quite amicable. He probably did want to make me into a jazz Liberace; that was his knowledge, experience and contacts. He wanted us to decide what we really wanted to be.

James already had a pretty good idea of what he wanted. 'I was becoming more a jazz musician,' he said. He certainly didn't see himself as a gaudy entertainer in a gold lamé suit doing the eternal Las Vegas circuit. 'We were quite successful,' he said, understatedly. 'We just needed bigger horizons.'

It was time for a new challenge, and his heart told him to go to New York. If he wanted to be recognised as a world-class player, he had to make it in America, the land of the jazz giants.

Chapter 13

New York, New York

James and John Morrison had learnt a great deal about the music game since their schooldays, but not a lot about making preparations for an important trip. Their first jaunt to New York in 1985 was planned with about as much forethought and attention to detail as their nocturnal voyage through the hazardous Heads in a two-man dinghy.

On that occasion, they took a compass, a street directory and a bucket of fast food. They set off for an extended stay in America's most intimidating city, with just $3500 wrapped in a sock, James' horns, John's snare drum, two didgeridoos and a pair of binoculars. The rest of the drum kit and the faithful purple Valiant had been sold to raise the fares and book just one night's accommodation in a city to which they were complete strangers.

But foolhardy, overconfident or both, at least they had a plan based on their own unique brand of common sense. New York is built on a series of islands. Islands meant inlets, moorings, houseboats — cheap living quarters. A simple line of logic for the Pittwater boys.

Their limited research also told them that the sightseeing Circle Line ferry went around Manhattan Island, where they figured they would need to live to be adjacent to the entertainment centre of New York. Consequently, early on the Sunday morning after their arrival, they jumped aboard armed with the binoculars, the *New York Times* classified section, and a notebook and pencil. While the tourists raced from one side of the ferry to the other, gawping at the Statue of Liberty, James and John studied the shoreline through the eyeglasses, scrutinised the small advertisements for boats and made notes on the pad.

James explained the modus operandum. 'We were both boaties and boaties can tell a boat where someone's living a mile off. I'm watching. I'm going, "No — fishermen; no — yacht club; no — too expensive." John was reading the boat classifieds, marking the best options.'

James identified the most likely spot, with the help of the ferry skipper who was beginning to suspect he'd taken two Russian spies on board. John thought he'd found a boat that suited their criteria for liveability. They'd decided they needed a fibreglass vessel with two cabins, a saloon, a living room undercover and a decent bathroom — a 'good head' to nautical types.

'What have you got?' shouted James over the noise of the ferry engine. It was a good news/bad news routine. First the bad: 'It's a wooden boat, no head, one cabin and a half-open cockpit — but …' cried John, 'it costs $2500!'

'That's our boat!' shouted James, throwing their criteria out the porthole because the price was right.

They rang the owner vendor in Jamaica Bay and hopped onto a subway train to Long Island, with their stash of cash in their pockets.

> Luckily, we looked so scruffy we were probably unmuggable! We quickly learned to dress down in New York, particularly for the Underground system. It's like a 'Don't mess with us' signal. Everyone dresses like they're dangerous, but they're probably all like us — quite scared. There's probably no-one dangerous down there at all.

The boys checked over the boat, said 'We'll take it!', handed over two-and-a-half grand and climbed aboard their new acquisition for the maiden voyage back to 79th Street, where James had spotted a likely berth. They asked Leonard, the boat seller, for directions back to Manhattan by water. 'Keep the land on your right,' said the Archie Bunker sound-alike. 'When you see "the necklace" — the famous bridge — go under it; that's Manhattan.'

How could it possibly go wrong? The boys even had a big tourist map of New York, with cartoons and a picture of Coney Island as a backup — nearly as reliable as a Sydway street directory for navigating the Northern beaches back home!

In the dark, without lights — there's the ring of familiarity to all this — the boys negotiated their new Owens 26ft cabin cruiser around the shallows and sandbars at Coney Island, and arrived in Manhattan at 10.30pm.

Inevitably, as they tied up they heard a voice saying, 'You can't park there!' It was Bung, the Royal Jester from The Wizard of Id comic strip or, if not, someone bearing a very close resemblance. He was a man perpetually tipsy, but able to function amiably. Bung was taken by the boys' accents, and impressed to think they'd just arrived from Australia in a cabin cruiser. It wasn't in the boys' best interests to disillusion him at that point, as he proceeded to find them a better spot to tie up 'just for the night'. 'Just for the night' became just over a year.

They had arrived in Manhattan, which could have been dangerous for two ingénues from Down Under, but Dame Fortune found them a berth in a rundown marina protected by a high wire fence with a population of boaties — 'some strange people,' said James, 'quite odd,' — who looked out for each other. Venturing outside the compound meant taking your life, or at least your wallet, in your hands as you ran across the park to the subway downtown. But behind the wire they could live safely and cheaply, if not necessarily conveniently. The *Koala Bear* had no fridge, heating or hot water, and the ablutions block was a good 200 metres away.

It would be natural to assume that the Morrison brothers, almost household names in Australia, had a few prospects to follow up in New York — several numbers jotted down in a diary. Doubtless, Don Burrows could have provided some, and their old encourager and benefactor, Horst Liepolt, now ran a club in their new town. But 'we had nothing,' said James. 'We didn't know a soul; we had no gigs lined up and we hadn't tried to make any contacts. Just didn't do it; never occurred to us.' John talked about 'the challenge of stripping themselves bare and starting from scratch' which, in this instance, meant taking their talents onto the streets. Maybe the young men assumed that New York would open her arms to welcome them, but she proved a more demanding mistress. She'd let them starve if they couldn't make enough to pay their dues.

The prospect of starvation concentrated the mind, though. 'When you're literally playing to feed yourself, you don't say, "Let's not play that tune, I don't like the changes." If the audience wants it, you play it!' They became adept at finding the best pitches, and other buskers steered clear of them. 'We were Australians, and we were loud!' smiled John.

James had his trumpet and trombone, and John merely his snare drum, but they played all their big club numbers. Bunny Berrigan's 'I Can't Get Started' was a winner. 'I could hear the orchestra in my head — we'd done it a thousand times with Tommy Tycho. John would play the drum roll and I'd take off as if I had a big band behind me.'

'You could hear it five blocks away,' added John, 'and then I'd do the 'Caravan' solo, ratatatting around the sidewalk fittings.' They played the didgeridoos they'd brought from home — 'circular breathing, the lot, part of my brass playing from Mona Vale Primary,' said John. 'I'd only do it for about ten minutes on the trot. That was plenty for me.' The cabaret show would stop the traffic in Bleecker Street until the police moved them on, since they had no licence.

Unfortunately, they never learned to be thrifty; they made money and they spent money. They saw every band in town, listened to the great players and, when they had cash in hand, bought movie tickets and a pizza. In the end they were reduced to eating beans and potatoes. 'We worked out they were the cheapest things. For six months we couldn't get any work at all. We couldn't get a gig; we didn't knock on doors. We probably didn't do enough, and no-one offered us a job.'

They did jam sessions at The Blue Note, where experienced trumpet-playing band leader Ted Curson sorted out the sheep from the goats by calling tunes only known to New York musos, or standards — Coltrane or Miles Davis — in outrageous keys. James passed the test and gained Curson's respect, but it didn't lead to any work. 'We'd expected to get something but, then again, I wasn't surprised not to,' said James philosophically. 'In the end I thought, *Well, that's New York.*'

The Morrisons were about ready to come home, even though the 79th Street boaties looked out for their battling Aussie friends by passing on their leftover spaghetti dinners in Tupperware containers, and Bung had allowed them to mortgage the *Koala Bear* back to him in exchange for a six-month extension on the marina rent.

When they least expected it, their luck took a turn for the better. They got into conversation at the local Burger Boy with the waiter, Arnold Cummins, who was working tables by day and playing reeds by night to pay his way through college. He spotted their instruments and the chat turned to music. 'He looked at us a bit sideways,' said John, 'but invited us to come down to Arturo's, a restaurant on South Houston Street.' With a loud, open atmosphere straight out of the sitcom *Cheers*, Arturo's offered jovial service and traditional Italian dishes to the patrons in the worn leatherette booths in the dining room, and gave free feeds to the musicians who turned up to play in the corner.

Arnold explained the hesitation that John had sensed in his invitation. 'They were the furthest thing from jazz musicians I had ever seen in my life; certainly unlike those in New York, not scruffy at all.' Don Burrows and Ken Laing would have been proud!

Arturo's suited the boys' appetites for music and meatballs, and they were soon turning up regularly, like two little Tommy Tuckers, to play and to eat. It wasn't a great band. There were singing waiters and Jimmy the pianist, who had lived above the shop for umpteen years, but other musos and vocalists walked in off the streets, as the

Morrisons had done, to sit in. Actor Timothy Hutton would drop by to play percussion and sing backup, and young Kate Ceberano, a sultry up-and-comer from Melbourne touring with the Australian band I'm Talking, smouldered through a poignant 'Cry Me a River' one night.

The Morrisons became popular regulars — patrons would ask, 'Are the Australians on tonight?' — doing Friday and Saturday nights, before moving on at about 2am to The Blue Note and the Jazz Cultural Theatre, carrying enough takeaway to see them through the weekend. There was no pay for a night at Arturo's, but the atmosphere and the food made up for it.

Some nights they popped into Bradley's, to listen to Kirk Lightsey and Ron Carter or Ray Drummond. Piano player Bradley Cunningham had opened his eponymous, intimate wood-panelled nightclub and restaurant on University Place in Greenwich Village in 1969. Seven nights a week it featured sophisticated duos. Players like Tommy Flanagan and Hank Jones would play there on a piano donated by Paul Desmond, the exquisitely distinctive, breathy saxophonist of the Dave Brubeck Quartet.

One night, they were approached by a man who asked James, 'Aren't you the guy who plays trombone at Arturo's? I heard you there when I was buying a pizza. You should sit in with these guys.' *Yeah, right*, thought James. 'It's okay,' said the guy, who turned out to be Angel Romero, an arranger for George Benson. 'I know these guys,' he said, and walked over to talk to Kirk Lightsey.

> I could see what was going on. Romero was saying, 'I've got this trumpet player from Australia here and I want you to let him sit in.' These two stately black gentlemen were shaking their heads. It was so inappropriate; an unknown Bleecker Street busker turning up uninvited to jam along with players who'd played alongside Chet Baker, Sonny Stitt, Dexter Gordon and every other member of the all-time greats' rollcall.

James underestimated Romero's clout. Eventually, they agreed to just one song. It was enough. James put aside his trumpet, assembled his more mellow trombone and with very little 'how do you do' launched into the first tune. *I'm going to get one chance at this and I'd better be ready*, he thought. He decided to take all the solos anyway. It was typical Morrison — once the instrument was on his lips he'd take on any challenge in the musical world.

When the song ended, the duo nodded to each other and to James. 'Stay,' they said. Recognition and acceptance in a single word. Morrison 'stayed' the rest of the night and as the gig ended was approached again, this time by agent Larry Clothier. Larry was a prolific record producer and manager, who had Carmen McRae on his books and used the two veterans now onstage in recording sessions.

John recalls Clothier giving James his card, saying, 'You're the next Rosolino — call me.' James had been compared to the most respected trombonist of his era.

They didn't follow it up then — they were out of money, the boat rent was overdue and a new Australian manager had gigs lined up in Sydney. They sold off John's return ticket to prolong the whole exercise but, after a crowded farewell party at Arturo's and promises to return 'real soon', James flew out and returned to the Sydney circuit to earn enough to bring his brother home some weeks later.

They left New York chastened, but not defeated. They'd done some basic living and survived without a steady income, on a barely habitable boat with few facilities, for over a year. Their playing and personalities had enabled them to eat. They hadn't cracked any professional gigs, but they really hadn't tried that hard to find them. James had never sought a job in his life; opportunities had always come to him. They hadn't this time, but he was sure they would next time — and he was determined there would be a next time.

Chapter 14

The Boy in Ipanema

James Morrison arrived back in Sydney, Australia 'under new management'. After the separation from Ken Laing, Don Burrows, in John's words, 'set James up' with Peter Brendle, a Swiss-born Australian whose name lacked the acute accent over the second 'e', which would have made its pronunciation, 'Brendlay', more obvious.

Brendle was 'more a jazz guy,' James said, 'than Laing. Peter knew the international festivals far better than Ken. It was a necessary change, which Ken understood.' Brendle's roots and interests were in the jazz scene, not the general entertainment industry. He was a manager, a promoter and publisher of *Jazz* magazine and, consequently, was the right man to handle Morrison's affairs for the next four years.

James took up where he left off in Sydney and in October, during the New South Wales Music Week, the 22-year-old was named Jazz Musician of the Year. His stature within his own country had not diminished during his absence, but already he was thinking about his return to the States.

When the American trumpeter Red Rodney toured Australia, Morrison played alongside him. Each had been impressed by the other. They had much in common: they were white guys playing 'black' music, they had both worked professionally in their early teens, they were both inspired by Dizzy Gillespie and they were both into bop and bebop styles. In one enviable area, Red Rodney — ginger-haired Robert Chudnick to his mother — was ahead of James. He'd played with the Charlie Parker Quintet after Miles Davis left, about as good as it gets, though he had to be billed as 'Albino Red' so he could work in the segregated southern states. It's a story James tells with great relish, having heard it direct from the Jewish trumpet player himself:

> In about 1949, Parker's Quintet was booked to tour the South. The fact everyone in the band, bar Red, was black didn't faze Bird one iota.
>
> 'We'll get you to sing the blues; the Southerners are so racist, they'll think if you sing the blues, you must be black!'
>
> 'But I've got red hair and freckles,' Red pointed out helpfully. 'That's okay. They've never seen an albino Negro anyway. If you sing the blues in a black band and we tell them you're an albino, they'll believe it.'
>
> They called him 'The Singing Sensation — Albino Red' and it worked, though in truth the ruse probably fooled nobody. Everyone accepted it in order to get round the racist attitudes of the Deep South.

Later, when the quintet got back to New York, Red got up to sing with the band.

> 'What are you doing?' Charlie Parker demanded.
>
> 'I'm going to sing the blues,' said Albino Red Rodney.
>
> 'You're not doing that shit up here,' said Charlie. 'We're back in the real world! Pick up your trumpet! You're not albino anymore, Whitey, and you're not singing anymore either!'

Red and James Morrison may have been alike in their musical precocity, their love of bebop and their white skins, but in other ways the two were totally dissimilar. Unlike James, who couldn't even drink, Red Rodney's career was blighted by almost predictable-for-the-era drug addictions, which led to theft and periods of imprisonment. By the 1980s, when he visited Australia, he had cleaned up his act enough to record five highly acclaimed albums.

Red invited James, some thirty-five years his junior, to come and play with him at the Village Vanguard in New York. James accepted the invitation and sold out several nights, before touring and making a big splash, particularly at the prestigious Dick Gibson Jazz Party in Denver. Here James, in the words of Richard Guilliatt in *The Times on Sunday*, was 'like a pig in the proverbial'. James said it was 'an incredible thing' to be onstage with great trombone players like Bill Watrous, Slide Hampton and Urbie Green, and it set his creative juices pumping to know that he could walk onstage and see Freddie Hubbard sitting in the audience. Red Rodney watched his young friend approach the daunting situations wearing, in another of Guilliatt's colourful phrases, 'his shit-eating grin, the smile of a buoyant personality'. At the time, Red said,

> I think James is tomorrow's superstar, I really do. The fact he can play trombone as easily as saxophone as easily as flugelhorn … his technique is awesome, awesome, and with maturity he'll learn what to leave out. Then, look out! Oh God, in another two years he'll be hiring *me*!

James was much better prepared for his second visit to New York. He not only had Red Rodney's offer, he had Larry Clothier's business card in his pocket. Peter Brendle rang the number on it. Larry, basically a recording engineer, passed him on to Edith Kiggen, who was a manager and player agent. 'When can he come back to New York?' she asked immediately. 'She was an older lady who looked after all sorts of acts,' James recalled. 'She was into taking new artists like me and building them up.' After receiving a very informed nod from Clothier about James' potential, she was ready to organise concerts, recordings and tours.

James also did some gigs without Rodney, and on one occasion borrowed the older man's car in New Jersey to drive for two hours to Philadelphia. He found the venue in an old warehouse, locked and dark. 'It was a very dodgy area — felt very dangerous.' James says of the night. 'We drove around, but there was no-one to be seen. We thought, *The gig starts in an hour; what's going on?*'

James rang his new American agent, Edith Kiggen. 'We're in Philadelphia,' James said. 'We're at the right venue, at the right time. I can see the name of the club painted on the warehouse wall, but there's no-one here.'

'James, the gig is next Friday,' she said, probably muttering 'you idiot' under her breath.

'We drove back from Philadelphia to New York, dropped Red's car off at New Jersey and caught the subway back to Manhattan,' James says. The irony was that by the following Friday, the gig was cancelled.

At the time of his remarkable farewell gigs at the Don Burrows Supper Club at the Regent Hotel in April 1987, James had a huge itinerary in front of him. He was off to New York, then on to a tour of the principal European jazz festivals, including the North Sea Jazz Festival in Holland, a trumpet feature night at Montreux in Switzerland with Clark Terry and Jon Faddis, and Umbria Jazz in Perugia in Italy, before returning to play in America at Red Rodney gigs in Chicago and New York. There was even a suggestion of a festival appearance alongside Dizzy Gillespie. It was a far cry from the 'let's buy a boat when we get there and hope for the best' plan from eighteen months previous.

In the months leading up to their departure, there were still many gigs to be done. An unusual one took James away from his normal backing groups in jazz venues and saw him accompanied by Adelaide's Polished Brass, a group of nineteen teachers led by Bruce 'Dizzy' Raymond, the conductor of the brass band at which this author first encountered Morrison a few years later. The singular feature of Polished Brass was that it was a versatile ensemble made up of brass instrument teachers employed by the South Australian Education Department, which covered big band charts by replacing the reed section with three French horns. The concert was the culmination of a week of promotional concerts for brass instrument students in Adelaide schools under Raymond's entrepreneurial leadership, featuring Morrison on all the instruments. The final public concert was a sell-out at Elder Hall. Morrison's performance in it indicated, a reporter said, that James 'would carry the flag of Australian jazz proudly on his forthcoming trip back to the States'.

In retrospect, the concert exemplifies three of the branches that were developing from the main trunk of Morrison's career. It brought together his ambition to be accepted in America, his growing interest in the promotion of music in schools, of jazz in particular, and his appeal to the brass band world and its practitioners, who understood and appreciated probably better than most what he could do technically, even if jazz improvisation was an unspoken language in their field.

In April 1987, Morrison said his goodbyes to his hometown fans with a unique series of jazz concerts, though Joya Jenson in the *Sydney Morning Herald* said he'd already done more farewells than Dame Nellie Melba and Gladys Moncrieff combined! He'd played already, she said, with 'Bob Johnson's 'Bones for the Jazz Action Society. Then, Bevy's and Kirribilli Ex-Services Club added their adieus, and at Soup Plus, James and John had the wall-to-wall crowd swinging from the rafters'.

Finally, at the Supper Club farewell week, James played with the Oz Bop Band on Tuesday; on Wednesday, he played with his own tuba consort (Morrison has a soft spot for the cumbersome brass bass and longs to free it from its 'oompah' stigma); on Thursday, the Big Bad Band featured; and on Friday, James headed his own quintet. He appeared again on Saturday night with Don and the Roger Frampton Trio (Frampton on piano, Craig Scott on bass and Alan Turnbull on drums). Jenson's report said Morrison was unusually subdued to start with, but ended up 'spitting out sixteenths and hitting the highs'.

It was a remarkable sequence of gigs. Many players play several nights in a row. Morrison's uniqueness was that each night presented a different style, a different aspect of his virtuosity, on different instruments from different sections of the orchestral and jazz families of brass, woodwind and rhythm. Few in the world play convincing jazz on tuba, but to follow that in successive nights with driving big band, confidential quintet and energetic bop is probably unparalleled. He played an evocative 'A Foggy Day' on the trombone one night and the Supper Club for a moment misted up, till he blew it away with breezy versions of his old standbys, 'Sweet Georgia Brown' and 'Basin St Blues' on trumpet. He had his flugelhorn, euphonium, alto sax and piano within arm's reach all night, too.

It was an exhilarating send-off for a major Australian artist, for whom big things were now planned in North America and beyond. Suddenly, Peter Brendle got a phone call, which changed the flight plans. It came from Felix 'Cappy' Capicchiano, who later became Shire Councillor Felix Cappy, OAM for services to the Castlemaine community in Victoria, at that time a real estate agent and James Morrison fan. Felix wanted to know if Mr Morrison might be available to do some work in Brazil. Peter was taken aback.

'What's the gig?' he asked.

'We don't know yet; we'd just like to take him to Rio to play some jazz.' Peter, sceptical and cagey, probed a little further and the story came out.

Felix had a friend, Ian MacNee, a business entrepreneur who was making a fortune in gold mines in the Amazon Basin in South America. They'd met when MacNee had asked the real estate man to find him a quiet property on the Loddon River out the back of rural Castlemaine. Ian was more than happy with the grand stone house Felix recommended, and the two became good friends.

It was natural that jazz fan Felix would want Ian to hear his favourite trumpeter, the one he had been so impressed with in the late 1970s at the Castlemaine State Fair, when the teenaged Morrison had played as a protégé of Don Burrows. When James returned a few years later, Felix and Sue Cappy took Ian and Bobby MacNee along to the local basketball stadium, which served as the concert venue, to hear him.

Ian was as impressed as Felix, not only with the music, but with the PR possibilities he immediately saw for his companies. Sue Cappy's feeling was that Ian realised that little was known about Australia in South America, and bringing a sensational jazz player to Brazil — he knew South Americans loved jazz — might raise the awareness and standing of Australia in general, and Ian MacNee's mining companies, as sponsor, in particular.

MacNee — Sue said he was 'a mysterious man in some ways; he was always dropping in for a few days, then flying off to Hong Kong or New York' — didn't have time to work out the details. He authorised Felix, a great organiser, to make it happen. MacNee may have been mysterious, but he also proved extremely generous. When Brendle came up with a figure for airfares, accommodation, gig payments and living expenses, Felix didn't bat an eyelid; he wasn't footing the bill! 'No worries!' he said happily. Peter suggested three or four gigs in a ten-day period was a reasonable workload, and hung up the phone. He told James about the proposition, still suspecting it would never happen. *Hope it does*, thought James, *I'd love to go to Brazil. Don's been and never shuts up about it!*

The sizable deposit Peter requested turned up, accompanied by an airline ticket. So Morrison was off to South America with people he'd never met to play gigs that, at that point, didn't exist: a typical Morrison Boys' Own adventure.

The Cappys had seen James on several occasions at concerts, but Sydney-based Morrison, trombone case in hand and trumpet gig bag over his shoulder, first clapped eyes on his hosts from Victoria at Auckland airport. There was an immediate rapport. Sue saw James as 'a lovely, fun-loving, gorgeous person', while Felix sat next to him listening to his stories on the long flight. He heard how eighteen months earlier, James, with his sister Kathryn, had been at LA airport waiting to fly home when they discovered they didn't have enough cash for the departure tax. James said,

> We'd done that clever thing you do; we had about $14.62 left in American dollars, so we got a drink and a chocolate bar. Then they say, 'The departure tax is $14.' You go, 'I just had $14!' I had a credit card, but they wouldn't take credit cards. I'd been over on gigs, so I had my trumpet there. I realised the flight was going soon, so I got it out from the case and started playing in the check-in area, where everyone is in line. I didn't quite get to $14; I got stopped at about eight bucks when the airport police came over. I said, 'I'm just getting the departure tax; I only need another six dollars.' They wouldn't let me play anymore, but they stamped our passports anyway and we got the flight. It wouldn't have taken much longer.

He added, almost regretfully, 'We were up to eight bucks! Only six to go. Once you get to the high note stuff at the end of the piece, you get five or ten dollars in no time!'

Felix laughed, too, when James recalled how he and John were once lost on the Japanese railway system trying to get to Tokyo. In frustration, John said to a porter, 'Do you like cream or ice-cream on your apple pie?' The syllables must have registered something, as the porter pointed to Platform 16. Needless to say, though, the train they took didn't go anywhere near Tokyo.

There were yarns of boating misadventures, of course, including the 'sailing to The Heads overnight' chestnut. Another James told was of how, when he was living aboard the *Tiki* in Pittwater, he got up to find the dinghy that he used for getting to shore had drifted away. He stuffed his music into a plastic bag and swam with a lifebelt, hoping that his clothes would dry out by the time he got to the Con that day.

Felix's first impression, noted in his diary at the time, was that James seemed to be 'an interesting and adventurous character who looks a lot older than his twenty-four years, yet has a loveable, boyish mischievousness about him.'

The ten days in Rio were a marvellous experience for the Australians. The Cappys stayed in the huge apartment of Ian MacNee's son Christopher, on the thirteenth floor of the Rue Garcia D'Avila, fifty yards from Ipanema. It had views over the beach in front, and the city and the skyline-dominating statue of Christ the Redeemer on Corcovado Mountain behind. Morrison's hotel was a stone's throw away.

They ate together — Brazilian barbecues with ten meat varieties, *bife com arroz e feijao* (steak with rice and the very popular Brazilian black beans), local fresh fish and fruit.

They shopped; Sue bought good shoes at bargain prices, James bought small Latin-American percussion instruments from a flea market, and a guitar. They explored the town, rode the cable-car up Mount Sugarloaf and basked on Ipanema Beach. Felix waxed eloquent in his travel diary:

> The girls are as stunning as the song might suggest. Deeply tanned, well-rounded and wearing the briefest of bikinis, they glide along the beach and nearly make your eyes fall out. As they get a bit older, though, the lithesomeness seems to turn a bit heavy on the middle-aged women.

It was a wonder James could drag himself away to play the nightclub gigs scheduled for him by Chris MacNee at his father's behest. It was easier said than done. The name 'James Morrison' didn't cut much ice in Ipanema yet, and club owners were reluctant to put an Australian unknown on in prime time. The clubs James was booked to play at were first-class, but his initial timeslot was support-act status. He started his first stint at Peoples, Rio's number one nightclub, at 3.30am when things were winding down. He was an instant success, though, and his second gig the following night was brought forward to 1.30am, main-event time, with the club's featured band. Again, Felix noted, 'He was well clapped and congratulated, and his fellow musos, all Brazilian A-listers, smiled their approval.'

The word spread. By the third night, James had 'the place rocking; patrons were standing up, clapping and calling out, "Bravo!"' The 1.30am gig ended at 5am.

By the end of the ten days, James was fitting in two gigs a night, racing between Peoples, Botelo Telo, Ragtime and the smaller Club One, an intimate venue that catered to the wealthy set. James was particularly taken by the vocalist there, Fatima Regina, likening her to Australia's own Kerrie Biddell — high praise indeed.

He played with a full samba band at Botelo Telo, but was a little wary of his first night at Ragtime. He heard the band practise and suspected they might want to show him up. Within two numbers, the ice was broken, the group really gelled and the pianist even offered James the keyboard for a number. Sue was amused to hear the bandleader, far from resenting the Australian intruder, say after the shortest of breaks, 'Come on, James, let's play some more!'

The biggest night was the fourth birthday celebrations at Peoples. The joint was packed — the Cappys and the MacNees had to stand most of the night — and musicians came and went in celebrity spots. 'James played with several groups and was very well-received,' reported Felix. 'In one bracket, he played with three different pianists, two drummers and two different trumpeters. James seemed to enjoy himself!'

The last sentence sums up the trip. After a hectic ten days, the Cappys flew inland to see the workings of MacNee's gold mine out of Manaus on the Amazon. James had three more gigs to complete over the weekend before heading to New York to meet up with John.

Felix wrote, 'It has been a great experience sharing ten days with James. He is a simple character; no pretension, very homely, likes company and has a spirit of adventure.' There appeared to be only one minor regret, and that in the mind of the chief benefactor and trip facilitator, Ian MacNee himself. He hadn't been around much, as usual, but popped in towards the end, promising 'to give the boys a night to remember'. He was disappointed twenty-four hours later, after a gig till 4am and a visit to a private disco called Hippopotamus, to run out of time to take the men to Barbarella's Strip Club. He had wanted to take James, he said, 'to have some entertainment'.

James didn't need it; he'd been vastly entertained by his twelve-gigs-in-twelve-days adventure, and he was keen to be in New York again.

Chapter 15

Another Bite of the 'Apple'

In early May 1987, James flew on from Rio de Janeiro to New York, met up with John, and the two young men were ready for their second assault on the jazz capital. It was a more mature undertaking than the first. The Morrisons were a little older and a great deal wiser. They no longer looked like two boys just out of their teens. James in particular was filling out. Back in 1985 he'd had, perhaps through his New York living circumstances, a 'lean and hungry look'. Now after eighteen months feeding in a better pasture, *The Bulletin* writer James Hall could describe him as looking 'more like a country parson than a late-night jazzman'. His hair, never very thick, was starting to recede and there was a fair amount of forehead above his balloon-cheeked embouchure. By the time I first saw him, a year or so later, he was even more Pickwickian, both his face and his tummy becoming increasingly round.

His changing shape didn't affect his performances, though, and there were plenty of them in the offing. The boys had even put themselves up in a hotel, The Belleclaire, a few stars short of five but a good deal better than a cabin cruiser — one cabin, and no head — moored out on 79th Street.

Larry Clothier and Edith Kiggen had engagements lined up, including a European tour with Cab Calloway, eighty-year-old veteran of big bands, and 'Minnie the Moocher' and *The Blues Brothers* fame. He was touring for a month and the instrumental soloist of the big band had fallen sick. It was probably someone like, James imagined, Buddy DeFranco, the bebop clarinettist. James tried to reason why he was chosen before all the known great players of New York. He figured

Clothier and Kiggen thought, 'I might as well get a nobody; someone no-one's heard of. That'll prevent resentments among the band guys.' Added to which, Morrison would come cheaper than a Buddy DeFranco. 'About a tenth as much,' laughed James. He took John along as 'his manager'.

Edith Kiggen would have known, through Clothier, exactly what James could do. He was thrown in the deep end; he had solo spots on the big Cab Calloway concerts. Edith warned her young protégé not to get ahead of himself. She said,

> As a newcomer, you can't come here looking like the new kid on the block who's going to blow everyone's brains out; you'll simply get killed. There are a lot of people who've been here for years working and, if they want to, in their own little way they can destroy anybody.

She quickly found that James had a very good sense of jazz etiquette, and respect for the legends of the genre. 'It was impossible not to like him personally,' she said. 'The musicians liked him.' James, for his part, felt well at home:

> I was back in the nightclubs of Ken Laing and Tommy Tycho, except now it was Edith Kiggen and Cab Calloway. I knew how to walk on, I knew how to work with Cab, I knew how to act and I knew how to talk to the audience. I could play up and put some comedy in. I just did my cabaret act, and Cab and everyone said, 'Okay, now I see why this guy was booked.' I played fours with myself on trumpet and trombone; I did the full shtick. If I could have, I'd have got John up to do the rounds with his drumsticks!

Kiggen continued to manage James' affairs as he and John travelled around Europe. They were a dream to work with, she found. 'Apart from James' talent, he also has a manner which is extremely important. He doesn't drink, he doesn't do drugs, he's always on time, he has a super sense of humour; he has all those things beyond talent. And he's also vastly assisted by his brother, John.'

Kiggen had stars like Calloway and Manhattan Transfer on her books, as well as her 'nurture artists' like Morrison and a young Polish piano player called Adam Makowicz, whom she later linked with James. She could pressure the European festival organisers by saying, 'You can have the Transfer or Calloway or Clothier's Carmen McCrae, if you take my two new boys.'

James got his spot on the Calloway concerts and later embarked on a tour of the principal European jazz festivals. They included the monstrous North Sea Jazz Festival in Holland, where he was introduced by jazz great Benny Carter and played in a special trumpet 'summit' with Wynton Marsalis, Woody Shaw and Roy Hargrove, and the Umbria Jazz in Perugia, guesting with Carter's Quintet.

The following year, James did the Festival circuit again — North Sea, Nice, Montreux, Pori in Finland and the Cascades in Portugal — as well as duo gigs with Makowicz, often playing euphonium to complement the keyboard. John said,

> The duo was great. Makowicz was an incredibly gifted classical and jazz piano player. He was crazy and awesomely talented. I remember at the North Sea Festival, they were playing 'Proclamation' and floating through the keys with surreal subtlety. They started laughing, the other musos started laughing, and the whole audience joined in, watching this amazing exchange of jazz minds.

John Morrison was enjoying himself, too, in his putative role as manager. Edith Kiggen even offered him an extension of it by asking him to consider taking care of Manhattan Transfer.

> For some reason, Ken Laing [back in Sydney] and others have thought I'd be a great manager, and I was sort of managing James in an indirect sense at the time. I would go with him and look after his stuff. I never did the Manhattan Transfer tour, but I did train two other guys from the Calloway band to do it. James

> and I had a car during those years and we saw a lot of Europe during the three or four months of touring. I played gigs myself. There was a lot of jamming and playing at the festivals, so I wasn't getting rusty. I felt a part of it all, and we made some great friends and contacts.

One of the contacts, through Clothier and Kiggen, was Nesuhi Ertegun who, with his brother Ahmet, had started Atlantic and Elektra Records. The Erteguns were huge in the recording business, to the extent that they became WEA Records (Warner, Elektra, Atlantic) when Warner tried to buy them out. Nesuhi's preference was for jazz and he signed Morrison to the Atlantic label.

The trumpeter recalled his first meeting with the mogul: 'I sat in his office overlooking Central Park. Not that long ago I'd been living with my brother in a cramped and decrepit cabin cruiser with no toilet. Now I'm in an office big enough to accommodate sixteen of us!'

Nesuhi was evidently as impressed by Morrison's talent as James was by Ertegun's office space. Nesuhi said,

> We'll do an album a year, a big album with anyone you want. Oscar Peterson, Count Basie — doesn't matter, anyone you want. But first we'll do one with Adam Makowicz. We'll put in a good rhythm with you guys. I'll pull a couple of guys off Herbie Hancock's tour in France, fly them to Montreux and we'll record a live album.

James was stunned. *This guy can do anything. In a jazz sense*, he thought. *I've just met God. He can dictate to the biggest jazz festival in the world!*

The fact that Ertegun had given director Claude Nobs substantial assistance in getting his festival up and running in the first place probably helped.

Morrison's career had reached a very high platform. He was undoubtedly Australia's best-known and most extraordinary instrumentalist and jazz player, with a personality that charmed audiences both live and on television. He'd challenged himself to take on New York, where his talent had been recognised and acknowledged by the city's finest, and conquered the European festival circuit. He'd signed for regular recordings with Atlantic Records, an offer most could only dream of, yet he remained relatively unsurprised by it all. He said,

> It made me feel lucky and blessed, but I'd always felt it was bound to happen, I just didn't know how. I realised that because Arnold had been working that day, I ended up at Arturo's. Because of that, I met Larry Clothier. Larry's guy was sick so I got the Calloway tour. All these things led me to where I was. I figured I was good enough, but then, I'd figured since I was seven I was good enough!
>
> There were lots of guys who could do it, but you don't just get where you're going because you can do it; everything has to fall into place, as it did for me. That was the path it took; I didn't know how it would happen but I always knew it would. It was certainly interesting to see it unfold, though!

It's unarguable that, as James said, everything did fall into place. One step seemed to follow inevitably after the other, but it's not true that 'a lot of guys could do it'. It's Morrison's innate modesty and apparent lack of appreciation of the uniqueness of his gifts that leads him to say such things. He seems to genuinely believe that the things he does are within the capabilities of most people: that anyone can play a variety of instruments at extreme ranges; that anyone can write musical arrangements as he did during primary school and high school; that anyone can progress from busking on Bleecker Street, New York, to the festival stages of Europe and an American record deal.

It's not the way things happen. A lesser player wouldn't have caught Larry Clothier's ear; a lesser personality couldn't have fronted the Cab Calloway band, and a lesser jazz interpreter and instrumentalist wouldn't have convinced the savvy audiences of Montreux, let alone Nesuhi Ertegun of Atlantic records. Nevertheless, that was, as James said, 'the path it took'. Not, though, by virtue of being a lucky bloke in the right place several times, but by the recognition of a very remarkable jazz talent by a series of very knowledgeable people.

James finished his 1987 American/European odyssey with stints alongside Red Rodney at the Jazz Showcase in Chicago and the Village Vanguard in New York, and when he was back in Australia reflected on it all: 'At home, I think of myself as a trumpeter — its flamboyance grabs the public's attention. In the US, I think of myself as a trombonist because that's what they see me as there. In the US there are lots of trumpet players, but trombonists are few and far between.'

He told James Hall of *The Bulletin*, 'People would say "Oh, that's nice," when I played the trumpet, but when I played the trombone it was, "Can I have your card? Let me call you tomorrow."'

Sometimes, James wondered whether he should just concentrate on one brass instrument and take it as far as he could. He tried it occasionally, but found himself pining for the others after two or three days. He couldn't do without the piano either. He preferred the keyboard when he felt 'orchestral' and wanted to play all the parts, which he couldn't do on the trumpet or trombone. 'I'll never stop playing the piano,' he said, 'Some nights it feels better than the brass.' He thought he might devote some time to it over the next few years and see if he could express himself on it as readily as he could on the trumpet. He quickly added a typical Morrison rider, though. 'It depends on what others think about it. I'm a great believer in the fact that it doesn't matter how wonderful you might think you are, if no-one wants to listen, you might as well go sailing.'

On 20 October 1987, *The Australian* announced, 'The Conquering Hero Returns Home'. That was the publicity theme used by Australian manager Peter Brendle for a huge 'welcome back' gig. Eric Myers wrote,

> When a concert featuring local jazz stars virtually fills the Sydney Town Hall, drawing nearly 2000 people, then there is something

unusual happening in what is still a minority art form. At this concert, the question which many were pondering was the obvious one: has Morrison's overseas experience made any difference to his playing?

On the basis of this limited sample, I venture to say Morrison's improvisations are now more focused, more controlled than ever before. He played his armoury of instruments with his brilliance and customary flair, but there was no sign of his Achilles heel, the tendency to let technique run into overstatement and vulgarity. Musically, he has matured.

The first half of the concert by the Morrison Quartet was measured and somewhat sedate. The second stanza, featuring the Big Bad Band, guest stars Don Burrows and singer Ricky May with John Morrison providing, Myers said, 'percussive fire', nearly brought the house down. The concert ended, the critic wrote, 'on a note of fun and mayhem. It was pure show business, which forcefully underlined the clout which a group of key jazz musicians have with a mass audience outside the narrow jazz community.'

The critics applauded James' musical growth, his versatility on his arsenal of instruments, and his ability to entertain and push jazz into the mainstream of public entertainment. As Myers pointed out, 'James had achieved what Australian jazz performers had merely dreamed of for forty years: being able to work in Europe and the US, in the top echelons of the art form for half a year, while maintaining a career in his own country for the other half.'

The late 1980s were momentous years for James. He was now so well-known at home that when his high profile was added to his much-publicised love of action sports, like sailing, abseiling and fast cars, it was no surprise that he was invited to drive in the Celebrity Race at the Australian Grand Prix in Adelaide. He accepted the invitation readily, not ever dreaming it would be a life-changing event.

Chapter 16

A Romantic Interlude

It was part of advanced driving instructor Jim Murcott's job to teach the drivers selected for the Australian Grand Prix Celebrity Race how to career around the Adelaide street circuit very fast without doing themselves an injury. After a week's training at the International Raceway, some of those invited didn't make the grade. It was Murcott's sad responsibility, then, to tell them not to race in case they ended up making fools of themselves.

Those who did pass muster in November 1987 included comedian Rowan Atkinson, author and TV presenter Clive James, cricket captain Ian Chappell, golfer Greg Norman, trumpeter James Morrison, and that year's Miss Australia, Judith Green.

In an article in the *Sydney Morning Herald*, Murcott described Greg Norman as 'a natural' and Chappell, by virtue of his highly developed hand-eye coordination, as 'very good'. Rowan Atkinson was petrolhead enough to choose to be a spectator at the James Hardie 5000. Behind the wheel, he was very quick, showed good control and said he was having a ball. Speed buff James Morrison didn't crack it for a mention.

The drivers took the event very seriously — at speeds in excess of 160 kph, they had to. Murcott said any one of ten celebrities could win the race held before the real Formula One event in front of 100,000 spectators. He wouldn't be drawn on a specific favourite. 'It all depends on who adapts to the track the quickest. It's a tricky circuit. It's like a tunnel and can be off-putting for new drivers. They only get a short practise, so it's not easy.'

'But if you want to have some money on it,' suggested the newspaper, 'back Miss Australia.' In the previous day's practice, while Chappell spun out, she came from behind to win.

That might have been the trial run where James claimed he was cut off by another driver. His chat show story goes that he became frustrated with the driver in front of him and when they both returned to the pits, James approached his rival to give him some much-needed driving advice. As he got nearer, starting to wave an indignant finger, the rival removed the driving helmet to release a cascade of long dark hair onto her shoulders. James was face to face with Miss Australia, and tongue-tied like a teenager on a first date. 'Nice driving,' he spluttered as his heart pumped faster than his Formula One engine.

John Morrison admits both he and James are 'great fabricators'. 'We could sell the leg off a chair and ice to an Eskimo,' he claims. James' sensationalist description of the event is at odds with an interview he gave to the *Brisbane Sunday Mail* in 1989, when he was looking back on his recent career, romantic and professional. James said then that he and Judi met at a barbecue at Murcott's house. 'I walked into the room,' he said, 'and I saw this very sophisticated-looking woman and wondered who she was. I thought, *It doesn't matter anyway, she looks like one of those types who wouldn't stop to talk to one of us.*' Judi had similar thoughts: 'I saw all these famous people and wondered what they would think of plain Judi from Perth.'

Despite her poise and not-so-plainness, she felt quite intimidated and ill-at-ease. She spoke to James briefly and tried to guess his age. His receding hairline led her astray; she estimated thirty-four when he was, in fact, almost ten years younger and close to Judi's own age.

Despite the gaffe, James was smitten. He says,

> I thought, *Oh, she's the one*, though now, looking back, I'm wondering what I was on. I remember thinking, *What possible chance does some trumpet player dag have with Miss Australia?*

Then I found out that, professionally, she was a paediatric nurse. *That's who she is*, I thought. *She's actually this wonderful person.*

The Miss Australia Quest ran from 1954 to 2000. Over 1000 young women from around the country entered each year in its halcyon days, and the State winners competed for the National title. In addition to being a beauty contest — in the days before such events became unfashionable — entrants also participated in fundraising and, in its 45-year lifespan, raised $87 million for the Spastic Centres of Australia. It's not a stretch to see that a committed paediatric nurse in WA would deem it justifiable to use her good looks and personality to help children struggling with such illnesses. It offered a huge amount of fun and adventure for a very worthwhile cause.

James was perceptive enough to divine Judi's inner qualities. 'She's gorgeous,' he realised, 'and she's Miss Australia, but there's something more about her. This is my wife, I can tell.'

James' previous history hadn't seen a string of romances; he was too busy onstage to have too many attachments off it. He was never pictured at a celebrity event with a pretty young thing on his arm. In fact, he'd once told his mother, 'I don't date anyone. I may not marry; I haven't got the time.'

He'd had girlfriends, but, in a vox-pop for *The Age Good Weekend* magazine, he reflected:

> **My first relationship was** ... a disaster. She left me because 'things weren't moving along quickly enough'. We were 12!
>
> **My most humiliating moment was** ... when I was 15 and took the beautiful Louise to a party. I thought it was going fantastically — right up to the point when her 23-year-old boyfriend turned up.

It's probably not advisable to put too much store by such responses; Morrison seems to have created his answers quite flippantly. Another response went:

At home I cook ... mostly raw things. I've tried cooking cooked things, but it's not as rewarding.

Nevertheless, the angst of his youthful love-life was reflected later in the column, when he was asked if he preferred cats or dogs. 'Dogs,' he answered. 'Cats are too aloof and fickle with their affections. If I wanted to be treated like that, I can just reminisce about dating as a teenager.'

When James met Judi, he had just about resigned himself to being single for the rest of his life. He'd decided his lifestyle made it impossible to meet someone, let alone develop a relationship. The way the relationship with Judi developed was the only way one could. Their courtship was like their Grand Prix driving (at which both still claim to have beaten the other) — very fast.

In December 1987, Judi was in Sydney for the launch of the Miss New South Wales Quest. She tracked James down to the ABC. When her call came through the switchboard, a secretary brought the message to the boardroom and read it aloud, much to James' delight, in front of the directors of ABC Records. 'Miss Australia would like to know if James can join her for lunch', was the message. James was suddenly the most admired bloke in the room which, surprisingly, didn't stop him from being two hours late for the appointment. He tried to make amends the best way he knew how: he took Judi sailing on his beloved Pittwater. They talked the night away and James returned her to her hotel at 7am, giving her just enough time to pack for her flight to Tasmania.

On Australia Day in late January 1988, the beauty queen was back in Sydney again. They made another date, and again James was two hours late! He was making a hash of this, and was fortunate that Judi also felt she and James were right for each other. She accepted both his excuses and his apologies. At the time she said,

I thought at first he'd be pretentious and snobby and big-headed, but he wasn't. I can't really say what it is about him. He's funny and I love his attitude to life, and his opinions. I realised he was someone who was able to live his dreams. He strives for something and achieves it, but is unaffected by it.

James certainly had something in mind that he was trying to achieve at this time. A couple of days later, Judi got a note at her hotel written, predictably enough, on manuscript paper, saying, 'Be at the airport at six in the morning. Tickets will be at the counter. I'll meet you in Brisbane.' The adventurous Judi was up for a mystery trip. It ended on Hayman Island, where James not only had a series of gigs, but had also managed to arrange for a dozen red roses in her room when she woke on her first morning.

When they returned to Sydney, James suggested she stay there for keeps. Judi remembers, '*I can't*, I thought, *I live in Perth*. But I knew as well as James I couldn't go back.'

Though their jobs kept them apart for long periods — Judi's year as Miss Australia involved as much air travel as James' gig touring — they were engaged and married within twelve months.

The ceremony, inevitably for James and the water-loving maternal side of the family, was on a tall ship; a romantic, square-masted schooner on Sydney Harbour in front of a hundred guests. They included painter Ken Done, and TV personality and occasional drummer Daryl Somers, as well as the Cappys from Castlemaine. After the vows were complete, they all headed off to the reception, which James predicted would be 'some jam session!'

Chapter 17

A Year to Celebrate

If 1988, the year of his marriage and the cementing of his reputation worldwide as a unique instrumentalist, was momentous for James, it was also pretty significant in the history of the nation. It was the year when Australia celebrated the bicentennial anniversary of the arrival of Captain Arthur Phillip and his fleet of eleven ships in Sydney Harbour and the commencement of European colonisation of the island continent.

Australia partied hard throughout the year. It held a World Expo, which thousands of Australians and international visitors attended, on the banks of the Brisbane River; it re-enacted the arrival of the First Fleet and sent a Bicentennial Exhibition touring the country. All schoolchildren received a Heritage Medal, and the New South Wales Roads and Traffic Authority issued 160,000 commemorative number plates at a premium. The Boy Scout Movement, ever taught to 'be prepared', got in early and opened its World Jamboree at midnight on New Year's Eve 1987. Later in the year, Queen Elizabeth II popped in to open the spanking new Parliament building in Canberra.

An Australian Bicentennial Authority was set up to plan and coordinate the myriad events, and generous funding was available for projects that emphasised the nation's cultural heritage. One of those was the Australian Jazz Orchestra (AJO), a thirteen-man combination of musicians, 'young lions and valued veterans', Joya Jenson wrote, the cream of jazz talent from Sydney and Melbourne. It included many of the usual suspects — players James had long worked with on the Sydney scene. Dale Barlow was there, Alan Turnbull on drums, Warwick Alder on trumpet and Bob Bertles on reeds, as well as newer acquaintances like Melbourne's creative pianist Paul Grabowsky, and its finest trumpeter, Bob Venier. The band directorship was officially shared between Dale Barlow, Don Burrows, Paul Grabowsky and James Morrison, but as Barlow pointed out, the group was 'made up of leaders'. 'It's very democratic,' he said. Bernie McGann was more cautious: 'If everyone puts their egos aside, it should work.' It was a once-in-a-lifetime combination, made possible by the national drive to celebrate and demonstrate the finest and most talented in the Australian culture in its birthday year.

The band toured Australia twice, and was probably unique in the annals of jazz history in that it was flown from one outback gig to another by one of its own musicians, James Morrison, and his brother, John. Paul Grabowsky laughed and declared,

> I never felt in any danger! It certainly put to rest any fear of flying! We had two twelve-seaters and we visited many out-of-the-way places, like Broken Hill and Geraldton. I remember we flew into Sydney on Australia Day over the huge regatta they had there to play in The Basement that night. It was incredibly exciting. I loved being in that band.

The AJO had kicked off in the grand manner on New Year's Day before an enormous crowd of over 70,000, including the Prince and Princess of Wales, at The Domain in Sydney. They played two gigs at The Basement to settle the line-up in, then took off on the 'Australia coast to coast' tour before flying to America for gigs in Chicago, New York, Washington, San Francisco, Houston and Los Angeles.

Initially James, through a clash of dates, was unavailable for the US leg, but he was anxious to be part of the distinguished line-up for the entire unique tour. So, when Peter Brendle managed to free up his diary, he put his hand up to go.

In a generous gesture, rather than push his replacement, the fine US-based Sydney trombonist Dave Panichi, off the squad, James put his hand in his pocket and paid his own fare. It was too good an opportunity to miss, even if it cost him a few bob.

James smiles when he recalls the recruitment policy of the group: 'They were very careful to make sure it was a mix of Melbourne and Sydney. I love it when they want to make sure it's inclusive. No-one ever considers Brisbane or Adelaide or anywhere else; it had to be an even mix of Victorians and New South Welshmen.' Alan Turnbull, the Melbourne drummer now living in Sydney, in particular loved to stir up the old intercity rivalries.

They never surfaced onstage, though; everything there was supportive in a wide-ranging repertoire. Everyone wrote for the band, so there was no particular style or musical direction. One minute it could sound like Paul Grabowsky's band, and the next like Bernie McGann's. Everyone had their own idea what a band should sound like, but everyone fell over backwards to fit in with others. 'So,' said James, 'out of arrogance and politeness, it never had a sound of its own. I'm glad it happened, though,' he added, 'just to get all those jazz luminaries together in one place.'

Paul Grabowsky disagreed somewhat: 'It's all a matter of expectations. I felt that the band, at its best, played extremely well. The critics really liked the band.'

He was right. *The New York Times* described it as 'an unusually strong ensemble, playing a repertory that comes primarily from within the band' while the *LA Times* noted that

> on a relatively poorly attended night at the Catalina Bar & Grill, though the publicity was limited and the weather abysmal, everything else was piping hot as the Australian all-star aggregation roared through a set of modern mainstream jazz that was always exciting and, occasionally, electrifying.

John Porter (*NYT*) added that the AJO's

> widely acclaimed young star, the multi-instrumentalist James Morrison, is a fascinating trombone soloist. In a warm, colorful arrangement by Mr Burrows of Fats Waller's 'Jitterbug Waltz', he slithered deftly through pools of darkness and light with sinuous phrasing that suggested Urbie Green, with an occasional touch of Jack Teagarden in his tone.

Zan Stewart (*LA Times*) said he

> exhibited wit and virtuosity where a bristling eight-bar ensemble wallop followed the soloist's spirited melody reading. Later, Morrison picked up the larger euphonium and blew mad, wonderful bebop at breakneck speed.

Morrison was doing what he generally did: surprising the most cynical American critics with his energies and versatility. His regular US successes led Leonard Feather, the foremost jazz commentator, to speculate whether Morrison would settle in the States. Don Burrows, who, while not the only leader of the democratic group but generally its spokesman by dint of his seniority, shook his head. 'James is like me and most Australians,' he said. 'We love to travel and visit, but Australia offers so much in terms of lifestyle that we always like to go home again.'

Once back home, the AJO wound up its campaign, with shows at the World Expo '88 in front of some of the 100,000 people a day who were attracted to Brisbane during the fair's six-month lifespan. Sadly, apart from ABC tapes for broadcast, the AJO never recorded. It was, as Paul Grabowsky put it, 'a golden opportunity missed to document a fascinating experiment in Australian jazz history'.

James couldn't stay long to reflect on the success of the AJO's extensive whirlwind tours, though. He was booked to return to America and Europe, to work with Adam Makowicz and make the first of the recordings Nesuhi Ertegun had promised to set up. *Swiss*

Encounter was recorded live from the Montreux Casino on 7 July 1988 and, true to his word, Ertegun completed the rhythm section with 'a couple of Herbie Hancock's boys', Buster Williams on bass and Al Foster on drums. Makowicz played piano, of course, and Morrison trumpet, flugelhorn, trombone and euphonium.

The quartet put down seven excellent tracks, all the more creditable since 'Herbie's guys' had arrived only one day earlier. Nesuhi flew them in from the Nice Jazz Festival in France on a scheduled night off. The recording opened with a Gershwin standard, 'S'Wonderful', and used Sonny Rollins' 'Oleo', Hanley's standard 'Indiana' and a sixty-year-old Sigmund Romberg tune, 'Softly as in a Morning Sunrise', for which James played euphonium. The latter was an extended ten-minute track exceeded in length by the almost thirteen-minute 'Blues for Judy', a Morrison original and a swain's lament for his fiancée, Miss Australia, 10,000 miles away! Morrison also penned 'My Delight', and Makowicz had a dedication to his own wife, 'For You, Irene'.

John Morrison remarked earlier on the pair's musical empathy, and the Polish pianist clearly enjoyed working with the trumpeter. He displayed the wonderful touch, tone and shading that had gained him a 'best jazz pianist' award from readers of the *Jazz Forum* magazine. He created clever solos that complemented Morrison's flights of brilliance and contrasting subdued colours. One critic compared the trumpet sound to the great Clifford Brown, master of the husky and intimate, a comparison not often appropriate to James.

Warren Wen, an online commentator, thought the arrangements were 'fresh and superb, and the interchange between the trumpet and the piano like two lovers breathing to each other. You find intelligent conversation between these two virtuosos, but no exaggeration and no self-indulgence.' Well, almost none. James couldn't resist some multiphonics and four-bar trading between trumpet and trombone on 'Blues for Judy'. It was, after all, a live recording in front of a big audience, and James' middle name is 'Entertainment'!

This was James' first real album in some ways — the first that had his puffed-out chops on half a record cover, alongside Makowicz. His playing had been recorded on numerous occasions on radio, TV and shared discs, but this was the first where his name was in the biggest font on the jacket. Ten years earlier, he'd soloed on the Young Northside Big Band pre-Monterey album. He'd been on Don Burrows' records, like *Jazz at the Opera House* and *Burrows at the Winery*, and the Big Bad Band had made two records for the ABC in Australia. But now he'd completed his first international disc for East-West, with distribution through Atlantic. It was a huge breakthrough, with more promised. 'A record a year,' Nesuhi Ertegun had said, 'with whoever you like — Basie, Peterson — you name it.'

A second record quickly followed the first. Within months, James had completed *Postcards from Down Under* for WEA (Australia), jazz settings to match and illuminate the paintings of his friend, Ken Done. Done was a very popular painter at the time, one whose penchant for bright colours and sunlit Sydney scenes was immediately recognisable, whether on a gallery wall or printed on tourist T-shirts and tea towels.

Mostly, the Morrison brothers collaborated on the tunes to fit the artwork, but a couple of times the process was reversed and Done completed a canvas based on his impressions of music already written. It worked as if Done was the eye and Morrison provided the ear. Of the nine tracks, four were credited to the Morrisons, while experienced American jazz pianist and co-producer Garry Dial, who played alongside James in the Red Rodney Quintet, wrote the rest. It covered a range of styles, from post-bop to fusion and jazz funk, and was generally well-received, though Scott Yanow, reviewing for the *AllMusic* website, rightly predicted that 'none of the individual tunes would catch on'. *DownBeat* magazine in the States was enthusiastic about the double release. Bill Milkowski said, 'Check them out and see for yourself if Morrison is, as Leonard Feather says, as sure a bet for superstardom as Wynton Marsalis was in 1981.'

A trumpet player, like a prophet it seems, is sometimes without honour in his own country's press. John Clare, who wrote on jazz for the *Sydney Morning Herald* throughout the 1980s and 1990s, mostly under the pen-name Gail Brennan, was not impressed. 'The new album, *Postcards*,' he wrote, 'is the sort of fusion music you might hear over an ABC filler of sunlight glittering on the Harbour.' He described James as 'a gifted, if sometimes vulgar mimic' and wondered whether there was not, 'rather than great creativity, a certain shallowness'. 'The playing is slick,' he continued, 'even by American standards. Some pleasant lines emerge; also some very banal ones.'

Perhaps Brennan could have, like Milkowski, reviewed the dual release as a package — the contemporary studio session *Postcards* aimed at Morrison's home and Japanese markets, and the mainstream *Swiss Encounter* at the US and European jazz buyer. Morrison himself said at the time, 'I've been attracted to so many styles of jazz that it's hard to capture it all in just one record. That's why they're releasing two albums so close together.'

Even this early in his career, James wasn't much exercised by critics, feeling they often failed to understand what his criteria were and what he was trying to do. They misunderstood his determination to make sure his audience, to use his favourite phrase, 'got it', whether it was Dixieland, swing or bebop. Instead of asking if the night 'happened', he sometimes felt critics carped on inappropriately about a lack of innovation or creativity where none was sought. What, then, if the journalists broadcast their lack of appreciation to the world? 'The people who were there, they got it. If they were there, they'll know the report's not right; if they weren't there, what does it matter?'

James didn't have time to stew on criticisms anyway. He had a wedding to attend, a short honeymoon to enjoy and a huge professional year in prospect. In 1989, he was scheduled to tour South America again, before going to Japan to sell *Postcards* there. Then it was back to the European festival circuit, where his profile was growing like Jack's beanstalk, for the third year in a row.

He was due to record with WEA Records, but the sudden death of Nesuhi Ertegun obviated all that. 'Once Nesuhi passed away,' James said, 'they paid lip-service to his artists, and I was one of many.' Nesuhi was mourned far beyond the jazz fraternity. He was a Rock and Roll Hall of Famer, a Lifetime Achievement Award winner from the Grammy Trustees, and the Nesuhi Ertegun Jazz Hall at the Lincoln Center was dedicated to him. Additionally, he and his brother, Ahmet, were inducted to the US Soccer Hall of Fame. They had set up the famous New York Cosmos club which, by signing up stars like the magical Pele and the imperious Franz Beckenbauer, had raised the profile of soccer in the States enormously.

Yet, suddenly, Ertegun was gone and 'the album a year with whoever you like' went with him. James played on the tribute album, *Nesuhi*, which featured many of the artists he'd championed over the years. Gillespie was on it, and numerous others who wanted to pay their respects to a man who'd done so much to, as James put it, 'legitimise the jazz scene'. Claude Nobs produced the album, so James' link with the Montreux Festival was maintained. Morrison was set to promote his dual releases there and Nobs, the Festival director, wondered who to put James onstage with in addition to the *Swiss Encounter* team. 'Dizzy's having some guests,' he said, 'I'll put you on with him.'

Dizzy Gillespie! The father of bebop; James' idol and inspiration since high school. 'I was thrilled, but anxious not to "jevver" him,' recalls James, remembering the old days with Don Burrows, when garrulous fans had outstayed their welcome after gigs.

So I didn't say to Dizzy, 'Oh, I've heard all your stuff.' What's he going to say? 'What? You and 50 million others!' Dizzy would have been gracious; he was that sort of man. He would have said, 'Oh, that's wonderful,' but by the time he'd said that to fifty-six people, you wouldn't want to be another one. So I just said, 'It's great to be here,' or something, and he said, 'It's good to have you.' He was terrific; very friendly.

James' favourite story recalls Dizzy with his clipboard, running through the set order in the dressing room:

> Now I'm going to come out and do something with the boys. Then Steve [the trombone player Steve Turre], you can come out [perhaps to perform his remarkable jazz feature on prepared conch shells]. Then Carmen [McCrae], will you do a couple of songs next? After that Mr Morrison will come on and … [the old maestro's faced turned to a snarl] if he brings his trumpet with him, I'm going to smack him in the mouth.

He wasn't serious; his face crinkled and he roared with laughter at his own joke.

Gillespie was always happy to give concert space to the next generation, whether it was Arturo Sandoval, Jon Faddis or the new Australian bloke, James Morrison. Nevertheless, in the first set James only played his trombone. Later in the night, he found himself duetting on the valved instrument with the world's greatest bebop trumpeter. James was over the moon, but not overawed; he was thrilled and not unnerved to be playing alongside his hero. He could hold his own in this company. He remembers:

> I was appreciative of the opportunity, but there was this dual thing. When you're onstage next to Dizzy, trading fours with him, you can figure you're really hot and should be playing with Dizzy Gillespie, which means you've got a big head. Or you can think, *My word, I don't deserve this*, in which case you don't, because you're not going to play well enough. Or you can think, *This is a huge privilege, but I deserve to be here*. If you don't deserve to be there, then it's not a privilege, it's a farce and it's all wrong. So you have to say, 'I deserve to be here. I'm privileged to be the one getting what he deserves.'

It was a remarkable achievement, whichever way you look at it: a country town Australian playing alongside the master of bebop at one of the world's greatest jazz festivals; akin to a boy from Baghdad batting alongside Bradman at Lords, or a girl from Katmandu singing Carmen at Covent Garden. It's possible, but highly unlikely.

Mr Gillespie was generous in his summation of the event. 'It's not surprising to me for James to be playing all styles of music and be very good at it,' he said. 'That happens in many places in the world, but he's one of the best.'

Dizzy forgot to mention that James had played Set One on trombone and Set Two on trumpet. It was a feat even Mr Gillespie himself couldn't have equalled, and it made James not just one of the best, but quite unique.

Chapter 18

Back to Rio

Early that same year, in February 1989, James had taken a second interesting detour through South America. He travelled first-class this time, having bewilderingly turned down the opportunity to ride up front with the Cappys two years previously. Again, the munificent Mr MacNee was picking up the tab.

It wasn't altruistic; MacNee had seen the benefits of promoting Australians like himself in Brazil, and wanted to push the PR into Bolivia. This was made easier by James' superb performances in 1987. He was invited to play with big bands at a series of monster balls, which preceded the four-day Carnival, with its colourful eye-popping parades and the incessant, insistent samba beat.

From a jazz-playing point of view, it wasn't the ideal time to be in Rio — the single hypnotic rhythm permeated everything — but from all other points of view, where else would you rather be? James lapped up the atmosphere at one of the most exciting events on the planet. He arrived three days before the Cappys to practise with his first samba band, and was glad to see his friends when they walked into Chris MacNee's huge new apartment at Ipanema. It could accommodate Chris, the Cappys, James and five more friends who materialised in time for the Carnival proper.

On the night of Felix's arrival, James was due to play his first gig. Sue cried off with jet lag, but Felix flipped on MacNee's best Mardi Gras shirt and was ready to samba. 'What a ball!' he noted in his travel diary. 'The ballroom had two levels; each floor had over 3000 people dancing the samba nonstop. The dancers stand in one spot and move or sway to the beat, rather than jumping around a lot. This makes it easy to join in; no-one needs a partner nor any dancing experience.'

Felix hadn't lost his eye for the girls in the two years since his last visit. 'The dress is predominantly skimpy. G-strings with stockings and suspenders are common, through to lavish outfits with feathers and masks.' Bars dispensed drinks, and many of the girls danced on the tables and chairs. 'The men would walk past and kiss them on the bottom,' wrote Felix. 'The thing that impressed me was that, despite the huge crowd and the crush, behaviour was very good; everyone was there just to enjoy themselves.'

James was due to play at 11pm with the group he'd rehearsed with. At 9.30pm, with typical young Morrison forethought and planning, he realised he needed to have a pair of black pants. No-one had any to lend him, so Chris MacNee drove him to Rio Sul shopping centre, where he picked up a pair just before closing time. They were much too long and, again typically, he pinned the cuffs up.

Just on 11pm, Chris dropped him off at the backstage door. When the doorman challenged him, he held his trombone case aloft and declared, 'Musica.' He was ushered into a room, where several other musos were getting ready. They, too, had black pants, and were putting on black bow ties.

James grabbed one for himself. Next, they passed around the tuxedo jackets. As James pulled his on, he realised he didn't recognise anyone from the run-through a couple of nights before. He remembered the bandleader's name was Nello. 'Nello?' he inquired. The other band members just smiled and shrugged.

James walked out onstage with them in front of 3000, worryingly aware that this wasn't the band he'd rehearsed with and that he had no idea of the repertoire. He played along anyway, without any complaint from band or audience. Felix and the local boys, Chris MacNee and his friends, moved through the crowd to the front of the stage to make sure James saw them. When he spotted them, Felix noted, 'his face sure lit up — though it might have been from all the girls that were jumping on the stage and dancing in front of the band,' in those skimpy G-strings and suspenders!

After the ball, when Felix mentioned there was another ballroom upstairs, the peseta dropped. James realised he'd been directed to the wrong band on the wrong floor. He'd enjoyed the spectacle and the playing anyway, and Felix thought it was 'a tribute to his talent that he played along so well in a totally unprepared gig'.

The boys left the ball around 4.30am and, since James was always hungry after playing, found a pizza place for supper and/or breakfast. The gang got home at about six in the morning, the first but by no means the last occasion when the boys fell into bed during daylight hours.

The highlight of the week and the Rio social calendar was the final shindig, the Sugarloaf Carnival Ball, which marked the official opening of the Carnival of Rio. Every year, 2500 partygoers in costume took the cable car up to Murro da Urca to dance to the samba bands, from 11pm till 'the sun rises next morning', as the tickets boasted. The theme in 1989 was 'Lenin and Marilyn at the Sugarloaf'. The patrons, including James who had a night off from performing, the Cappys, Chris MacNee, and his mates and their girlfriends, dressed as an American pin-up or a Russian dictator, and pretty much anything in between. 'It was amazing,' said Sue. 'You had all these rich people from around the world, beautiful women; it was mind-boggling.'

It was evidently too much for Felix; he ran out of words and his diary stopped abruptly after describing the men in their red Lenin hats and the girlfriends, Giselle, Anna and Myra, in their matching silver, sequined leotards. He noted, faithfully, that his wife Sue, in her 'long, sequined skirt with a full-length split, matching top with bare midriff, and a headband with red feathers' held her own among the local beauties.

Finally, Ian MacNee provided grandstand tickets for the great Carnival parade. 'They cost a fortune,' said Sue, 'just a little bit of space where you could stand and soak up the entire spectacle' of about two million revellers in colourful and revealing costumes, dancing a joyful and energetic samba through the streets of Rio.

Then, for the Cappys and Morrison, the Carnival was over. The entire South American adventure, however, was not. Ian MacNee's mining tentacles were stretching into Bolivia and he thought a corporate gig with President Victor Paz Estensorro, with his wife in attendance, wouldn't do his standing any harm. So La Paz appeared on the itinerary.

At over 13,000 feet above sea level in the Andes, La Paz is the highest national capital in the world, and that generates its own problems. Even just flying up there was stressful for Sue Cappy:

> We were in this dodgy old aeroplane and the engine started making a funny noise on the right-hand side. It sounded very sick and I was getting nervous. James was sitting across the aisle. He lifted his head from his book and listened. 'Oh well,' he said, 'nothing we can do about it.' His head went back down and he calmly started reading again. It was typical; he was a man of adventure and nothing fussed him much.

The altitude was one of the few things that did, however. Visitors are advised to take precautions before flying into La Paz. The Cappys and James took nothing, and suffered for it. Sue was violently sick for several days and James spent twenty-four hours living on chicken broth.

He collapsed leading up to the big performance. 'We were very worried about him,' said Sue, 'his fingers turned blue and he was out of it.' He took no medication, but after a while, maybe an hour or so, he came good, jumped up and played his trumpet as if nothing had happened.

Curiously, Felix was largely unaffected by the rapid change in altitude. He was a man from Italian stock who enjoyed a glass of wine or three, but he gave it up temporarily, knowing it could be a problem at high altitude. James noticed that he was still able to function quite normally from the outset. This lead to the 'Morrison First Principle of Intoxication': the amount of wine consumed by the average Italian is equal in depletion of oxygen to the bloodstream to living at 14,000 feet above sea level! This valuable contribution to the store of human knowledge tickled his fancy, and still amuses him greatly. Felix could eat steak, go sightseeing and do everything normally — no better and no worse than if he'd partaken of his normal quota of red wine.

Another problem James experienced, once he acclimatised, was with the language — not translating Spanish into Australian English, but in music, the lingua franca James normally spoke like a native. James' back-up band for the President's gig were local men. Even trusty John wasn't on hand to play the drums. 'What sort of music do they play?' James asked his translator, whose English was only marginally better than James' Spanish. 'Traditional,' was the answer.

Okay, thought James. '"Saints"!' he called, and they were away. They were good musicians and James was comfortable, though not stretched, during a very enjoyable first half of trad jazz.

During the break, James got a message from the President's wife: 'Could the band please play some bebop?' *Hmm, hip lady*, thought James. He knew he could oblige; he wasn't sure about his sidemen. He went to the band and said, '"Anthropology"?' with a raised eyebrow. It was as though he'd asked if they wanted to win the La Paz lottery. 'Sí, sí.' '"Dexterity"?' Their collective thumbs went up and they grinned broadly. James hadn't cottoned on to their music-speak. 'It was the same as New York,' he explained later. 'Trad jazz to a New Yorker is bebop; trad jazz to us is Dixieland. If they want Dixieland, they call it Dixieland or New Orleans. When I was told they played 'traditional', they meant 'bebop'. James had spent the night thus far calling Dixieland tunes when they were Bolivia's best beboppers, specially hired to suit the musical preference of the wife of the President. The band who had, uncomplaining, churned out an hour of 'trad' were delighted and exhilarated by the sudden turn of events she'd instigated.

'It would have been interesting to be in the audience, though,' reflected James afterwards. 'The first half the band sounded like Preservation Hall, and the second like the Dizzy Gillespie Quintet! "Geez, what happened in the break?"'

Ian MacNee was unsighted during the second South American adventure. He left the organisation and arrangements to his son, Chris, who looked after his Latin American business affairs while he turned to new enterprises in mining in Russia.

While the Cappys have kept in touch with their trumpeter friend over the years — they were invited to James' wedding, and other Morrison family events — MacNee faded from the picture. His generosity remained, though, and he offered James and Judi the use of his Knightsbridge Mews when they were in London a few years later for James' sell-out appearances at Ronnie Scott's Jazz Club. It was a pretty well-to-do setup; 'We went there,' said James, 'and a doorman let us in.'

Down the track, in October 2004, when Ian MacNee took a former adviser to court, he was exposed by the accused's lawyer, David Hammerschlag. It was for, as *The Sydney Morning Herald* reported, having 'a propensity to avoid paying bills on time and putting his name to rubbery cheques'.

The silk said he planned, later in the day, to submit that MacNee had 'lied deliberately in the witness box'. The case was settled out of court during the lunch break.

James has no reason to remember MacNee as anything other than 'a lovely man, not some billionaire big shot. He's actually very humble … he got things done.'

Chapter 19

Superband Tours

During the second half of the 1980s, while Morrison was building his reputation in the US, South America and Europe, Andrew Whist, jazz fanatic and Executive Vice President of the Philip Morris Corporation, was putting together Superbands of the finest players in America. This was to spread the jazz message under the advertising banners of his cigarette company.

In 1985, Philip Morris had set up an eponymous Jazz Grant to bankroll jazz ensemble tours. Whist was President and chief recruiter. He declared that 'more people are listening to jazz than ever before and more large corporations are sponsoring jazz'. He neglected to mention that cigarette companies were at the forefront of arts and sports sponsorships, as their opportunities to advertise in print and on billboards dried up. 'There is,' Whist continued, 'a heartening renewal of interest in familiar artists and eager acceptance of young jazz musicians experimenting with bold new ideas.'

The early Superbands were mainly quartets and quintets, and Whist enlisted the Ray Brown Trio — Ray Brown (bass), Gene Harris (piano) and Grady Tate (drums and vocals) — to his stable after hearing them at the Bern Jazz Festival. It was not surprising; the three were jazz masters who could together have been the finest trio in the world at that time. Four years later, when Whist decided Philip Morris should take a big, swinging eighteen-piece band round the world, it was Gene Harris he called to pull it together.

Harris was a great pianist. Leonard Feather had asked whether there was anyone 'who can outdo Harris in hitting and sustaining a jazz groove'. 'No-one comes to mind,' he added. Nevertheless, for all his experience, Harris had never led a big band and was quite nervous leading up to the first concert, which was to be recorded live for a tour CD. He recruited well; his friend Ray Brown was one of the first to sign, and players of the calibre of James Moody on sax, Urbie Green on trombone, Harry 'Sweets' Edison on trumpet and Jeff Hamilton on drums were added to the ranks.

The band was all American, bar one. Andrew Whist had spent eight years in Australia, had married an Aussie woman and heard from friends in Sydney of James Morrison. 'Word filtered back to me in New York about this young genius,' he said, 'He visited me here and I took him to a late-night jazz session and listened to him. I thought, *Hell's bells! This guy's got it!* Speaking as someone who knows hundreds of the world's top musicians, he's up there.'

Bandleader Gene Harris didn't need any convincing either. He'd played with James at the previous year's Denver Jazz Party in Colorado. He was warm in his appraisal and had predicted,

> He's going to be one of the great performers of our time. I think right now he's as good as anything I've heard. Every instrument I've heard him play he's excellent on, which is extremely rare; and he's so young. He stands out in many ways, but firstly as a person; on meeting him, it seemed like we'd known each other for years.

So Morrison was on the team, perched on the trombone stand next to the golden-toned Urbie Green. There was a week of rehearsals leading up to the first concert. Harris' concerns about leading a big band faded when experienced Basie sidemen, Jerry Dodgion and Frank Wess, took over responsibility for cueing in and cutting off the band when the leader's hands were engaged on the keyboard.

Janie Harris, Gene's wife, recorded her thoughts on the opening night in New York City. She gushed,

Eighteen musos with one soul. Eighteen voices blowing in harmonies and creating dynamics that raised goosebumps and brought tears. On the night, the boys were dressed to the nines in tuxedos. For two-and-a-half hours they took us to big band bliss and back. The record was cut; the New York audience was blown away, responding with standing ovations, and we were on our way to Casablanca.

Not just Casablanca, though. The band toured fourteen countries in ten weeks — almost around the world in eighty days. This was a Superband tour in every sense of the word. Janie Harris called it 'a whirlwind of cultures, smells, languages, politics and sights'. The sights included Jeff Hamilton on a camel in Cairo, James Moody Cossack-dancing in Russia, a belly dancer springing from a gift box in Istanbul to mark Mike Mossman's birthday, and an old Soviet musician leaping onto the stage in tears in Moscow, having been recently released after serving a fifteen-year prison sentence for playing decadent Western jazz.

The Babel of languages was most apparent to James when he tried to explain in Casablanca what jazz was, firstly through a French interpreter, who had no understanding of musical terms. She was replaced by an Arab who fared marginally better. James could never be sure how much of his message, about the young bloods in the band taking the baton of big band jazz from the Ellington/Basie stalwarts to pass on to the next generation, got across.

The band was feted everywhere. In Warsaw, it featured at a huge jazz jamboree before an audience of 10,000 people. The crowd in Budapest was smaller; only 7000 turned up!

'Russian, Polish and Hungarian audiences were very vocal,' James remembered. 'They stood on chairs, yelling and screaming as if they were at a rock concert. They even cheered the mistakes!' Following Casablanca, the band moved on to Rabat, where it played for HRH Princess Lalla Meryem and HRH Sidi Mohammed, Crown Prince of

Morocco in a concert that raised US$15,000 for the Princess' charities. In Cairo, Judi Morrison joined the tour for ten days, and the young couple spent their first wedding anniversary in Turkey.

In early November, the band reached Germany and made its way by bus slowly and cautiously through Checkpoint Charlie, into East Berlin. The guards were pleasant enough, but seemed uneasy. In the concert that night, tour manager John Ellson burst into the dressing room in the Metropol Theater in Friedrichstrasse at halftime, with the news that the East German Cabinet had resigned, and travel restrictions between East and West Berlin no longer applied. As the Philip Morris Superband played its second half, joyous Berliners were starting to dismantle the Wall. The next day, when the band made the return trip through Checkpoint Charlie, a lone guard cheerfully waved them through.

James tried to explain the inexplicable. It was great to be there on such a moment in history, but the thing that struck him most was the irrationality of it all:

> Earlier the same day, if a man crossed that line, not for espionage, not to bring down Communism, but to visit his daughter, he would be shot. What he's doing is wrong enough, bad enough, that they've got to kill him. Tonight, what's changed? Now everyone can wander back and forth, and we're all fine. Because some guy signed a piece of paper, they've had a change of heart. That's the most stark example of the insanity of humans.
>
> Most laws have a reason; they won't be changed on a whim. Like, you can't speed in a school zone because you might kill someone. That's not going to change. In three weeks' time, we're not going to say, 'Okay, you can drive fast.' The law has a reason to it.
>
> But here nothing changed, yet everything changed; there was no reason for it and it seemed to me starkly insane. This was

the law, the government, the country — it was all insane.

It was like two kids sharing a room, and one drawing a line down the middle and saying, 'If you cross that, I'll kill you!' We can all do that; countries do it, too.

That was the big thing for me, not so much the historic moment. I thought, I've got to remember that anytime I look at anything humans might or might not do and think, *Surely not?* I've got to go, 'Oh yeah, there are no limits to man's stupidity.'

James can talk at length about most things — mouthpieces, playing with Dizzy, fast cars — and he was at his most passionate talking about his reaction to the fall of the Wall. He spoke with the natural rhetoric of a son of a preacherman. It was perhaps a tribute to his upbringing and family principles that his main reflection wasn't as an eyewitness to one of the most unforgettable dramas in twentieth century history, but an incredulity at man's inhumanity to his fellow man, anathema to the standards he'd been taught from his earliest years. It says a lot about James Morrison and the kind of human being he is.

Janie Harris, in her book, reflected how appropriate it was that as Communist rule was crumbling, the Superband was playing jazz in an East German theatre, jazz being the music that best symbolises a personal freedom of expression. The 1989 tour was so successful it was followed by two others in the next two years. They got progressively shorter. The six-week tour in October and November 1990 went to Taiwan, the Philippines, Korea, Japan, Australia, Turkey, Germany, Holland, France, Italy and New York, still a pretty horrendous schedule for Gene Harris, who never overcame his fear of flying.

There were some personnel changes for the second tour, the most remarkable being James Morrison, who had been featured trombonist on the first. Now he was about to be lead trumpet in the same all-star group. This is worth thinking about for a moment. It wasn't some makeshift outfit, where near enough would be good enough; this was a band of jazz champions like Edison, Green and Brown, whose playing had graced just about every great recording and big band concert over a number of years. They were first-call players, and when replacements were required they came from the same top drawer. Kenny Burrell, for instance, was joining on guitar, and Harold Jones on drums. In this sort of company, James had proved himself more than capable of playing either lead trumpet or lead trombone. It was a marvellous compliment to his instrumental prowess and musicality.

Two other superstars joined the Superband in 1990: Ray Charles and B. B. King, both major figures in American and international popular music. It was a wonderful line-up for the singers to work with, the band to back and the audience to thrill to. The concerts promised to be a spectacular treat for everyone, but the enterprise was not without its moments in rehearsal.

Ray Charles had a reputation for being hard to work with; a perfectionist who demanded precise tempos and strict adherence to his written parts. That would have been okay if the music had been legible. The manuscripts, probably unbeknown to the blind blues veteran, were in very poor shape from constant use. Nevertheless, Charles was relentlessly paying out on the drummer, who was having enormous trouble deciphering the dots. The rehearsal was itself almost in tatters as Charles began another rant. Suddenly, from the trumpet section, 'Sweets' Edison's voice rang out. 'Ray, sit your greasy ass down and shut the hell up!' There was a stunned silence; the future of the tour was on a knife edge. Then Charles started laughing. Obediently, he sat down and shut the hell up! As the practice continued, a grateful Gene Harris got up from the piano, walked across to the 'Sweets' man and kissed him full on the embouchure.

The previous day, B. B. King had breezed into the room with a few sheets of foolscap paper. It was his entire repertoire for a three-month world tour. 'You guys, we'll do a blues in F, you know the one I do, and there's some figures you can play. You've all heard my stuff, just play what's on the records. Maybe then I'll do "The Thrill has Gone" in E-flat. I'll take a chorus, you can take some solos, whoever wants to, and I'll take it out.' That was pretty much his rehearsal, recalls James, the lead trumpet. 'We were busking the riffs we'd heard on the albums. We all knew "The Thrill is Gone", so we played the riffs we'd heard on that. The guys on the recordings hadn't had parts either. They'd made up their riffs and we copied them.'

There was a tradition of that; it reminded James of what he'd heard of the Basie Bands, as opposed to the Duke Ellington Orchestra. Basie's arrangements were written out note for note, Ellington's weren't.

James explained what he'd been told by a baritone player who 'depped' in the original Ellington Orchestra. 'I couldn't wait to play all those beautiful lines I'd heard Harry Carney play,' the stand-in said, 'but when I saw the parts, they were very simple. The guys had embellished them themselves, and anyone who sat in was expected to play them the same way.'

For the Philip Harris Superband, it was a tremendous contrast in style on two successive days: B. B. King, easygoing, with his 'we might do this on the night' attitude, and Ray Charles, dictatorial and, 'Drummer, that's not what's written!'

And the contrasts didn't end at the practice room door. At plane take-offs, after everyone else was seated, Charles' limo would cruise across the tarmac, and the singer would climb the stairs and take his seat. When the plane landed, everyone was asked to remain seated while Mr Charles disembarked and got into his car. B. B., on the other hand, arrived hours early like the band members, sat on his luggage and played poker with the boys.

'It was chalk and cheese,' said James. 'Ray's in the limo; B. B., an equally big star, is hanging with the gang. B. B. came and did school workshops with us; Ray wouldn't be seen from one gig to the next.'

When they hit the stage, the differences in approach were unnoticeable. The band backed both equally well, both were equally musical, and each was as soulful and electrifying as the other. The audience couldn't tell any difference in their levels of preparation, organisation and personalities. They only knew they were hearing two of the great entertainers of the twentieth century.

The tour itinerary was pretty much alternate days of travelling and performing, with a few master classes and press conferences thrown in. The longest time in one country by far was the nine days in Australia, where the entourage visited Perth, Brisbane, Sydney and Melbourne. The extended time was used to record a second CD, *World Tour '90*. Later, the two recordings *Live at Town Hall NYC* and *World Tour '90* were re-released as *Big Band Soul*, a double CD bargain for the price of one.

The CDs are a good guide to the music of the group — Basie-style arrangements that showcased the keyboard work of Harris himself more than the fantastic array of soloing talent in the sections. Kenny Burrell had but three brief solos, Edison two, and others, including James, only one. James made a good fist on trombone of the Christmas song 'When a Child is Born'. In the end, the recording didn't do justice to the 'climb on seats and yell like a rock concert' atmosphere the live gigs engendered.

Neither B. B. King nor Ray Charles graced the recordings. A video of King and the band at the final concert in Apollo Theatre back in New York called, prosaically, *B. B. King and the Superband Live at the Apollo*, won a Grammy for the best traditional blues album. Charles refused permission for his part of the performance to be recorded.

Morrison had had a great time on the first two Superband tours (there was a third, only four weeks long in 1991, which he didn't participate in). It certainly wasn't a normal Morrison vehicle, with James himself front and centre. He was a team player in a very fine side.

He soloed from the bench, but there was no opportunity to showcase his multi-instrumental talents once the tour was on the road and he had established whether he was required to play trumpet or trombone. There was no trading fours with Gillespie, no abseiling into venues as he'd done earlier in the year at the Sydney Town Hall. There was certainly no necessity to blow up a storm to draw a crowd, as he and John had done on Bleecker Street in their busking days.

This was James working hard with his peers, the best in their fields, playing classic big band parts in a rich ensemble; a champion player in a team of champions. The solo spots he had, he covered with great credit; *The New York Post* had noted that 'brief, choice solos came from [three others] and James Morrison in crisp, confident, punchy statements.' In an ensemble of this calibre, James was content with that — being recognised for fulfilling his role.

He was gratified to find his recording of *Swiss Encounter* selling well, not only in Poland, Makowicz' home country, but in Paris, Tokyo, Istanbul and Berlin. He was delighted to sign autographs because of it, but really, this tour wasn't about James Morrison. It was about the music, the tradition and big bands. It was about complementing and respecting the pioneer big band musos he felt blessed to be playing alongside, and keeping the flame burning bright for the next generation. James was more than happy to be part of that. At the same time, he didn't miss the opportunity to enlist the band rhythm section, while they were in Sydney, to work with him on a new CD, which stretched James' multi-instrumental skills to places they'd never been before.

Chapter 20

Snappy Doo

In November 1989, James Morrison and a rhythm section, consisting of Superband mates Herb Ellis, Ray Brown and Jeff Hamilton, turned up at Rhinoceros Studios in Sydney to make a big band record. That was it, just four of them to put down seventeen-piece arrangements. Ellis played guitar, Brown bass, Hamilton drums and James Morrison everything else — all the trumpets, all the trombones, all the saxophones, and some piano for good measure.

It had never been done before and, to my knowledge, never done since — well, not till Morrison recorded the long-awaited sequel *Snappy Too*. On that, since Brown and Ellis were gone, James himself also played bass and guitar. In addition, he contributed flugelhorn, bass trumpet — his new 'favourite instrument' in 2011 — clarinet and banjo.

These are two outrageous projects and, if playing virtually all the instruments was not enough in itself, James also did the lion's share of the arranging. He wrote the *Snappy Doo* parts while the Philip Morris Superband was on the road. James says, 'There was no Sibelius [computerised music program]; then it was all pencil on paper. You can see on some of the original scores where I finished a score, I'd sign it with a date and Milan, or wherever it was. It was written in hotel rooms all over the world.'

'The Shadow of Your Smile' was finished in Russia, 'The Old Rugged Cross' in Manila, and 'Le Belleclaire Blues', a tribute to the hotel John and James stayed at early on in the second trip to New York. Len Barnard, the experienced old drummer and washboard exponent extraordinaire who wrote the sleeve notes, summed it up: 'I know these hotels: butts, dust, tired bottles, hookers and a man at the front desk who looks like a bottle of milk with shoes on!'

James arranges without recourse to a piano keyboard; nowadays he writes straight to computer:

> You get to know what things are going to sound like when you've been playing that much big band. I arranged the charts, then we put down the rhythm with the boys and myself, and then, when I got back from the tour, I overdubbed all the rest of the parts. I did first trumpet, first alto and first 'bone — got them all working well together, then fleshed the sections out.

James enjoyed the experience and has overdubbed himself on several albums, including *Manner Dangerous* and *Snappy Too*, since. It gives him the opportunity to

> write some stuff that could only be done if one guy overdubs it. You can write things for other people, but you can't include certain tiny inflections, bending and squeezing of notes. It's far too personal a sound. When a trumpet really stylises a line, putting too much breath on this note, not enough on another, it sounds so human, so 'jazz'. What if a voiced section of trumpets did it? I've never heard it done before, so now I'm looking for what musicality there is in overdubbing, not just for fun.

Six of *Snappy Doo*'s eleven tracks are big band and five are quintet. James arranged ten of them; the exception was John Clayton's 'Jitterbug'. Clayton was a bass player and arranger with the Superband, and James recruited him to bring his overdubbed baby into the world.

James was so keen to get into action with his new producer that he drove him straight to the studio from the airport — no shower, no feed, no normal courtesies. 'I was so excited,' said James, 'I only thought, *Let's get into it; let's do it.*'

Ray Brown's little blues riff in B-flat became the title track when the team was scratching around for a catchy name to put on the cover. *Snappy Doo*, explained Ray, means precisely nothing. There was a more substantial reason behind another original title, 'A Brush with Bunji'. It was a reference to the nickname the Superband boys had for Morrison the abseiling trumpeter: Lord Bunji. The track featured Jeff Hamilton's expert brushwork on the drum kit.

The album was issued in early 1990. It received a spectrum of views, ranging from cautious praise to euphoria, though all admitted tremendous admiration for the doubling, nay, quadrupling skills of the young Australian.

Kevin Whitehead in *DownBeat* spoke of his 'high note pyrotechnics', 'fat trumpet sound' and 'dark, burnished, ballad sound on trombone', but thought 'he hadn't quite developed independent approaches to different axes'. It described his lead sax solo in 'Shadow' as 'limp'. 'For better and less gimmicky Morrison, try his live *Swiss Encounter*,' Whitehead suggested.

All About Jazz's Bill Swanson was beside himself with excitement:

> James is a phenomenon. What he can't do isn't worth doing. And the fact he arranged all but one of the charts is another creative jewel he possesses. Whether he's playing here in a combo context or as a one-man big band the result is the same, 'I can't believe my ears!' I suggest you remove your shoes before you play this monster CD; it will indeed blow your socks off!

Even Gail Brennan in the *Sydney Morning Herald*, always Morrison's most trenchant critic, gave credit where it was due, though he couldn't resist putting down, in passing, Morrison's two previous recordings.

> When I heard that Morrison had overdubbed a complete big band (except for bass, guitar and drums) my immediate response was, 'But to what end, dear boy? *Tubular Bells Goes Jazz*?'

In fact, the big band tracks are not only impressive but well-arranged and enjoyable. Despite the excruciating title, at last Morrison's outstanding competence on a number of instruments has been channelled into a good, mainstream to middle of the road album. This is the product of intelligent planning.

It really didn't matter what the critics wrote, the public loved it; not just jazz lovers and brass players, but the wider CD-buying public loved it.

It wasn't long before James could observe that the single of the week was a song by Prince and the album of the week *Snappy Doo*. James was surprised; he had considered *Postcards* a much more commercial album. Certainly, Morrison gained more exposure on Australian TV and radio than your regular jazz player. His extrovert personality, ready wit, ability to spin a yarn and his musical performances made him a desirable guest on everything from breakfast TV to chat shows to *Hey Hey It's Saturday*. He even played a duet with guitar-strumming soapie hunk Craig McLachlan for the 500th episode of *Neighbours* — you can't get more high-profile than that in Australian pop culture!

JazzChord reported that *Snappy Doo* had sold 70,000 copies, a phenomenal number for a jazz album. Warner presented James with a Gold Record in recognition of its success. It remains James' best-selling album to date.

Early the following year, in February 1990, James won three categories in the Australian Mo Awards, in its heyday the entertainment industry's most prestigious recognition. He won not only Best Jazz Performer of the Year — he became accustomed to that by winning it four years in a row, from 1988 to 1991 — and Male Jazz Performer of the Year, but also the Australian Performer of the Year Award. This was an elevated plateau generally occupied by the likes of John Farnham, Kylie Minogue and, during the years when classical music also featured in the Mo Awards, Dame Joan Sutherland, the great operatic diva. It was the most exalted company in Australian entertainment, company that James, who had proved himself a world-class instrumentalist and entertainer, was entitled to be in.

During the period between 1988 and 1993, James Morrison had put in place all the building blocks to reach this high point in his career. He'd become the best-known jazz personality in Australia, just as comfortable performing live on the *Steve Vizard Show* as at the Dapto RSL, was recognised in the US as a brilliant multi-instrumentalist, and played the great European jazz festivals. He'd soloed alongside Dizzy Gillespie, sat on endchair in a globe-trotting Superband, produced his own best-selling big band recording almost single-handed, set up a jazz scholarship for secondary school musicians and married Miss Australia. Morrison was in a pretty good place — two as a matter of fact; he had a house in Adelaide (which he rarely saw) and an apartment at Milson's Point in Sydney.

There was some to-do with his manager Peter Brendle — ill-advised words, threats of litigation and settlements out of court — but it didn't inhibit the momentum of Morrison's trajectory.

The Brendle break-up came when the relatively new Mrs Morrison, with a much shrewder business brain than James, queried some expense deductions. 'I'll take it up with James,' said Brendle, 'I won't be questioned by a woman.'

'I knew from that moment that he wasn't going to be my manager much longer!' James says. 'I thought, *Mate, you just don't know the woman you're dealing with; you'll be more than questioned, you'll be fired shortly!*'

James suspects, in retrospect, that the manager thought he would take Peter's side in the debate and ask his wife not to intrude into 'men's business'. 'Even though I'd only been married three years, I knew which side my bread was buttered on. In a dispute between your wife and your manager, it's "Goodbye, mate!"'

James thought, somewhat naively, he could shake hands with Peter and they could go their separate ways. Peter calculated that he was entitled to not only his percentage for jobs already completed or booked by him for the future, but a share of James' income for the foreseeable future, maybe indefinitely. In a colourful phrase, Brendle claimed he'd 'transformed Morrison from a corner hamburger store into a McDonald's empire'. In reality, while he may have found the empty premises, it was James who was producing and selling the entire hamburger, sauce and all, which the public was lapping up.

James took the matter to the Industrial Relations Commission to have his 1988 management contract declared 'harsh, unconscionable and against the public interest'. Brendle asked the Federal Court to affirm the contract and order damages.

They could both argue they were responsible for the other's success — Morrison was bigger because Brendle had introduced him to European markets and the Superband tours; Brendle gained career kudos for being the manager of a virtuosic instrumentalist in huge demand.

'You'll continue to get gigs for years through the work I've done,' argued Peter, 'and I should be rewarded for that.'

'But you haven't booked them yet and I'm the one who'll do them,' responded James. 'You're going to benefit from being able to say, "I managed James Morrison," and I benefit from having had you look after me. Aren't we kind of square on that?'

Eventually, James settled out of court. 'It all coincided with me getting a large advance on a Warner Bros Records deal, and I passed it on to Mr Brendle to make him go away. It was a pity it ended that way; Peter had been good in many ways.' The *Sydney Morning Herald* reported the sum to be around $250,000.

Lisa Davis, a career businesswoman and friend of Judi, stepped into the managerial role for a while, but with a major shift of emphasis. Whereas previously James had been a client of an agent, now James became the employer, and master of his own musical fate. 'After Peter

Brendle, Judi and I decided, rather than have a manager who I worked for, we would do it the other way around. I'd employ someone to work for me and I'd make the decisions on what I wanted to do next in my career.'

When Lisa moved on, James thought back to an old friend from his New York days, Roy Ferin. Roy was a band booker and trombonist, who rang James in desperation one night looking for a trombone player for a small gig. Someone had heard James jamming and busking around town, and recommended him. Roy was sceptical that an unknown busker would be any use to him, but time was running out. He rang James, who ran to the office of the boat marina to take the call. A conversation followed, which only multi-instrumental Morrison could give rise to.

'I'm Roy Ferin; I'm booking for the Barry Harris Big Band tonight. It only pays $20.'

'Great,' said James, 'I'll do it.'

'Be there at seven. Can you read alright?'

'Big band? Yeah, fine. What instrument do you want me to bring?'

'Just tenor,' said Ferin, thinking James was asking 'which trombone?'

James thought he meant tenor sax.

'But I've only got a trumpet and a trombone with me,' he explained. 'I didn't realise you wanted tenor sax.'

'No, no,' said the befuddled Ferin, 'Tenor trombone.'

He put the phone down, wondering what sort of crackpot or egomaniac he'd been talking to — one who thought he could play sax, trumpet or trombone on a professional Big Apple gig. He wondered, too, whether Barry Harris would ever trust him to assemble another big band for him.

There was much relief when Roy sat next to James on the stand and found the young foreigner could really play the trombone. The band booker and the Bleecker Street busker became good friends, and

Roy appealed to James as the ideal person to become his new manager. Timing is everything, and at the time when James' office chair needed filling, Roy was making plans to leave America and move to Sweden, where he had family. James said, 'What about Australia? I've got a job for you and a cottage down the road in Balmain. I'll set up an office there.'

Ferin took two seconds to decide, and has lived in Australia ever since. It was a straightforward job in some ways. James was so well-known and in demand that Ferin, who had good contacts in the States and Europe, just had to introduce himself as James' manager to get things started. The other advantage was that James could, and often did, pop his new manager, the very able Roy Ferin, into the Big Bad Band to play trombone. None of his other managers had been able to do that!

Chapter 21

Careering On

Under his own direction, with Roy Ferin overseeing the diary and finances, Morrison began increasingly to diversify himself during the 1990s. He still played jazz festivals at home and in Europe, and small group gigs in clubs and jazz joints. He also spread his musical wings to fly into other genres and activities, like orchestral concerts and the promotion of jazz in education.

The seeds of both had been sown long before. He'd played a very legit Haydn 'Trumpet Concerto' with orchestras more than once and, during his stint as a university lecturer, been Musical Director of the Pan-Pacific Jazz Camp, which Ken Laing had run, as far back as 1983. These interests burgeoned. He started to play with Lalo Schifrin, the Hollywood composer and pianist, in a series of *Jazz Meets the Symphony* concerts around the world and, after being a guest artist at Generations in Jazz in Warrnambool in 1987, became increasingly involved in its efforts to promote jazz among secondary school students.

The brass band world pricked up its ears, too — the idea of one player with mastery of all its instruments, and more, flabbergasted its technically proficient aficionados. Even gospel big bands, encouraged by his 'clean' image, background and affinity for the old hymns, were encouraged to seek him out and invite him to grace their stages and the occasional tour.

Calls for James' services came from everywhere. In January 1990, he and Judi holidayed in the Whitsundays with Don Burrows and his wife. They played every night at the resort. He crossed the Bass Strait to Tasmania for a music festival, school performances and tutorials, before flying to the Gold Coast to play with his own band 'some richly satisfying jazz', in which 'he abandoned much of his accustomed theatrics', Neville Meyers said in the *Sydney Morning Herald*. He went back home to play two nights at the local Avalon Cinema, where sister Kathryn, once an usherette but by now a member of the cast of *42nd Street* and about to fly off to Germany for a season, came to the party with a Cotton Club routine in front of her brothers' Big Bad Band.

Next minute, James was himself jetting off round the world with B. B. King, Ray Charles and the Philip Morris Superband. Back home, at the Montsalvat Jazz Festival 'he won the crowd with his unaffected humor,' *The Age* reported, 'and a couple of spectacular displays on the trumpet. But he left no room for disputing his worth as a jazz player, with plenty of swing, spontaneity, warmth and taste in his solos on a variety of instruments.' Then he was back in Sydney at the Real Ale Café, where he played alongside his old mate Dale Barlow. 'We haven't rehearsed,' said James, which is usually a preface to a shoddy performance. 'It means we can play tunes we haven't played for ages. Anyone can solo as long as they like.'

'There was a looseness and camaraderie onstage,' Kevin Jones of *The Australian* wrote. 'It was a great night for jazz.'

Not long after, James was opening the Sydney Spring Festival in the Art Gallery of New South Wales, playing 'a commanding and heaven-slicing version' of 'Spiral', Karlheinz Stockhausen's avant-garde piece for soloists, with a shortwave receiver and some free improvisation. He played with classical pianist Roger Woodward, inspired by a specially commissioned Ken Done painting, *Playing on Magenta Reef*. Woodward said the artwork suggested the key of G-sharp to him, while critic Roger Covell thought Morrison's 'instrumental peacock cries were particularly vivid'.

One gig James was most excited about was the Laser and Jazz

Spectacular he staged at the Sydney Opera House. The hall was pitch black — 'I even got permission to turn the exit lights off for a few minutes' — as Morrison appeared through a hole in the ceiling and descended, bathed in green laser light, playing the trumpet. As he dropped lower, the band hit the groove and James' signature appeared behind him in huge laser-lit scrawl.

James is accustomed to a standing ovation at the end of a two-hour gig, but having the crowd on its feet two minutes in is something else. The concert was off to a flying start, almost literally, and never looked back as the laser lights danced and capered in a backdrop to a sparkling repertoire, ranging from Dixieland to rock'n'roll to funk.

James was everywhere — even on the front of the L-Z White Pages of the Sydney telephone directory, alongside Joan Carden, the operatic diva with whom he performed 'Let the Bright Seraphim' in a private performance at Parliament House and in public concerts in the Brisbane City Hall.

By 1997, Channel Nine deemed him celebrity enough to be worthy of a *This is Your Life* program. Eric Myers, the editor of *JazzChord*, saw it and wondered whether James, whom he described as 'a very nice guy, and very modest despite his considerable success', might be

> embarrassed by the hyperbole that was employed by some on the program. Is James really 'the greatest musician alive', as he was described by [guitarist] Tommy Emmanuel? Was he, by 1990, 'largely responsible for the rebirth of jazz in this country', as the compere Mike Munro claimed?

Myers felt that Ray Brown, James' bass-playing friend,

> had a better handle on reality. He remarked that he really loved James very much, otherwise he wouldn't be standing with his wife Cecilia outside his house in the American heat [105 degrees Fahrenheit] wearing make-up, speaking to a television camera!

'You are a very special person to me,' Ray said to James. 'You are a talented man, and I think you're one of maybe a dozen individuals in the entire world who are able to do what you do on so many instruments.' Warm, truthful praise.

The 'Life of Morrison' was evolving even as the story was being told on television. His wife Judi stood by his side with sons Sam and William until the show was over. Then she rushed back to the hospital, twenty minutes drive away, where the Morrisons' third son, Harry, born only six weeks earlier, was recovering from a worrying bout of pneumonia.

It's not sensible, valuable or even feasible to list all James' performances, but the diversity as well as the aggregate is remarkable. The visa stamps in his passport would have filled umpteen pages as he travelled the world. He toured Japan and Indonesia for the Australia Council for the Arts, a group from whom, unlike many others in the jazz field, he had never sought grants or funding. He took his own groups to Europe — Jonathan Zwartz on bass, the faithful and ever-present Steve Brien on guitar, John on drums and Glenn Henrich on vibraphone. 'What was I thinking taking a vibraphone player to Europe?' reflected James. 'The overweight bill at airports was unbelievable!' He sometimes took Don Burrows as his guest, the wheel turning full circle: the ex-student could now invite his old professor to join his quintet on an international tour.

He formed the Hot Horn Happening in Europe, a seven-piece outfit of two Americans, two Brits, a German and the Morrison brothers. He toured Australia and America with Ray Brown, and played the Albert Hall in London and the Royal Opera House — in the presence of Princess Anne — at Covent Garden.

That wasn't his first brush with royalty; the Queen, after all her hundreds of Royal Command Performances, can still probably remember the night an abseiling trumpet player dropped into the Sydney Opera House to serenade her. He played for Her Majesty and

Prince Philip on four occasions, and for Prince Charles and Princess Diana twice. He played for President George Bush Sr in 1992, and President Bill Clinton came within a few minutes of playing with James! James recalls,

> We had a chat with Bill and he was going to play with us. He was keen and we had a spare saxophone set up. At the eleventh hour, during the dinner, he's going to get up and play. Just before we were supposed to invite him onstage, I got a message. The Secret Service said, 'No, he can't play. We haven't got the equipment here to sweep the saxophone. We can check it for bombs, but we can't check it for chemicals so, sorry boys, the President can't play tonight.'

Clinton was apparently disappointed and not a little annoyed; it would have been his biggest saxophone gig since he played 'Heartbreak Hotel' on the *Arsenio Hall Tonight Show* during his 1992 Presidential campaign.

Officially, James played for two presidents, but unofficially it's three. One night, while playing at the New Morning club in Paris with the Hot Horn Happening, the French President, François Mitterrand, arrived quietly with a young woman said to be his niece. 'He just arrived out of the blue and sat down; that was nice,' said James. He seemed 'very, very friendly with his niece,' he added.

James smiles at the suggestion that playing in front of presidents and royalty might make him nervous. He says,

> It's significant to be asked. It's a recognition that the people organising the event are of the opinion you're the most appropriate person, so that's a compliment. But no, I wouldn't get nervous. What would they know? You'll get nervous if you're playing alongside Joe Lovano [the post-bop saxophonist] because he'll know!

His feelings about gaining awards are similar:

> It's not about the award itself. For instance, one of the Mo Awards is the Ricky May Performer of the Year. That might mean more because I still miss Ricky. But really it's about the recognition. What it means is someone appreciated your work, valued what you were doing. Because I don't place a different value on people, I don't put a different value on their awards. If I won the Nobel Peace Prize — which is not on the cards! — someone might say, 'That's much more important than an ARIA.' But what they're saying is the people on the Nobel Board are more important than the people in, say, Oodnadatta who might give me an award for being the best at the Oodnadatta Festival. They're actually not. It's more of a career boost to win the Nobel Prize but, when I look at them on the shelf, both awards say the same thing: they're acknowledging what you're doing. The people of Oodnadatta would put as much thought into it as the Nobel Board. In that sense, I don't think of them any differently.

This at a time when awards were coming thick and fast. He won Mo Awards in at least one category each year from 1988 to 1991 inclusively, was musical director of the ceremony in 1993, and Jazz Performer of the Year again in 1998, 2000, 2003 and 2006. From 2007 onwards, the Mo Awards declined in status as the ARIA Awards grew. Jazz, along with several other categories, was dropped from the Mo as it turned to focus on performers in the New South Wales club scene.

James was nominated for ARIAs for best jazz album in 1992, 1993, 2002, and 2008, before finally winning with his collaboration with the vocal group Idea of North in 2010. He was nominated again in 2012 for the *Snappy Too* album

Oddly, his most successful recording in terms of sales, *Snappy Doo*, was never nominated for either a Mo or an ARIA. He did, however, receive the Vierteljahrespreis der Deutschen Schallplattenkritik from Germany's most distinguished critics.

In 1997, James was appointed a Member of the General Division (AM) in the Queen's Birthday Honours List for 'his services to music, particularly jazz, and the sponsorship of young musicians'.

It was an unusually high honour — the second level of the four-tiered Order of Australia — for a 35-year-old jazz musician. 'I thought you received something like that when you're sixty or sixty-five,' James told the *Sydney Morning Herald*. 'To see a younger contemporary musician receiving it is great. It says something about the view the establishment has of the arts in general, and jazz in particular.'

He reflected later:

> Someone nominates you. I have no idea who recommended me; it could have been a school principal or someone I've been involved with in education. You go to Government House and the Governor-General puts the big medal around your neck. That's to be worn at viceregal occasions and above. You get a little replica to wear at official functions, and a lapel pin that can be worn whenever you put on a collar and tie. I wear mine nearly every night; it's in my dinner suit all the time, looking like a Rotary pin.

In 2000, James was awarded an Honorary Doctorate from Griffith University in New South Wales. It wasn't the most predictable of outcomes for a high school dropout who was granted his secondary school certificate in preference to being allowed to return to the school to finish it in person.

Chapter 22

Fun and Games

For a bloke who avoided sport at high school — like he avoided most timetabled lessons on the curriculum — and who used physical education time on Tuesday afternoons at Mona Vale Primary for band practice, James goes to a lot of major sports events.

He's been a celebrity driver at some, of course, but he's also played at grand finals of both the nation's major football codes, and performed at the Olympic Games of 1984 and 2000 at Los Angeles and Sydney respectively.

In the jazz event in LA, where drummer Shelly Manne had acclaimed him so boisterously, Morrison did his country proud. Leonard Feather, the jazz guru who had previously expressed admiration for James' talent and described the musician as a 'teacher from Australia', said, 'He left himself and his listeners breathless with a stunning trumpet solo. Later, he proved himself no less brilliant as a trombonist.'

But the finest Olympic moment for Morrison was on his own turf in Sydney 2000. He was first asked to write a fanfare for the Opening Ceremony, a momentous assignment musically, summoning the eyes and ears of the world to focus on Sydney for two weeks. James remembers how the Musical Director, Ignatius Jones, outlined his brief: 'We need a fanfare. I want you to use elements that are recognisably Australian. I don't want you to quote but I want Alf, sitting in his lounge room in the US, to turn to his wife and say, "Listen, Marj, that's 'Waltzing Matilda' they're f---ing with!"'

Morrison came up with a fanfare, which started with a lone,

exposed trumpet playing a very high note. James said, 'Now we just need someone to play it!'

'Yeah, and who'll that be?' said Jones.

'So,' reflects James, 'I wrote a fanfare and got myself a gig!'

On the night, a huge Ken Done-painted drape of the Opera House dropped away to reveal a huge three-tiered wedding cake structure. James Morrison fronted the lowest tier dressed in a white tux with a black bow tie, and was flanked by a semicircle of trumpets and trombones, including the members of brother John's Swing City Big Band in yellow, red and blue jackets.

Morrison squealed a dramatic high G into the expectant silence, then soared on for forty seconds, before the rest of the band on all three tiers joined in for what the voice-over commentator described as 'the most jazzy fanfare I've ever heard'. Morrison's heavy swing arrangement lasted exactly ninety seconds, and clearly suggested 'Waltzing Matilda' to Marj and Alf back in the US, as requested.

Morrison, mission accomplished, stood back and held his breath as the flame, lit by Australia's favourite athlete, Cathy Freeman, slowly and apparently reluctantly made its way to the cauldron. He found the wait for the flame to catch alight far more nerve-racking than standing alone and screeching out his upper register signal to the world.

> The trumpet doesn't know how many people are listening. The air pressure and the speed of vibrations required for high G are identical, whether you're doing it in your room or in front of a million people.
>
> It doesn't make any difference to how hard it is. The rest is in your head, so get it out of your head. Just play the G; if you can play one, you can play one. I'm at two levels. At one of them I'm thinking, *Wow! This is huge, this is amazing!* At another, *I'm James the trumpeter. I play high G every night.*
>
> Same thing when you play with Dizzy Gillespie. You don't

want to just think, *Okay, he's just another trumpet player, just a guy, just relax.* Then you miss out on, *I'm playing with Dizzy G! This is amazing. This is history. Wow!* The other half of me is going, *He's a trumpeter, he's taking four, I'm taking four. He's pretty good!* and you play.

You've got to believe you should be there. I think in life you're rarely anywhere you shouldn't be. If you should be there and you're called on to play high G, chances are you can. And if you're there trading fours, chances are you're supposed to be. I believe these things work like that, otherwise you start to think, *What am I doing?* That's not going to end well!

Morrison counts the Sydney Olympic fanfare as one of the highlights of his career. It might almost have erased any remaining embarrassment from a couple of lowlights. There were times when things weren't perfect. He didn't, for example, enjoy his first trip to Russia in 1989, where it was hard to find good drinking water and he didn't drink vodka, the locally recommended alternative. It was near the end of the Soviet era so the ambience of the whole tour was a bit unsettled. He remembers thinking at the time, *I don't think I'll come back and do this again.* But totalitarian regimes change eventually, and Russia has reappeared on the itinerary.

The night of the fire in the cheap hotel in grubby Birmingham in England wasn't so much a bad gig, as a bad experience for one band member, and a good laugh for the others. The quartet of James, John, Steve Brien and Jonathan Zwartz had finished playing and were tucked up in bed, when the fire alarm went off.

Hotel guests poured out into the streets in their assorted nightwear; old couples in fleecies, young backpacker girls in flimsies, young men, like the Morrisons, in their jocks. But only one was wearing a strategically placed musical instrument like a member of the Daly-Wilson Big Band in the old *Cleo* centrefold. Steve Brien had woken, heard the clamour, smelled the smoke and grabbed the most important thing in the room — his guitar — and rushed, half-asleep, into the alley before remembering he always slept in the nude. It was a memorable night for Steve, and a funny one — luckily for the guitar player, long before the days of mobile phone cameras — for his three mates.

There was the time James and John turned up sopping wet after their trip through the Heads, and another when James got stuck in traffic on the Harbour Bridge and could hear the band he was supposed to be playing in already pumping it out in a rotunda near the Observatory. There was even a report in a Canberra newspaper of a 'no show'. But once onstage, James' gigs go without a hitch, or at least without anything that can't be covered with some amusing patter, or a segue to the next number.

The gig that went really haywire, where a witty comment couldn't cover any embarrassment, was the Davis Cup final between Australia and Spain in November 2003, when the Spanish people in the crowd started booing as James began to play. James finds it hard to think of really bad gigs, but the opening of the Davis Cup was a doozy. 'The Spanish Government has demanded a federal inquiry into yesterday's right royal stuff-up at the Opening Ceremony,' thundered the *Herald Sun* the next morning. 'The Spanish team, the country's Sports Minister, its Ambassador to Australia and hundreds of patriotic fans were outraged when trumpeter James Morrison played the wrong anthem.' It was a 'diplomatic fiasco' another outlet said.

James was unaware that the tune he was given to play, 'Himno De Riego', had not been the anthem for over sixty years. It had been the official theme of the 1931 to 1939 Second Republic, when King Alfonso was forced from the throne. To exacerbate matters, the current King, the popular Juan Carlos, was Alfonso's grandson.

The Sports Minister waved frantically at James to stop, but the fanfare-focused trumpeter didn't see him. 'I was looking at the Spanish team; I was playing their anthem, so I thought it would be respectful to look at them.' He was surprised by the fiery looks on their faces as he played, but assumed they were getting 'into the zone' for their forthcoming matches.

The Sports Minister, Juan Antonio Gómez-Angulo, and the Spanish Tennis Federation President charged angrily from the stands. Gómez-Angulo demanded a formal apology and expressed 'absolute indignation at the offence' that the Spanish delegation felt it had been subjected to. It was 'an offence to the Spanish nation,' it said. The Spanish team, visibly upset, refused to take the court unless the correct anthem was played. An offer to 'play the correct one tomorrow' was not enough.

A frantic search ensued, until eventually somehow, from somewhere, the music for 'March Real', the authentic anthem, was relayed to James. A public apology was rendered by Craig Willis, the courtside announcer, and the crowd cheered as he asked them to 'please rise for the playing of the Spanish National anthem'. James, sight-reading like never before, negotiated the 'March Real', and play got underway.

Geoff Pollard, the President of the Australian Lawn Tennis Association, apologised again to the Spaniards. 'We believe the error arose because the CD of world national anthems supplied to Mr Morrison by Tennis Australia contained what we have subsequently been advised is not the current anthem,' he wrote.

Morrison himself was mortified, and said he would write to the Spanish team. Though he was in no way to blame for the horrendous gaffe, when he was invited to perform in Spain later, he joked that he hoped it wasn't just a ruse to get him into the country to be punished suitably for his crime.

It all probably just confirmed to James that he and ball games were not an ideal mix. He'd realised that as far back as grade 5 at Mona Vale, when he happily went to band practice rather than running around in the heat chasing leather.

Sailing was a much better leisure time alternative. From the moment the family moved back to Sydney from the country in 1970, boats had been a part of his life. He messed about in dinghies with John as a kid, won the New South Wales under-15 sailing championship when he was fifteen, and puttered out to forbidden islands to be brought home by the police. He'd gone on an ill-advised jaunt through the Heads for a gig, lived and rehearsed on an old trawler on Pittwater, berthed at a shabby marina in New York, and even celebrated his marriage ceremony aboard a yacht in the Harbour. There was water, water everywhere.

James and his brother-in-law and former manager — and champion wind surfer — David Green owned a boat business for a while. It's in the Morrison genes, and James says he could happily go back to it if he wasn't a musician. He's also said he'd like to take six months off to sail around Australia, but that's not likely to happen anytime in the near future, while Morrison's diary is so full of international engagements.

He still loves to relax by taking his *Flying Dutchman* up to Pittwater after a gig in the early hours of the morning, when Harbour nautical traffic is at a minimum.

The early hours after an interstate gig, though, are more likely to be spent in the cockpit of a light aircraft. James dreamed of being a flier ever since his father who, while not engaged as a pilot learned to fly during his RAAF days, took him and John on their first flights. As a little boy, he used to make planes of his own in the garage and draw a windscreen with a far horizon on it to fly to. 'I'd sit in front of it and do very long flights. Mum used to bring me dinner and I'd say, "Not now, I'm between Tokyo and London!"'

John got a commercial licence first, and James learned by watching him during overnight flights to Hobart delivering the mail. James admits he could fly long before he ever took lessons. Coincidentally, he started flying lessons in 1986, just as his musical career with Don Burrows was also taking off. Consequently, it took James four years to find time to complete his formal flying qualifications.

The first plane he owned was a Beechcraft Baron, a twin-engine craft well regarded in aviation circles. James moved up to the bigger ten-seater Piper Chieftain after a few years, and carried himself and his bands all over Australia, and to New Zealand and to New Guinea, too. New Guinea was not always without its perils. One night, after playing a gig at a resort, one of the band cars was held up at gunpoint and the locals took potshots at the plane as James hurtled down the runway for a swift getaway. By and large, though, the ability to fly himself home in a Piper Chieftain was very expedient; it saved transfers and connecting flights to the major city airports after concerts in larger country centres and seaside towns.

For a few years it was economic to carry the band interstate himself, but when deregulation was introduced to the industry, fares plummeted and suddenly promoters who had cause to be grateful to 'Morrison Airlines' for reduced expenses discovered it was cheaper to fly the band on commercial airlines. The large aircraft, which had been a boon, became uneconomical, particularly for trips Morrison undertook by himself. 'It's like driving a bus around on your own, burning huge amounts of fuel.'

He sold the Piper Chieftain and spent a couple of years without wings of his own, till he encountered the state-of-the-art *Cirrus*. It seemed perfect, with its modern avionics and digital flight displays. James, who had learned in analog planes, was fascinated by the new technology.

He bought a second-hand one and loved it. 'No gauges, two computer screens, no wheels beside the joystick. After I've done a flight plan, it's just a case of plugging in a USB stick. Yeah, I'm going to like this; it's a great plane!'

He liked it so much that at the start of 2012 he splashed out on a new one. 'It's economical enough that I can drive myself anytime, but I can also carry a trio and all my horns. I can treat it just like a car.'

It doesn't bother James that several pop stars, not to mention band leader Glenn Miller, have had their careers drastically foreshortened by plane crashes. 'They weren't the pilot,' James says confidently.

The flight back to Bankstown in the early hours holds no fears for him either. He can switch from free-wheeling jazz entertainer to meticulous pilot without effort. In fact, one state of mind complements the other. 'With jazz, you're trying to stretch your limits; with flying you can't be too calculated. It would be much more difficult for me to go down to an early hours jazz club as some players do; I've already given everything.'

Most of James' other preferred pastimes — like his late-night flight from New Guinea — have an element of high speed and risk. He's happy to hop into a fragile-looking hang-glider and, for a time, loved to abseil; he'd often be seen in the press and on the TV news descending a rock face or city building. He's dangled on a rope for both pleasure and publicity many times. He certainly did it for his own Big Bad Band concerts in 1983, as part of *Hey Hey It's Saturday* hijinks (whereupon exuberant jazz singer Ricky May instantly 'shot' him on the way down!) and in the presence of Royalty at a Command Performance.

A couple of James' more imaginative rope trick ambitions failed to get off the ground. He toyed with the idea of dropping from a helicopter onto the Melbourne Cricket Ground to play the anthem before an Aussie Rules football Grand Final. He suggested to the organisers of the celebrations, to mark the opening of the new luxurious Regent Hotel in Sydney, that he and his band could abseil down the side of the nearby Qantas building with their instruments, pausing to play the new Regent jingle and — wait for it — tap dance on the wall! The group did some training, but Qantas, like the AFL, wouldn't be in it for insurance reasons. Undeterred, Morrison approached the Harbour Bridge authorities for the same stunt, only to find it had the same obdurate insurance company

James hasn't played the trumpet suspended in midair for a while now — it's probably not dignified for a fifty-year-old international star — but there was a time when, even if he wasn't the only abseiling trumpeter in the world, he certainly gave the term 'swing music' a whole new meaning. 'I like to be in control and doing these dangerous things makes me feel totally in control, totally alive. Once the stunt is over and the excitement of it is over, it's just great to go and play some jazz.'

He abseiled into the Sydney Opera House before Occupational Health and Safety, let alone insurance company misgivings, reared its cautious head. Back in those pre-litigious days, you took responsibility for yourself; if you wanted to dangle from the end of a rope playing a musical instrument, well, good luck to you!

It had all changed by April 2007, when trucking magnate Lindsay Fox hired out Sydney's prized venue for his private, but very extravagant, seventieth birthday party. Fox wanted James to abseil in. The Opera House backstage team insisted on putting Morrison on a motorised winch and lowering him, playing all the while, to the ground. The Fox party was a remarkable affair anyway. The millionaire's birthday fell on a night when the Opera House was already scheduled for an orchestral concert. Fox bought all the tickets, which had not yet gone on sale, and gave the orchestra the night off while he turned the country's most iconic auditorium into a ballroom for a single night's knees-up.

It's not surprising that James, whose penchant for speed, thrills and adventure is well-known, should be a fast car driver, abseiler and pilot. What is surprising is that a man who dislikes sport and describes himself as 'basically lazy' should decide to take on an extreme athletic pursuit. Not jogging, or cycling round the block; not even a regular swim at the sea baths. No — all three together! In the late 1990s, in a successful attempt to lose weight, James Morrison became a triathlete — an Olympic-distance triathlete.

It started when his wife Judi, worried by his increasing girth, encouraged him to get fit; perhaps jog or ride a bike. James went to the gym and spoke to a trainer, who recommended a program of healthy exercise. It wasn't enough for the obsessive trumpet player.

'What would you recommend that a bloke in my condition doesn't do?' he asked. 'What's too extreme for someone like me?' The trainer cast a practiced eye over the self-confessed couch potato. 'Well, you probably shouldn't attempt triathlons,' he said wryly.

'That's it then,' called Morrison. 'I'm a triathlete! Now, what are triathlons?' Morrison was unconcerned as the coach explained the parameters of triathlon performance and training to his unlikely student. That's when Morrison got excited about it. 'I found out about it and I got into it. I trained for a year before I was ready to do one.' It's a tremendous feat to start from scratch and, in the portly musician's case well behind scratch, and compete as a triathlete within twelve months. James says,

> I can't do just 'a bit' of anything; if I'm going to be fit, I'm going to be a triathlete. I don't need to be the best in the world at what I do, but I do need to be the best I can be. I ended up training five hours a day and thought, *This is no good. This takes too much time from everything else* — my family, my music. I had to find something I could do and fit into my life that was good for me.

He wasn't going to be an Olympic representative anyway — the only way he could do that was as a musician — but he did compete in and finish nearly a dozen races. 'One of the advantages,' he said, 'of being near the back of the pack is that when you come to find your bike, it's easy. All the others are gone!'

Now, Morrison has returned to his former ways; doesn't jog, doesn't do press-ups, doesn't ride a bike, doesn't powerwalk along the beach. When he stopped doing triathlons, the idea was that he'd continue to exercise an hour a day. 'That was never going to work, was it? You've got to be a triathlete or you do nothing!' Judi says every now and then. 'Couldn't you do something moderately and normally?' Then she catches herself. 'I know you can't, so don't worry about it.' And, of course, he doesn't.

Chapter 23

Cars and Cameras

It's hard to dispute the fact that James Morrison has led a charmed life. He has a tremendous musical talent, which has earned him enough money to be able to indulge his passions. Sometimes, he can enjoy them almost simultaneously. It's not impossible to imagine he could abseil into a standing ovation at an interstate gig, fly himself back to Bankstown airport, drive home in a Ferrari and wind down with a gentle sail across the Harbour in the early hours. He loves to do all these things, but music must be paramount. James says he was born to be a musician; even if he laid bricks, as he did for pocket money one student holiday, he'd still be just a musician who laid bricks. Cars might sneak into second place in his list of favourite things. He's had more cars than a centenarian has had birthdays; a telegram from the Queen must be imminent.

He owned his first car when he was fourteen and has bought them, old and new, ever since. In an interview when he was thirty, he was asked if he made a lot of money. He whispered, 'Gee, I don't know, but I'll tell you — I bought a Ferrari!' It was the car, not the ability to pay the price, that excited him.

He's owned and, latterly, been loaned all sorts of vehicles, from the legendary purple Valiant he sometimes slept in on the streets around the Sydney Con, to the Lamborghini he chauffeured the incredulous conductor of the Black Dyke brass band in down Geelong Road at high speed for a concert. He's had multiple Ferraris and Rolls Royces, an E-type Jag — 'the V12 convertible with the manual box' — BMWs, a

Commodore, a Mercedes, a Land Cruiser; he's even had a motorcycle with heated hand grips! He had a night job in his teens driving trucks for an engineering company. It lasted a couple of years before he had to give it away. Truck drivers start very early, jazz musicians finish very late; the two jobs were incompatible.

He loves the mechanics of cars, restores some and tinkers with others. His idea of socialising is 'visiting my mechanic and talking about exotic cars'. He once said,

> I travel a lot. People think I'm mad because I do things that others don't consider sensible. Like tomorrow, for example, I have to fly to Adelaide for a performance. Now, if the Ferrari wasn't in hospital I'd certainly cancel my ticket and, just for the fun of it, just for the adventure, drive through the night and arrive in Adelaide, the motor still sizzling.

James drives fast. 'I love controlling a piece of machinery and I don't mind the risk if it's entirely up to me.' On *Talking Heads*, the ABC's interview program, he told Peter Thompson, 'I like being in control — just! The beautiful thing is that unlike the car, where you don't want to go over the edge, in music you want to be on the edge, and occasionally step over, just to see where it takes you.'

The unexpected upshot of James' passion for mechanical things was that, in 1995, Channel Ten offered him a job as presenter of a 'new lifestyle program' called *Behind the Wheel*. It made very little use of his musical skills, but relied more on the broad appeal Morrison had through his musical appearances in a great variety of shows.

The program, produced by Tim Kupsch, who was formerly with *60 Minutes*, would be 'broad-based', the publicity material said. It would feature not just cars, but anything with a wheel: planes, boats, trains, even 'how to steer a submarine'.

The pilot episode opened with Morrison careering down a dirt road and skidding to a halt in a cloud of red dust.

'I'm James Morrison. What am I doing in a car show? I love cars.'

He sat in the driver's seat, while a monster truck approached at a right angle.

'There wasn't a car program that told you what you wanted to know about cars; now there is,' he intoned, as the vehicle rumbled closer. 'This week we'll test drive a Lamborghini Diablo; we'll show you which cars are good ones, which cars are bad ones; what's easy to fix and what are lemons.'

He kept talking while the huge wheels of the truck lurched over his sedan, crushing the hood and the boot. This, while forcing James to take evasive action, didn't stem the flow of his introduction. He was obviously having a whale of a time.

His co-host, glamorous mini-skirted Monica Trapaga, later sashayed around on high heels, asking 'the questions people like you might want to know'. One was, 'Do you think a car is an extension of the male anatomy?' She claimed no motoring expertise — in fact, she had learnt to drive for the show.

The program would also deal with car safety and legal issues — what to do, for example, if you got hit with a speeding ticket. James had one solution: when he'd lost his licence early in the 1980s, he'd thought it was a good time to head to the US for an extended period!

There was little music in the program, which is perhaps surprising because Monica Trapaga — an ABC *Play School* presenter and, coincidentally, sister of Ignatius Jones, musical director of the Sydney Olympic Games — was a jazz singer. She first met James when they did a national tour together to launch the new Ford Capri in 1987.

James, who looked remarkably comfortable in his role, mused on the irony of a musician presenting a motoring lifestyle show. He said,

> To tell the truth, I'd probably have Buckley's chance of getting a jazz show on TV first up. I felt confident that, done the right way, one could make it very well. But before I do something like that,

> I need to establish myself as a TV person, apart from guesting on other people's shows and playing a bit of trumpet. If that works, then maybe I'll be able to go to the networks and say, 'Well, I think we can try something else now.' In the meantime, a lifestyle program like this, which is a lot easier for them to come at, is a good way to start.

So it was *Behind the Wheel* not *Behind the Trombone* that ran for eighteen episodes at 7.30 on Tuesday nights in 1995, attracting an audience of over 2 million viewers. It didn't lead to *Jammin' with James* as he might have hoped, but perhaps someone remembered Morrison the Motorhead when, in 2008, a replacement was sought for Englishman Charlie Cox in the second series of *Top Gear, Australia*. James had made a bright appearance in episode six of series one as the 'star in a bog-standard car'. He introduced himself in his new co-presenting role, alongside Warren Brown and Steve Pizzati, by playing 'Reveille' on a Volvo dipstick. Brown proved that, while James had an expert's grasp of automobiles, his offsider's knowledge of music was limited: 'Ah, the fox-hunting tune,' he cried.

Top Gear, Australia ran for only four seasons — two on SBS and two on Channel Nine. While Morrison got good reviews, the show lacked the cheek, pizzazz and, dare one say, the drive of its British original. Its ratings dropped from 650,000 for the first series to 577,000 in the second. It was taken over by Channel Nine for series three in June 2010, and Morrison was replaced by the actor Shane Jacobson for an Australia versus England Special parallel to the cricket Test match series.

Morrison was ambivalent about leaving the show; it was enjoyable, but very time-consuming:

> You can't get much else done. It's hard to do gigs, let alone write or start new projects. People said it must be fun driving all those cars, but you're obliged to have fun for TV. There's actually a lot

of sitting around. You drive, you back up; you do it again. It's not just jumping into a Lamborghini and going for a bat around a racetrack. There's a bit of that, but mostly it's lots of drudgery and waiting around.

Morrison's media exploits didn't end there, though. He continued to be the jazz presenter on Qantas in-flight programs, and in 2006 wrote his autobiography, *Blowing My Own Trumpet*, in which, by and large, he wasn't. It's an entertaining read — strong on anecdotes and sailing adventures, and light on his musical career and achievements. Bernard Zuel, the *Sydney Morning Herald* reviewer, reckoned 'you come away little wiser about James Morrison, the jazz musician', a sentiment that was echoed by Leon Gettler in *The Age*. He called it 'a collection of funny yarns that keeps the reader entertained, without much sense of what drives Morrison to music'.

The remarkable thing was that he wrote the autobiography in six weeks. The publisher, Murdoch Books in Sydney, gave him a year to write it. With just nine weeks to go and nothing to show, Morrison worked out mathematically how long it would take to type out his 90,000 words. He estimated that if he could knock it out at fifteen words per minute, he could finish the assignment in just six weeks — and promptly decided, therefore, he didn't need to start for another three! He handed the manuscript in at 5pm on the day it was due — an amazing effort for a guy who at high school not only didn't hand assignments in on time, but mostly didn't hand them in at all!

After such a long catalogue of disconnected extracurricular activities that Morrison makes a better than average fist of, nothing much else would surprise, you would think — but then it does. Just when you reckon you know the full extent of Morrison's myriad accomplishments, along comes another that stretches credulity even further.

In the credits of the 2006 Hollywood film *Abominable*, the name of James Morrison is listed alongside Ryan Schifrin as scriptwriter.

Schifrin is the key to this unlikely and unexpected career deviation. He is the son of Lalo Schifrin, the Hollywood pianist and composer with whom Morrison has a long-standing musical relationship.

Staying over at the Schifrin's, James met Ryan, and the director listened as James shot the breeze and spun yarns in his normal enthusiastic manner.

'You should write a script,' said Schifrin Jr.

'I don't know anything about film scripts,' protested the jazz player.

'You're a natural storyteller — I'll help you,' replied Schifrin.

James invented the tale of a Yeti-Bigfoot-type monster terrorising hunters and five sexy girls on a hens' trip in the mountains, with a wheelchair-bound hero impotently watching it all. There are gallons of blood and a rising body count, as the horror/thriller plot — which one critic said 'excels in spite of major plot holes' — unfolds to a grisly finish.

The film, which went straight to video, was never likely to be up for an Oscar, and its *Abominable* title proved too tempting for some. The film 'wasn't quite aptly titled, but came close,' said the *LA Weekly*. Some reviewers were more charitable. Quotes like 'undeniably entertaining' and 'a rip-roaring monster movie which doesn't try to be anything else' balanced the ledger. Sixty-three percent (of only thirteen) critics gave the film a favourable three stars or more on the popular *Rotten Tomatoes* website.

The film starred actors Matt McCoy and Jeffrey Coombs, and had a score by Lalo Schifrin. It should have featured the Englishman Malcolm McDowell, but he had to drop out at the last minute. His role as Dr Seussberger was played by one James L. Morrison. Again, James had protested his inexperience, this time as an actor. 'You wrote the part,' said Ryan Schifrin, 'You can play the part!' and he did, in a Hitchcockian cameo the old director would have been proud of.

Chapter 24

'Flash Harry' and the Jazz Police

Despite, or maybe because of, his many triumphs in many fields, including his primary one as a jazz artist extraordinaire, James' career and modus operandi have never been beyond criticism at home.

It wasn't so much the extracurricular interests, the scriptwriting, the triathlons or the high flying. It was more the abseiling with trumpets, the high-note pyrotechnics, the humorous patter — 'You may know this song and want to sing along; please don't, you'll spoil it for everyone else!' — and the self-duelling trumpet and trombone finales that caused a proportion of the jazz population to refuse to treat James Morrison as a bona fide exponent of the art. The criticism raised its po-faced head many years ago; it still reappears from time to time.

He was aware of the 'jazz police', as brother John calls them, in the mid-1980s. 'I'd be accused by certain critics — not many, really — of playing to the masses or having gimmicks and therefore not being, strictly, a jazz musician.' It's not a new idea; Herbie Mann once said, 'If you're in jazz and more than ten people like you, you're labelled commercial.'

Around 1990, Morrison told Andrew Watt of *Inpress* magazine,

> They say I use too much levity, and I'm not being the stereotypical serious — and a little bit introverted — jazz artist. Their point is, 'If you're going to be a real jazz musician then you have to be a bit more true to the music,' but I think the single greatest thing about jazz is expressing yourself and being you. That being the case, I might turn around and design something to be more

commercial. But that is me; that is, in fact, what I'm like. The more showy I become, the more jazz I'm getting because I'm allowing myself to come out.

If I'm selling out, I'm selling out to decency and holding back a bit of what I'd really like to be. My real idea of a jazz concert is much wilder than anything I've done yet! If I came out and did a Miles Davis impersonation and was very serious, I'd probably get a lot of applause from some of my peers and the serious jazz critics. But, in fact, I'd be selling out; I'd be selling out to peer pressure! For me, the day you see me arriving by helicopter, parachuting out while playing the trumpet and landing on a stage with fireworks going off, then that's when I'm being really true!

Chopper-landing a jazz player in a shower of Roman candles would be anathema to many a jazz lover, though it may introduce the genre to a whole new audience looking for a fun night out — which is what James aims to provide.

He's had other trumpeters, less flamboyant than he is, ask whether he gets tired of being expected to scream up the octave every night. He says,

They don't realise that's what I want to hear. I can't wait to go up or play double time. I love that sound. I'm not arguing that my taste is impeccable, but at least you're hearing honest sounds. I'm a showman, and it's fair to say that some of my colleagues — though not the audience — may feel there's too much showmanship or flashiness when they want introspection.

James was right on the button. His most widely read critic, Gail Brennan, expressed that very sentiment while describing James as the 'Flash Harry of Australian jazz'. 'He can play tastefully and he can play really musically, but it was a long time before I heard him play like that,' he said, justifying his criticisms of James' earlier career. He went on to say,

> So many times when I heard him, he'd play almost the same solo as a demonstration of his range and technique, and I just tired of it. People would go nuts when he played his high notes on the trumpet. It's a bit like Pavarotti; Pavarotti was a beautiful singer, but when he got bigger and bigger he'd often take a note up another octave just because it was showier. I felt James was playing like that.

Brennan also felt that James was highly promoted — 'over-hyped' was the word he used. 'It was said he was the first to play trumpet and trombone, but Maynard Ferguson played the trumpet and the trombone.' Brennan asserts that James Greening, a fine trombonist from Sydney,

> picked up the trumpet and began playing beautifully in a very short space of time. I thought the hype about Morrison just wasn't true — his range and everything. Back in the 1940s nobody much played that range, but now there's tons of players who can play up there.
> There are all sorts of myths — like it's impossible to play the saxophone and the trumpet, but Eddie Shu in the Gene Krupa Band played trumpet and saxophone. 'Splinter' Reeves in Australia made a big band recording of himself over-dubbing all the instruments. James is not the only one who can do all these things, and he's not the greatest trumpet player in the world. When the Philip Morris Superband came out, their lead player, whose name I can't remember, a modern guy, could play everything James could play, only better. Nobody applauded him; the crowd went nuts for James.

All Brennan says could well be true. Others have indeed played two instruments — like instruments, as in two brass, or unlike, as in brass and woodwind — but few have played four, five and six, including reeds, brass and keyboards. Morrison is unique in that he has shown that he can play at professional standard virtually every instrument in the standard big band, with the possible exception of the drums.

Brennan gave *Snappy Doo* a very favourable review. He talked about 'intelligent planning' and 'not only impressive but well-arranged and enjoyable' big band tracks. He concluded, though, 'the album does carry Morrison's customary cornball compendium of gee-whiz clichés on trumpet, which, like paintings of blue Eurasian ladies and flights of china ducks, are beyond my aesthetic comprehension and therefore none of my business.'

Brennan, having decided Morrison wasn't for him, hasn't been to hear him in the last twenty years or so. However, he wasn't a lone voice in the period during which James' profile grew and he spread himself over the general entertainment scene. Bob Sedergreen, the well-known Melbourne pianist, had his reservations but was more restrained in expressing them: 'He doesn't bother playing anything challenging in concert. He is a pioneer, both in maximising the audience for jazz and young Australian musicians. The guy is a genius, but it's a pity he only chooses to play 'St James Infirmary'.

But that's the thing; James chooses to play his saintly namesake's tune where some, thinking it beneath them or 'uncool', would not. James says that he would choose to play that particular melody because firstly, he likes it, and secondly, it might be totally appropriate to the audience he's playing to. Just as a good teacher guides students from the known to the unknown, so Morrison maintains that he takes the listener from where they are to where he wants them to be. He has said,

> For example, at the Supper Club I felt we should start off with 'Meditation' and a nice bossa nova beat, but at the end we were playing 'Anthropology' flat out. And all the crowd was saying, 'Yes, great!'
>
> So they were taken to hard bop, gradually. That was a new experience for many of them, and they got a lot from it. What

you're doing this way is making that nucleus of jazz listeners a little bigger each time.

Morrison can play a wide variety of gigs in a short space of time: a corporate function, a dedicated jazz venue, an RSL club, a symphony concert and a private birthday party. He prepares for each like a comedian seeking local colour and information before a stand-up routine. He admits,

> I've always been a person who goes for the popular. I want to communicate something. It doesn't matter whether it's Dixieland or bebop or classical or slamming a door! Some styles I get into and I think, *I really love this song*, but only on a particular night. There are others where I go, 'I just don't want to hear chords; I want to play free.'

But it's picking the right time for each that's important to James:

> You don't go to your grandmother and say, 'I heard this f---ing great band.' She'd be offended. She wouldn't hear about the band, she'd just think, 'Why are you swearing at me?' But you wouldn't go to the guys in the band room and not say that; unless you put the expletive in, they won't get the message about how good the band was.
>
> That's communication. You talk to people so they will understand and get the message — if you're concerned about getting the message over. There are people like Miles Davis [who sometimes played with his back to the audience] who spoke the same way to his grandmother, the band and the press, so he offended some, endeared himself to others and befuddled others. What he communicated was, 'Here's what I'm saying; if you get it you do, if you don't get it, well …'
>
> The difference between Miles and me is I'm concerned that you get what I'm saying and understand it. I will put it in a way so that you will understand it. The real James Morrison is the person

who's concerned about real communication. While I play music, I'm not really interested in the sounds; I'm interested in the effect. When I first heard a band I went, 'Ahhh.' I just got that feeling. Some people get it when they hear Mozart's Requiem, some when they hear Metallica. They get moved by it. I want to create that feeling, and to make it you have to be in every style because it depends who you're talking to.

Gail Brennan once described James as 'playing like a performing seal, with masterful imitations of great Americans'. Many musicians believe that there's no shame in copying the best and striving to be their equal early on. Morrison developed musically, not by playing soulless exercises, but by listening to the best. He heard Gillespie, and worked till he had a similar technique; he heard Ferguson, and strove to acquire his range; he heard Erroll Garner, and fiddled around on the piano till he understood and could match some of his progressions. He was inspired by Armstrong, but

> would never compare myself musically as an innovator with such a great man as Armstrong. I wanted to play music other than traditional jazz, so I thought that if I could study his sound, approach and swing feel, and then imagine he'd been born forty years later, I could ask myself, 'What would he have sounded like?'

Gillespie was James' greatest hero — to play alongside him was perhaps his greatest thrill. Gillespie 'would be taking it easy, then leap in and hit you with a flurry of notes. I wanted to hear that sound again, so I tried it myself.' That James got close is undeniable; that he could perform similarly on the trombone is astonishing. Leonard Feather, one of America's greatest jazz writers, described James as 'awesomely gifted', and Gillespie himself had declared him 'one of the best'.

Though both comments diminish the impact and any pain caused to James by the nitpickers back home, another area that has drawn criticism is his stage persona, which includes his wisecracks, impish leg-pulling and endless quest to engage with his audience.

Jim McLeod, the former long-time presenter of jazz on ABC radio, used to regularly ask his guests whether jazz is art or entertainment. It never seemed to strike him that it could, even should, be both. Professor J. Neville Turner, an academic lawyer whose wide interests included jazz piano playing and Australian Rules football and cricket, wrote, 'It is still common for jazz musicians to condemn a player who clowns or plays up to an audience no matter how well he is playing. Think Dizzy Gillespie, James Morrison or even Don Burrows.'

James has never disguised the fact that his mission is to entertain and educate while enjoying himself. From the time he started playing out the front of Coles with his first schoolboy group, through busking on the streets of New York, to playing the club circuit for Ken Laing, fronting Cab Calloway's band in Paris and exploding onto the stage in laser light, James has been about grabbing an audience's attention and holding it, through great music and fun. He says,

> Presentation is the key to whether people accept the music or not. Jazz used to be the popular music of the day, and back then there was a lot more presentation involved. That went out in the modern era; people would just play the solos and that was it. I think presentation had a lot to do with rock'n'roll becoming popular music. People won't identify with the music if they just see notes coming out — though, if you're good enough at what you do, the music will come across anyway.
>
> For too long, jazz players have been intimidated by the thought that their music might be called 'commercial', or they might be accused of not taking it seriously enough. I want to play music that jazz buffs enjoy, and to present the music so that other people are going to come and hear it and enjoy it, too.

Humour is an important part of the package because it comes naturally to him. Perhaps listening to his preacher father gave him the timing necessary to crack up an audience. Tommy Tycho, the late Sydney bandleader and presenter, had to learn the craft himself and pointed out, in his own words, that 'generally musicians are "dumb" onstage. They tend to talk with their music, but few of them are eloquent speakers as well'. Tycho nominated as two exceptions Don Burrows and James Morrison.

James loves to tell an extended yarn about the background to a tune or a 'funny thing that happened on the way to the theatre'. He rags his brother mercilessly with drummer jokes, banters with his vocalists and teases the audience. Much of it is practiced and polished these days, but every gig throws up fresh opportunities for his ready wit and self-effacing good humour.

It doesn't please all the critics, some of whom claim he plays down to local audiences with routines he wouldn't dare try in the serious jazz festivals of Europe. But it's horses for courses — the right mood for the right audience. In Australia, he's more the big venue entertainer and TV performer Ken Laing always dreamed he might be; in Europe he's the ultimate jazz pro Peter Brendle encouraged him to be.

In the end, it doesn't really matter; James plays the music he wants in the style he pleases. Gail Brennan and other critics confirm it's often not for them and they go their separate and, in James' case, often unexpected ways.

By the beginning of the twenty-first century, and closing in on his fortieth birthday, James was an established force to be reckoned with on the international jazz stage. He was in demand at venues and events most Australian players could only dream about. But by then, his stage persona, flamboyance and fluency at the microphone and indisputable instrumental ability had made him attractive to concert promoters separated by several degrees from dedicated jazz venues.

He was wanted, not only by Europe's great festivals, but by symphony orchestra programmers, the brass band fraternity, and high school and tertiary educators, in addition to his normal TV appearances, recording sessions and extra-curricular activities. His current career encompasses them all, swinging from one to the other with dizzying speed. But there is no sign of jetlag; a band concert, a school workshop, a flight to the North Sea Festival and an orchestral concerto world premiere in a matter of days is not unusual.

James' career now seemed to be in three confluent sections: in jazz, in education and in the concert hall. His arrival as a performer on the symphonic stage is quite unexpected. For this, he owes a great deal to the emergence in his life of Lalo Schifrin, perhaps the finest 'crossover' composer of them all.

Chapter 25

Mission Made Possible

The Spanish name 'Lalo' means 'to sing a lullaby'. It seems an appropriate nickname for the son of the concertmaster of the Philharmonic Orchestra of Buenos Aires some eighty years ago.

Luis Schifrin hoped his son, Boris 'Lalo' Schifrin, would become a writer of music. He encouraged him to study with Enrique Barenboim (Daniel Barenboim's father) in his native Argentina, before moving to Paris to continue his classical musical studies and piano techniques with Olivier Messiaen, perhaps the most highly regarded of twentieth-century French composers. To help keep the wolf from his Parisian door, Lalo Schifrin played jazz in clubs and, having a real feel and talent for it, formed his own big bands for which he wrote and arranged.

Lalo's talent was spotted early and by 1958, still only in his mid-twenties, he was invited to become resident pianist and arranger for Dizzy Gillespie himself. Their association was long and fertile.

To describe Schifrin as prolific is like saying a monsoon brings a light drizzle. Schifrin has written thousands of jazz arrangements, not only for Gillespie's bands, but also for almost every prominent jazz outfit in America. Names like Coleman Hawkins, Stan Getz, Quincy Jones, Al Hirt and Johnny Hodges glitter on his CV.

His first film score, for the Argentinean film *Cachibache* in 1957, would have been heard by relatively few. His later work for *The Man from U.N.C.L.E.*, *The Cincinnati Kid*, *The Exorcist*, *The Planet of the Apes*, and dozens of others, have injected mood and excitement into popular films for cinemagoers the world over.

His particular talent seems to be for thrillers and action movies. He helped make Clint Eastwood's day in *Dirty Harry*, and its sequel *Magnum Force*. He added musical tension to kung-fu grandmaster Bruce Lee's *Enter the Dragon* and Jackie Chan's thrill-a-minute *Rush Hour*, as well as his son's feature *Abominable*, for which Morrison wrote the script. The tune that will perhaps always be most associated with Schifrin is the edgy, hard-driving 5/4 theme for *Mission: Impossible*.

Yet, while Schifrin continued to play piano, compose and arrange for big bands and compile a huge compendium of film scores, he still found time to write in the Latin American traditions he grew up with, and the classical genres he trained in. He wrote and recorded tango albums in Argentina, and has over sixty orchestral works to his credit; works with titles such as 'Three Pieces for Percussion and Strings', 'Double Bass Concerto', a cantata simply called 'Psalms', as well as the lyrically named 'Variants on a Madrigal by Gesualdo' for large chamber orchestra.

The man is a musical polymath — a jack of all genres and master of notation. He is neither a jazzman who dabbles in the classics, nor a symphonist who syncopates a few bars. He understands what are often thought to be two related but separate worlds. Rather than stepping like a dilettante from one to the other, he melds the two seamlessly together, drawing pop enthusiasts to the symphony and classicists to jazz improvisation. It was Schifrin who arranged 'Nessun Dorma' for the World Cup final in 1990, just as it was Schifrin who introduced the music of Miles Davis and Bix Beiderbecke to the concert halls. James Morrison has said that

> Lalo is the only person I know who understands the piano and classical music and jazz to the nth degree. If you get a classical composer who knows a bit of jazz, my part's not going to be great. If you get a jazz composer who can write for the orchestra, the straight parts aren't going to be great. You need someone who actually lives in both worlds. Lalo's the only one who can do it.

Morrison and Schifrin have worked together since 1993, when Morrison played flugelhorn on the second recording in Schifrin's ongoing *Jazz Meets the Symphony* project. The first recording in the series had featured only the London Philharmonic Orchestra (LPO), with an added rhythm section of Ray Brown on bass and Grady Tate on drums.

Morrison got his guernsey on *Jazz Meets the Symphony #2*, also recorded in London with the LPO, in December 1993. The American trumpeter Jon Faddis, though, played the main trumpet solos in the Miles Davis and Louis Armstrong tribute medleys Schifrin wrote. The same line-up was retained for volume three, *Firebird*, in 1995.

After that, Morrison comes into his own, and is the featured brass player, both trumpet and trombone, on the albums *Metamorphosis* (LPO 1998), *Intersections* (live with WDR Radio Orchestra, Cologne 2000) and *Kaleidoscope* (live with Sydney Symphony Orchestra, Sydney 2005), the next three issues in the series.

One reviewer, Doug Payne, finds Morrison to be 'way-too-Dizzy-like', which may or may not be a compliment, but admires the fact that on Schifrin's 'wicked "Peanut Vendor" arrangement, he launches into a trombone solo that begs to dance with the Devil'. Schifrin, Morrison and *Jazz Meets the Symphony* appear to be an ideal combination. The series sets the music of Gillespie, Davis and Armstrong on par with Bach, Mozart and Copland. The two expressions coexist under Schifrin's arrangements. It was Ray Brown who succinctly summed it up for Morrison after they read through a new chart. The African-American leaned over his bass and said admiringly, 'Man, he's a real bitch with a pen.'

In July 2007, the 'bitch' and the brassman were in Australia visiting Perth, Melbourne and Sydney, presenting *Jazz Meets the Symphony* in live concerts. The Perth and Melbourne programs consisted predominantly of music familiar to Schifrin and Morrison from their collaboration on the *Jazz Meets the Symphony* recordings. Sydney scored the bonus of a world premiere of Schifrin's 'Double Concerto for Jazz Trumpet and Piano'.

Morrison explained how composers writing for the trumpet approach it in different ways. He recalls taking his instruments from the boot of a car in a parking lot in Sydney, in order to demonstrate various riffs and possibilities for Allan Zavod, an Australian writer preparing his piece for symphony and James' jazz trio.

Lalo Schifrin, however, 'just needed to hear me play quite a bit,' he said. 'He doesn't talk to me about it at all. He ascertained what I could do from hearing me play. When I first worked with him I played a trumpet part, but now when he writes something he writes specifically for me, not just a trumpet, because he knows what I'm capable of.'

Schifrin has written copiously for trumpet over the years anyway, not only for the great jazz exponents, like Gillespie, Al Hirt and Doc Severinsen, but also for the flawless *Trompettissimo* recording of the French classical and baroque master, Maurice André.

The understanding jazz musicians enjoy created some difficulty for the pianist Ambre Hammond, who was the other soloist in the Sydney premiere and whose experience was almost exclusively in non-improvising areas. 'I need a cue for my entry there,' she said after James took off on another of his high-flying experimentations. 'Is that what you'll do on the night?'

'Don't know!' said James. 'What did I do?' he added, unaware of where his free-flowing ideas had taken him, and certainly unable to re-create it note for note. It would be left to conductor Schifrin to give the clarifying downbeat for the perplexed pianist.

It struck me that it would be educational and informative to see the interchange between the triangle of talents — trumpeter, conductor/pianist and orchestra — in rehearsal, even without the beautiful Sydney-situated Ambre, so I applied to Trevor Green, the orchestra managing director, in Melbourne for permission to attend. Fortuitously, he misread my request and promptly arranged free tickets, front and centre, for the concert. As it turned out, I couldn't have attended the rehearsal anyway, but I was at the Melbourne Town Hall bright and early and not a little excited on *Jazz Meets the Symphony* night.

The stage, empty when I arrived, gradually filled, orchestra members filing on haphazardly and informally. They prepared their instruments, the scratchings and burps reminiscent of a 'Tubby the Tuba' recording awaiting the arrival of Señor Pizzicato. The tiny piccolo and the bass trombone cut through the increasing noise of warm-up and pre-concert chat.

Unannounced, silence broke out. The oboe sounded its solitary note, the orchestra tuned and was ready. The lights dimmed theatrically, and it felt like a concert with a difference. I wondered how the bubbly and affable Morrison would approach the sometimes subdued atmosphere of the classical performance.

The question was left unanswered for a while. Schifrin entered, flanked only by Morrison's sidemen, drummer Gordon Rytmeister and bassist Philip Stack. The combined musical forces, after first claiming they 'Don't Get Around Much Anymore', took the 'A Train' around a kaleidoscope of Ellington hits.

Schifrin welcomed the audience in a delightful, lilting South American accent unflattened after years in the States, and then introduced Morrison with a plain statement: 'One of Australia's finest musicians.'

The well-bellied artist pottered on lightly, picked his flugelhorn from a rack of four instruments centre stage and blew. It was not a huge high C, but a plaintive and dreamy solo to commence Schifrin's arrangement of Villa-Lobos 'Bachianas Brasileiras #5', which the maestro translated helpfully as 'what Bach would have written if he'd been a Brazilian!'

There was no applause following Morrison's first improvised solo; this was not a jazz club after all, and Morrison himself seemed respectful, almost reverential; at pains not to upstage Schifrin's evening.

Morrison returned to the platform for 'Peanut Vendor', demonstrating Doug Payne's 'dance with the Devil' description. Schifrin took a solo, Morrison watched intently, relaxing as the rhythm moved his left leg. He smiled benignly. The pianist acknowledged the younger man's appreciation, counted off 'one, two, three, four' to cue the full orchestra entry. Morrison became trumpet section leader, playing the written line, albeit up the octave. Then, almost imperceptibly, he wrinkled his face in a familiar manner, and prepared the high, squealing finish.

Schifrin moved on to preview 'Madrigal', an original piece, and Morrison approached his piccolo trumpet, the instrument that gave the Beatles hit 'Penny Lane' its distinctive high note fanfares many years ago. 'Madrigal' called for extreme register acrobatics and a lip of steel, but Morrison pulled it off, apparently without a semblance of strain or a hint of a mispitch. It appeared to be a totally notated part yet, though the music was on the stand, Morrison seemed to play from memory. It was a highlight, in every respect, of the evening.

At halftime I thanked my ticket supplier, Trevor Green, for his beneficence — my seat adjacent to the VIP row he occupied. He declared Morrison 'one of the finest musicians in the world'. Green can claim some authority on this, having played trumpet in, and managed, some of Europe's best orchestras.

He thought Morrison 'used the dots purely as a roadmap', and as the night proceeded, it became clear that James knew the route pretty well, never missing an improvised solo or a written line when playing in unison with the orchestral players.

Morrison played the trumpet, flugelhorn, piccolo trumpet and trombone in the course of the night, and I wondered how they organised *Jazz Meets the Symphony* gigs elsewhere. It would take three or four soloists to fill James' shoes if he were unavailable.

It was a lengthy but thoroughly enjoyable evening. The combinations of music — Ellington beside Villa-Lobos, Fauré following Gershwin, Copland between Schifrin originals — were succeeded by the inevitable *Mission: Impossible* encore.

Morrison took his bows before Schifrin, allowing the sprightly septuagenarian the final spotlight. His respect was obvious and admirable. Never at any stage had he tried to overshadow the maestro or interject his own exuberant personality. It was a Schifrin night and the master of the dots was given his dues.

When they were fully paid, Morrison was granted the last fifteen minutes to figuratively loosen his dicky bow and dinner jacket. He played his party piece — multiphonics on the trombone, four-bar exchanges with Schifrin's piano, four-bar exchanges with himself — trumpet in his right hand, trombone in his left. He imitated the increasingly rapid trumpet riffs with his trombone slide till it couldn't keep up anymore. James shook his head ruefully; it's always a crowd-pleaser. Then he played pedal notes on the trombone as the trumpet climbed ever higher. People whooped like an American political rally, forgetting their concert hall etiquette. Morrison linked hands with Schifrin, and they acknowledged the crowd rising to its feet.

Then Morrison backed off, pushed Schifrin forward and started to applaud with the audience. It was an unusual role for James in some ways, playing second banana, but he had played it well and sincerely. His musical manners had been as impeccable as his performance.

James first met Lalo at a North Sea Jazz Festival in the Netherlands, when James was playing in the quartet of the late Ray Brown. Ray was a good friend of Schifrin, and had been his bassist on the *Cool Hand Luke* and *Mission: Impossible* recordings, among many others.

Schifrin went to hear his pal play on a night off, and was

'overwhelmed,' he said, 'by James' playing, by the way he presented the music and by his energy and sensitivity.' The two became instant friends; they had much in common, including the realisation that music should never be compartmentalised and separated into exclusive genres.

And Schifrin wouldn't have a bar of the snooty conception that symphony players can't play jazz. They can play anything that's written on a page, he argued, so it was just a case of notating his arrangements so that, when played accurately, they swung and created a jazz feel. He also expounded his own theory that all the great classical composers were improvisers. Mozart, for example, 'never wrote a cadenza for his concerti. He improvised them. In later years, when the soloists started to play larger and more diverse repertoires,' he theorises, 'the skill of improvisation was lost.'

Morrison was one of the men, Schifrin felt, who could help to bring it back. The composer had written extensively for Gillespie, so he was quite comfortable writing for James, whether it was exquisite short pieces, like 'Madrigal' for piccolo trumpet, extended works like 'Portrait of Louis Armstrong' or the Gillespie tribute 'To Be or Not to Bop', knowing that James could handle it all. These were times when James' ability to play in diverse styles — his 'masterful imitations of great Americans', as Brennan had put it — was more than useful and roundly applauded.

One of the finest Schifrin/Morrison collaborations — apart from the trumpet feature in 'Scheherazade Fantasy' on *Intersections* (*Jazz Meets the Symphony #5*, 2001), which received a Grammy nomination for Best Instrumental Arrangement — was the world premiere of 'Rhapsody for Bix', a tribute to the legendary cornet player Bix Beiderbecke, in 1996.

Schifrin was commissioned by the Beiderbecke Memorial Society and the Quad City Symphony Orchestra Association to write the piece, which included references to Bix's tunes 'Davenport Blues' and 'In a Mist'. It's gratifying that Morrison, an Australian, should be chosen before all the American trumpeters to perform the Beiderbecke solos in his hometown of Davenport, Iowa. Bix, who lived twenty-eight short years and died of pneumonia brought on by his alcoholism, is now regarded as one of the most influential of trumpet players of the 1920s, after Armstrong.

It was a huge honour for James to play the Beiderbecke role. A crowd of 3000 turned up to hear him do it in Davenport, the heart of the Quad City region, where the Rock River meets the Mississippi.

Quad City Times reporter, Shirley Davis, described the all-Schifrin program as 'an evening of extraordinary, take-your-breath-away jazz and pop music'. Morrison, in the 'Rhapsody for Bix', played cornet, trumpet and flugelhorn. Davis wrote of his 'clear, strong and sweet' tone, with some clear triple tongue passages that really delighted the audience. He brought the house down with his interpretation of the horn passages in 'Rhapsody', particularly when he swung into 'At the Jazz Band Ball'.

The reviewer was captivated by James' non-Bix items, too; when he came to the orchestra's big finish on Cole Porter's 'Begin the Beguine', she 'wanted to giggle because he was just so confident and so darned good!'

The partnership between pen and trumpet, which began with a meeting of minds in a hotel room, complete with grand piano at the Dorchester in London in 1993, shows no sign of running out of steam yet. The seventh in the *Jazz Meets the Symphony* series, *Invocations*, was recorded in Prague in late 2010.

The Argentinean and the Australian have taken their confluence of jazz, and classical writing and performance, round the world. They've recorded them in London, Sydney, Prague and Tel Aviv, and performed in more cities than you could poke a baton at. It's a productive association, and Morrison's most enduring, but by no means his only, foray into the orchestral auditoriums of the world.

Chapter 26

More Jazz at the Symphony

Morrison has made, and continues to make, all sorts of excursions into symphonic halls over the years. Back in the Con days in the 1970s, he played the grandaddy of all trumpet concertos, the 'Haydn', a couple of times. 'Not sure why I was asked to do that,' he says in retrospect, 'but I thought, *Okay, I'll have a go at it!*' He tried hard to play it 'legit' (as Maurice André, the French nonpareil, might do) rather than bring jazz features, such as lip trills, to it (as the American trumpeter Al Hirt ill-advisedly did some years ago). James passed muster, but he had no ambition to pursue the principal trumpet chair in a symphony orchestra — far too restricting!

Since then, he mostly stands in front of the large ensembles to play original pieces written for him. Australian composers David Stanhope, Mark Isaacs, Allan Zavod, Sean O'Boyle and Brenton Broadstock have all matched their creativity to Morrison's virtuosity.

Stanhope's piece, 'Battle Lines', presents James alongside leading symphonic trumpeters, in an intriguing comparison of their skills. The Melbourne Symphony Orchestra's principal, Geoffrey Payne — no slouch himself, with a recording of his own of Rafael Méndez's technique-stretching solos — produced immaculate tonguing and impeccable style in a mock-contest with James' soaring improvisations. The written part in D-flat major had, in one 11/4 bar, groupings of seven, twelve and ten notes, while screaming to high G natural. James noted, before its second performance at the International Trumpet Guild Conference in 2010, that though he'd played it before he didn't remember how difficult it was. He said to his Twitter followers that, unusually for him, a little preparation might even be called for.

Mark Isaacs, a classically trained jazz pianist, tried to 'bring together European classical music and the jazz-rock and blues dialects of the twentieth century' in his *Canticle: for trumpet*. Martin Ball's (*The Australian*) review spoke of Morrison 'putting notes under intense pressure so they split and burst like an atom undergoing fission, that's the sort of energy that this man puts into his playing'. Clive O'Connell (*The Age*) found the work 'rather staid' despite 'James vaulting into the instrument's stratosphere and staying there'. 'The whole house greeted the new work politely,' he added, 'which was my response, too.'

Allan Zavod, another jazz keyboard player and composer for whom James once played some instructive riffs in a Sydney car park, wrote a concerto for trumpet, jazz trio and orchestra for him. Judy Bailey, James' onetime harmony teacher at the Sydney Conservatorium, constructed two pieces especially for him. First, she wrote 'Two Minds, One Music' for James, his big band and the Hunter Symphony. Later, in 2000, her erstwhile student and fellow Con lecturer gave the premiere of her 'Four Reasons', a multi-instrumental piece that runs for about twenty minutes.

Bailey made no collegial concessions to her former student. She said,

> He is a trusting soul. He doesn't have the faintest idea what I have written. I just pray he likes it. As well as giving him room to exhibit what people have come to expect from him, I actually wanted to place him in a position where he was going to be led into different areas; areas that would challenge him in a different way, areas that I am sure he is going to adapt to successfully. It's a fine line to tread, because you don't want to place the performer in unfamiliar territory to the point he feels uncomfortable. It's challenging. He's not getting off scot-free.

It sounded a bit like a good schoolteacher pushing a talented protégé to be the best he can be.

Morrison was unperturbed, saying, 'Judy is a person whose ideas I find I can share. We have had some good collaborations.' In the event, Morrison was quite comfortable with the material, and reviewer Sam Millar said he was 'the ideal frontman for archetypical big-band-style cadenzas'.

Isaacs wrote his piece for James' trumpet; Bailey expanded the demand to include more of the brass family. But it was Sean O'Boyle, New York-based Australian composer and conductor, who gave James his first solo spot as a concert pianist. 'Fantasy on a Theme by Mozart' begins with references to 'Eine Klein Nachtmusick', before settling into variations on 'Twinkle, Twinkle, Little Star'. It's entertaining — it includes improvisation, a blues variation and a cadenza — and remarkable, in that Morrison doesn't at any stage reach for a brass instrument. It's a short but bona fide concert piece for piano. O'Boyle later wrote 'City Shift', a work in five movements, with sections called 'Blues Shift', 'Swing Shift', 'Night Shift', and the like, which featured Morrison on all his familiar brass family.

Morrison played both pieces with the West Australian Symphony Orchestra and the SBS Youth Symphony Orchestra. SBSYSO, in fact, put out a DVD, with James performing the two O'Boyle pieces, and Judy Bailey's 'Four Reasons'. The only orchestral composer who has written for James as a sax player is Dr Brenton Broadstock, for over twenty years Professor of Music and Head of Composition at the University of Melbourne, who was composer-in-residence of the MSO in 2009. Brenton is a very versatile, prolific and imaginative writer, who I first knew when he cut his baby teeth writing for a gospel big band we played in, which took both of us to the Sunbury Rock Festival in the 1970s. He's come a long way since then.

I became aware of the concert featuring Dr Broadstock's new

concerto at a tram stop, where a poster, complete with a large photograph of James Morrison, advertised the event. I didn't recognise him at first — some disrespectful graffiti artist had given the trumpet player glasses, a moustache and a snotty nose. It didn't suit him.

Later, I got an email from Brenton inviting me to the 'premiere of *Made in Heaven*, a 26-minute multi-instrumental concerto for James Morrison (playing trumpet, saxophone, trombone and flugelhorn) conducted by Boston Pops director Keith Lockhart. It is a homage to the iconic Miles Davis album *Kind of Blue*.

I started playing the album in the car and was struck again by the mellowness, the Harmon mute passages and the connecting motifs, in contrast to Davis' earlier hard bop style. It has been cited by many jazz writers as perhaps the best-selling jazz album of all time, and certainly one of the most influential.

Brenton Broadstock invited me to the final rehearsal, and I was looking forward to hearing how he would approach both his homage to Miles and writing for James. The artistic planning director of the MSO, Huw Humphreys, about two years previously had suggested Brenton might think about penning an anniversary tribute to coincide with the visit of the Boston Pops chief. The composer immediately reasoned that Morrison would be the man to play such a piece.

Broadstock had immersed himself in the classic *Kind of Blue* recording:

> It was always in the family collection, perhaps more through my brothers Harvey and Lyndon. I started listening to it again to refresh my memories. *Kind of Blue* has five movements; my concerto has five movements and has other melodic and rhythmic connections to the album, though my fifth movement has almost a rock'n'roll finale.

Broadstock hasn't written much rock or jazz since our long-ago, long-haired musical association, but he hasn't lost the knack:

James suggested a multi-instrumental piece, perhaps including movements on piano and drums. I decided to use B-flat trumpet, alto sax, trombone, flugelhorn and C trumpet. I've written it so the orchestral parts will stand on their own without a soloist. I think it's the first concerto for multi-instrumentalists, and it was a pleasure and a challenge to write.

Broadstock is not a man short of musical ideas, some of which take him to unexpected places, saying, 'My piece later in the year ['Tyranny of Distance', a 38-minute symphonic work for orchestra, chorus, soprano, didgeridoo and visuals] started as something and grew into something else. *Made in Heaven*'s parameters were set by *Kind of Blue*, to some extent.'

I was excited by the prospect of seeing, close up, Broadstock, Morrison and Lockhart putting the new work together. I met Brenton and another of his friends — pianist, composer and TV big band director, Peter Sullivan — at the stage door. Brenton nodded us past doormen and reception desks, and we '*Spinal Tapped*' through a maze of backstage dressing rooms and corridors, to the front rows of the audience-bare Melbourne Concert Hall. Brenton handed me a score the size of a broadsheet newspaper, fat as a phone book, to follow musical proceedings.

The orchestra, Lockhart and Morrison were ready to go. Brenton sat in Row A in the auditorium under the conductor's elbow for convenient consultation. Though he'd had dozens of extensive works, including six symphonies, performed by orchestras around the world, he feigned biting his nails nervously as he prepared to hear, in full and glorious orchestration, what he'd committed to paper for the first time.

The music captured the moods of Davis' work and hinted broadly at its melodic lines. When Lockhart stopped the group to explain his proposed baton work for some complex time signatures, James, dressed in a loose shirt and pants, with pointy-toed lizard skin shoes, sang his part *sotto voce* while beating a gentle rhythm on his ample tummy with his right hand. He was not well pleased with himself; he missed an entry and fluffed a couple of measures that were tricky, to say the least. He was sight reading, but doing it remarkably well. He nailed the phrase the second time around.

Peter Sullivan got a surprise at the beginning of the second movement. 'I didn't know he could play saxophone,' he whispered, but James certainly can. The movement had lots of improvisation and difficult chromatic runs, giving the lie to old mate Dale Barlow's tongue-in-cheek response to the question, 'How good is James on the saxophone?' 'About as good as I am on the trumpet,' he'd answered, laughing, 'and I mean that in the nicest possible way!'

The score instructions said 'fragmented', 'quirky', 'with energy and joy' and 'long lyrical notes' at various points, most of which James captured in this run-through. Movement Three, moody and introverted, concluded with a gentle cor anglais, horn and James-on-trombone coda. 'Beautiful!' he mouthed to Brenton as it ended, and it was. I'd have liked to have heard it again straight away.

But the rehearsal flamencoed on into the fourth movement 'with the exuberance of a Spanish dance', the composer instructed. Morrison improvised around given notes, took on the optional cadenza — of course! — and tremoloed into the final presto section.

It was all happening there, as the cricket commentator might say; James, on C trumpet for brightness of tone, shook his head as if momentarily lost, then plunged back in, concentrating hard. Squealing high notes, a frenetic finale and a three-octave swoop downwards; it was a crowd-pleasing finish, and Lockhart and his musicians applauded the writer and performer, enthusiastically tapping violins with bows.

There was no second run-through. If James was lost, he didn't say so. He had a brief discussion with the conductor, then picked up a wobbly rack of five instruments and carried them offstage himself.

Later, the composer declared himself happy with the rehearsal, and hoped the audience liked his piece. They will; I told Dr Broadstock, sometimes accused of writing 'difficult' music, that he'd sold his soul to the Devil by writing something that will be instantly acclaimed.

Made in Heaven was introduced to the general public three days later, as the major work in the second half of the *Swing, Swing, Swing* program. During the interval, Morrison took the stage briefly to inspect his 'space' and make sure his instruments were in position. He surveyed the scene in Pickwickian posture, fingers interlocked in front of him. He unlocked them to sign an autograph. He was obviously quite relaxed and ready; the impossible runs in bars 142 and 143, and his short disorientation in the frenzy of the finale, weren't causing any ulcers. Most instrumentalists facing difficult bars would sit down with the part, play it over dozens of times, slowly at first, gradually accelerating to the required speed. Morrison doesn't work that way. He later said, about his approach to a tricky passage,

> I certainly had to have a look at it, look ahead and see what was going on. I don't know that I did a lot of what you'd call practice. These days, I've got enough ability on the instrument that I only need to sit with the music, perhaps when I'm on a plane somewhere, and read through it a few times, so I'm rehearsing naturally. I'm working it out, but actually doing it is not really necessary.

Thus he will study it, visualise it and play it over mentally. Then he's able to perform it onstage. It doesn't work that way for most of us, but that's how Morrison makes it happen.

Later, Lockhart introduced the new work, its composer and the performer, and James came onstage to huge applause. I wondered whether he hadn't become more popular in Australia in this forum than he is in the jazz scene.

He was in great form and the audience, in a break from concert hall protocol, applauded at the end of each movement. The orchestra produced a fine big band feel for the second section as James played Q and A alto duets with it. He exchanged a cheeky smile with Lockhart at the end. The American conducted the third movement with a sinuous, batonless hand. Morrison smiled across the orchestra as he rested in the fourth. He is as at home onstage as a dolphin in the ocean or an eagle in the sky. It's his domain; he controls it and shares it. He enjoys what he does, and takes pleasure in what others are doing around him.

The sustained flamenco chords led to the big horn unison, which opened the finale. James went to town over Brenton's driving rock rhythm. He did a roller-coaster improvisation, soaring up, cascading down, and ripped the mouthpiece off his chops with a theatrical flourish.

All three celebrities — composer, conductor and performer — took umpteen bows to prolonged applause. It was the winner I suggested to Brenton it would be.

James then approached the mike for the first time, to acknowledge Brenton's very effective and intelligent homage to Miles and to inform the audience, as if it wasn't planned, that he'd like to sit in with the orchestra for Ellington's 'Harlem — A Tone Parallel to Harlem'.

He certainly lifted the orchestra with his big band sound from the back corner in the trumpet section, and improved its jazz styling with nuances and shakes. *The Age*'s music critic Clive O'Connell declared it 'the best performance I've heard of the work'. Morrison had worked hard, and patted his 'assistant principal', Shane Hooton, on the back at the end. He was evidently having a good time.

O'Connell also said,

> the night centred on Broadstock's concerto, written for James Morrison, who oscillated between five instruments with unflappable mastery and gave this score a memorable premiere. Broadstock's orchestration is packed with deft points, but its focus lies in a wealth of laid-back, long, lyrical lines and some fire-spitting pyrotechnics for his splendid soloist.

The composer was more than happy with his work, its performance and reception. 'James got better at each gig,' he said. This was the final in a series of three. For the second, in Geelong, James had torn up and down the Princes Highway in an Aston Martin courtesy of *Top Gear, Australia*.

Lockhart was keen to present the piece in the States with the Boston Pops. Such plans often depend on Morrison's availability, however. He's in demand in many places, not only in orchestral arenas. The brass band world, smaller but very musically aware and with highly accomplished practitioners, especially in England, has also discovered that Morrison can bring much talent and dynamism to its concerts and celebrations.

Chapter 27

James and Brass Bands: From Dizzy to 'the Dyke'

James Morrison and Bruce 'Dizzy' Raymond go back a long way. Bruce even gets a page of his own in James' autobiography, first up in the chapter on 'inspirational people', where James writes admiringly of his energy, his optimism, and his ability to motivate and inspire. Dizzy is the sort of guy who sees lemons as an opportunity to make lemonade. 'The sky may be falling in,' said James, 'but Dizzy can say "This'll be good! I always wondered what was behind there!"' James went so far as to write 'I decided many years ago that I wanted to be like him, as much as I could.'

James mentions in his book that Raymond grew up in The Salvation Army, but doesn't refer to his popularity in Adelaide as a grade cricketer and League footballer. Internet bloggers still remember with fondness Dizzy's performance in which his one-handed pick-ups on a gluepot at the Adelaide Oval were a feature of his side, Sturt's, victory in the 1970 Grand Final. Dizzy, who may have won his nickname for his football skills as much as for his non-stop lifestyle, is a well-known character in the Adelaide scene.

James also claims Dizzy is 'one of the few great entrepreneurs of the brass band world'. That may be less so now, but was certainly valid in Australia in the 1980s, when their paths first crossed. Dizzy was consultant to the Mersey Valley Festival in Tasmania and James, just in his twenties, was making his initial marks. 'We met down there and then I toured him back to the Adelaide Festival of Arts here in South Australia.'

Dizzy at the time was Senior Instrumental teacher in the South Australian school system, and had formed the group Polished Brass from outstanding students and the talented personnel on his statewide teaching staff. It was mainly to promote music education, particularly brass playing, in high schools, but also to give public performances in leading city venues.

It's therefore no surprise that in 1986 the article 'Brass at its Brilliant Best' appeared in *The Adelaide Advertiser*, after a concert with Polished Brass under Bruce Raymond had featured his new friend, James Morrison. It was the finale of a week's tour when the jazz player, conductor and group had taken their music to the Riverland district schools. 'Rarely, if ever, has Elder Hall resounded to the stratospheric high notes emanating from the trumpet of Sydney's James Morrison,' concluded the *Addy*.

Polished Brass was unusual in that its instrumentation was mainly brass, with three French horns taking the place of a reed section, giving the group a unique sound. James was back where he'd started — in a brass band, although this one probably had the edge on Mona Vale Primary circa 1962!

James treasured those early experiences, but had moved away from the band scene. 'I thought brass bands just played in schools,' he said. Dizzy Raymond nurtured him back into it. He told James of the great band traditions of England, Wales, New Zealand and Australia. He talked about the Black Dyke Mills Band, the great North Country English combination, and used him as a soloist with his own band, Kensington and Norwood, National Champions in 1992 and 2002 during tours around South Australia and to Victoria.

When Dizzy brought the euphonium virtuosi duo, the Childs Brothers, from England to tour Australia, James sat in with them. I, for one, was surprised that our own multi-instrumentalist was not overshadowed by the world's two greatest exponents of a relatively obscure instrument. Only in pure 'brass band' sound quality did they appear to have the slimmest of edges. For some of us, it was a Damascus moment: given his performance here, James Morrison could, perhaps, be considered the equal of any brass player in the world on any instrument, save maybe the French horn, which he seldom plays.

Dizzy's promotional roles involving James were not limited to mere brass band programs. At the end of his sports-playing careers, Dizzy was well-placed and in demand to organise many pre-match and halftime spectaculars at big field events. Everything Dizzy reports is bigger than Ben Hur. He says,

> For the Grand Final, the year after I retired from footy, I had thirty timpanists and hundreds of woodwinds, brass and trumpets all over the ground. It was fantastic and it took off from there. I was on the board of the Adelaide Rams [a short-lived Rugby League team] so I did the Rugby League entertainment, too. I remember bringing James over to do a Grand Final — didgeridoo and trumpet for the National Anthem; it was astonishing!

At the Adelaide cricket Test match dinner one year, in front of the official party and the West Indian and home teams, he arranged for a dramatic James Morrison entry in full batting gear — whites, pads and the precious 'Baggy Green'. James rifled through a voluminous cricket bag to produce a trumpet and start the evening's entertainment. The Morrison/Raymond routines seemed endless. 'There was a time,' said Bruce, 'when I had him blowing this fifty-metre piece of tubing, from the top of the Hyatt foyer deep into the rooms downstairs, for the start of a plumbing convention!'

Bruce is indefatigable; a man who survives on three or four hours of sleep a night. 'People used to say, "How do you do all these things?" "Well," I said, "my last sleep's a very long one, so any time I'm awake beforehand, that's a real bonus!"'

It was Bruce who, as representative of 'SA Great!', a South

Australian state promotion, offered James Morrison to Dale Cleves in Mount Gambier for a night of jazz. Within a year, Generations in Jazz was up and running as an annual event. It was Bruce who took James on a schools tour to Port Lincoln immediately after the Adelaide Grand Prix of 1987, but then had to find a light aircraft so the lovestruck trumpeter could fly back to the capital to reacquaint himself with the bewitching beauty who'd cut him off in the event's practice run. But most of all, it was Dizzy who showed James that the brass band world was another market, perhaps the most appreciative of all, for his substantial instrumental skills.

In some ways, the brass band is an anachronism, a nineteenth century idiom struggling into the twenty-first. But where it is strong in its traditional homes in Northern England, Wales and The Salvation Army, it is remarkably so. Notwithstanding its oompah image, leading brass bands play incredibly complex and demanding works from high-quality composers, with musicality, finesse and startlingly impressive technique.

All brass band parts, bar one, are written in treble clef, a piece of musical jiggery-pokery that enables a cornet player to become a tubist or a baritone player a trombonist, almost overnight. Bandies know, however, how damnably difficult it is to immediately make a convincing sound on a new instrument. Not many bandsmen and bandswomen play jazz. For many of the old school, it's beyond their ken — they can play anything written on the page, but nothing that's not annotated.

Consequently, the sight and sound of James Morrison improvising on every instrument in the spectrum without flexing his chops is a thing of mystery and amazement. He did it to me way back in 1980 in a concert with Dizzy Raymond and his band. He's continued to do it ever since, in every corner of the brass band world which, in spite of its apparent archaism, has pushed into Europe, Japan and the US in the last few years. James' diary is dotted throughout with invitations to play with the humblest and the highest.

Reynold Gilson's Advent Brass, the band of the Seventh-day Adventist Church in Melbourne, were somewhere in between at the time, neither the highest nor the lowest in band contest classification. They were game enough to put themselves up as a backing band in concert with him. It worked so well the first time that they did it again.

It was not without soul-searching. The conductor reported a conversation with a couple of old hands in his band:

> 'Do you know what you're doing? We're just a C-grade band,' they said. 'We've got three months to put it together. I'm one for a challenge,' I told them. 'You think we can pull it off?' I worked my butt off organising the program, doing the visuals, the PowerPoint and some audience participation.

The whole night was pretty much built around James and was a huge success, an absolute crowd-pleaser, with standing ovations for guest and band — not a result a battling C-grade band generally deserves or expects. A risk-taking and ambitious conductor, and a touch of Morrison talent, can make all the difference.

Morrison has performed concerts with bands worldwide now, but none was more memorable than a gig with the National Band of New Zealand, a composite band of that country's finest players put together for touring purposes.

James worked with the 2007 version in what might have been described as a ground-breaking tour of the 'Shaky Isles'. No-one realised how accurate that description would become. The band was brilliant, but the offstage effects were even better. In the opening concert at Wanganui, Mount Ruapehu started to erupt during Peter Graham's 'Journey to the Centre of the Earth', and in the closing gig at Invercargill, an earthquake rumbled during the final number, 'The Entry of the Gods into Valhalla'. James says of the night,

> If you wrote it as a film script everyone would say, 'Too clichéd; not going to happen.' We were in the old concert hall. The band

was playing a huge Wagnerian grandioso, and the chandeliers started to sway. I'm thinking, *Whoa! The band is putting out some sound. Wait a minute! That's not just the sound; the building's moving! I've heard of 'rockin' the house' but this is ridiculous.*

The band played on unperturbed, perhaps unaware.

Later that same night, James retired early while the band celebrated in the bar, as bandsmen often do. On the upper floors, he felt the earth move again and, seriously alarmed, literally tripped down the stairs and hurt himself trying to get outside into the clear. 'I was the only one injured in the whole earthquake. Everyone else was so pissed downstairs they didn't even know!'

James' renown quickly spread through the brass band movement. He played with the Melbourne Staff Band of The Salvation Army more than once, and worked with the Cory Band in Wales and several leading North of England institutions. It was inevitable he should end up playing with the Black Dyke Band, generally accepted as the finest brass band in the world for over a century. The inevitability was particularly imminent once Nick Childs became its band director. Nick was the younger of the two Childs Brothers, the euphonium virtuosos who Dizzy Raymond had introduced to James and Australia some years earlier.

When Black Dyke celebrated its 150th anniversary in 2005, Nick said, 'It didn't take me long to work out who I wanted to be our guest soloist.' James was equally enthusiastic, recognising both the history and the current standing of the band, saying,

> Once I began to work with the band, I realised that although there is an institution known as Black Dyke, the band I was playing with is not about the reputation or past glories. Instead, it is very much about the people who are in the band now, and are some of the finest musicians one could hope to meet — none more so than their leader.

The band, ever at the forefront of innovative programming, premiered new pieces like Philip Wilby's Northern Lights, which utilised a modern dance troop. Iwan Fox wrote,

> It was a night where a capacity auditorium was treated to something very special indeed — and we are not just talking about the band who were on cracking form all night. This was the musical phenomenon that is James Morrison, the Wizard of Oz. It is no exaggeration to say that this was a once-in-a-lifetime experience, for he simply brought the house down.

Fox talked about the 'collective sound of jaws dropping to the floor' at Morrison's wizardry. 'We were hearing a genius at work, albeit an absolutely freakish, bonkers genius who looked like a small Welsh prop forward, with a round face, engaging smile, waspish humour and a lip made out of titanium armour plating.'

It was the beginning of a beautiful friendship between conductor, band and instrumentalist.

In 2007 they did it again — twice, filling Cadogan Hall in London and, a week later, Bridgewater Hall in Manchester. This time the program had choirs, and the Mighty Zulu Nation Theatre Company, replete with leopard skins, spears and ornamental shields. British Airways managed to lose James' bags and instruments but, said Fox again, he did 'not disappoint — a remarkable achievement given he was playing on unfamiliar instruments and in a suit that just about snugly fitted'.

Fox made a crack earlier about James 'not being cast as your regulation Bondi Beach surfer'. Less unkindly, he noted,

> whereas with even the most gifted of brass players, the listener (and especially listening players) can make a connection with their own musical abilities to what is being delivered by the artist, it is almost impossible to do so with the Australian. Playing

instruments as varied in pitch, tone and timbre as the trumpet, trombone, euphonium, flugel and tenor horn, at times within a second or two of each other, defies the laws of musical physics (not to mention physiology) and you are left agog with admiration and bemusement in equal doses. Even if you hear him time and time again, you are left with a permanent bewildered smile on your face.

Two years later, in 2009, the band toured Australia, packing eleven concerts into fourteen days with eight interstate flights. Nick Childs delighted in two Morrison motoring stories. Firstly, when the band travelled by luxury coach from Melbourne to Geelong, Childs and Morrison hurtled up and down the highway in a six-litre DB9 Aston Martin. Then, after the Sydney Opera House concert, Paul Duffy, the band's lean soprano player, hid himself in the boot of the Bentley Silver Spur Morrison was chauffeuring the conductor in, intending to leap out and surprise his conductor and guests. They got wind of the young player's stunt. James jumped into the driving seat, slammed the Bentley into 'sport' mode and, à la *Top Gear*, did a 360-degree burn. The only thing squealing louder than the tyres was the terrified prankster in the boot!

The tour was a huge success, with Australian audiences wallowing in the magnificent Dyke sound and technique. 'They confirmed their place,' I wrote at the time, 'as the pacesetters, the nonpareil, the paragons of brass banding.'

In 2012, the Dyke/Morrison combination was together again for the 125th anniversary concert for the *British Bandsman* magazine. Morrison was in top form. Iwan Fox's pen ran hot again. He claimed 'if show-stealing was a criminal offence, then James Morrison would be doing ten years in Strangeways Prison after his amazing performance'. Nobody minded, least of all the Black Dyke bandsmen. They'd grown accustomed to James' impish wit and patter, and his musical in-jokes ('water key emissions are merely worker's condensation') but still remained in awe of James' abilities, which many of them considered freakish and inexplicable.

Chapter 28

Back to High School

It's paradoxical that James Morrison, a man who spent large parts of his adolescence avoiding classroom learning, should spend so much time in his middle years in schools and educational environments, encouraging students. He sees the irony himself at home when he's asked to reinforce his wife's requests to their sons to do their homework.

But enlightening and inspiring future generations with the history and social importance of jazz is a different matter. He verbalised his philosophy during a press conference when he was on the road with the 1989 Philip Morris Superband. He was talking about the legends he was playing alongside and how he came to be keeping company with them. He explained,

> Some years ago, these gentlemen (many now in their seventies) were the young guys in the band themselves. They had the opportunity to play with such greats as King Oliver, Louis Armstrong and Roy Eldridge.
>
> The reason the music of those greats lives today is because it was passed on to the young players on the bandstand. Jazz is an aural tradition; it can't be written down. And while it's great to listen to recordings, nothing replaces standing next to the original and soaking up the sound. Sadly, one day these men will be gone, so I'm here to make sure the music stays.

It's not just verbiage for an eager press corps. James demonstrates his belief in music education for young people in the most practical ways he can; he talks about jazz, demonstrates it, plays it with them, gives awards for it and writes arrangements for young players.

James is seriously into jazz education, and he's good at it. His old sax playing friend, the late Tom Baker, reckoned that 'James is one of the best teachers I have ever seen, both with children in a classroom and with an audience. He is giving jazz a whole new following'.

Opportunities to pass on the flame come thick and fast. James' management fields calls from schools around the country requesting Morrison's now-famous workshop and concert package. Some are accepted as a one-off; others are bunched together in a two-week tour of several schools in, say, outback New South Wales or Queensland. One way or another, he ends up playing at several each month.

I witnessed one such event at Camberwell High School in Melbourne. The school's music department was fundraising to take its senior stage band, wind ensemble and chamber strings to Canada at the end of the year. A successful night with James Morrison would bring in more revenue than dozens of lamington drives and barbecues at Bunnings, as well as give the ensembles 'match practice' in a memorable event with a fine musician. It would be a winner all round — all they had to do was sell out the capacious Hawthorn Town Hall.

At 2.30pm on the day, James arrived for rehearsal in the wood-panelled school assembly hall, passing under the gold-lettered honour board of school duxes running back sixty-odd years. He carried a takeaway coffee in one hand and his trombone case in the other. His vocalist, Emma Pask, in sunglasses, trailed slightly behind with James' trumpet.

The kids in the hall — music students from all year levels — burst into applause and excited chatter despite a teacher's earlier threat, 'If you talk, you'll be thrown out!' The expectant buzz was perhaps natural — after all, the kids felt a celebrity was in their midst.

Morrison himself chatted briefly to the Director of Music, Kathryn Cooper. He obviously had only a sketchy idea of the program. Now, in this public rehearsal, he was being introduced to the detail of the repertoire for that night's concert for the first time. He unloaded his trumpet case as the Director talked through the score, pointing out the solo spots and tempo changes.

Morrison took it all in, then disappeared up the back of the wind ensemble to sit among a row of teenagers. The Director brought the baton down, and the group launched into a bold piece of American concert band music.

Morrison's trumpet bell was raised above the horizontal, unconsciously or not, exemplifying good posture and projection to the youngsters around him, who sat round-shouldered and with instruments pointed down. It was the first silent lesson in an afternoon of rehearsal and musical education. The year 12 lad alongside Morrison, Chris Langden, spotted a friend across the band as James swept the group along. He rolled his eyes in delight and admiration. Later, he told *The Age* newspaper, 'I was nervous playing next to one of the best trumpeters in the world. It's pretty amazing.' He said some of his friends hadn't heard of Morrison, 'And I said, "It's *James Morrison!*" He was sitting next to me and I was like, "Why? How is he here?" It was a pretty surreal experience.'

The next band choice featured Morrison as soloist. He was handed his part — written for alto saxophone, and Morrison had brought no reed instruments. The transposition to trumpet was no problem, but the pitch was. Morrison had to decide which octave to transpose the part to: if he 'read it up' it would sound too high, if he 'read it down' it would get muddy and lost in the body of sound from the ensemble.

'Leave it with me,' he said, 'I'll work it out,' and experimented, hopping from octave to octave.

It was a recurring story; the music was written to suit the ensemble rather than as a vehicle for the guest.

One string piece, arranged by the group leader, was an odd combination of Finnish and Irish folk songs. There was no trumpet part. Morrison was just expected to fit in where he could. It was like asking Geoffrey Rush to appear in a school drama, giving him a script in German and asking him to play the role of a ten-year-old girl after only one rehearsal. Doubtless Rush, like Morrison, would not only cope on opening night, but steal the show.

As Morrison moved from one ensemble to the next, changing from trumpet to trombone to flugelhorn, he invited questions from the floor. They came readily.

'Do you ever get sick of practising?'

Morrison, a chubby unathletic-looking man not keen on ball sports, chose a soccer analogy:

> No, because I make it fun. How would it be if you went to football training, and the first week you just practised pumping up the ball and the next tying your laces? The third week you wouldn't go back. You wanna play! Music's the same. Don't spend nine hours practising for a one-hour match. Change the ratio — go half and half. Practise making a great sound and practise songs at least as much as you do scales and exercises.

Another lad asked, 'Can you play *The Godfather* tune?'

'Not sure,' said Morrison.

'Well, I can!' chortled the kid confidently.

'When did you start to learn?' came another query.

'I began piano at six and trumpet at seven, so I've been playing about eighteen years,' he laughed, his wisecrack soaring over the heads of kids who have no idea how old adults are.

Later, he explained how the prerequisite to get into Jack Akhurst's band at Mona Vale Primary was to be able to produce a note at the first attempt. If you failed, you became a drummer. He talked about 'spitting' an imaginary hair or — in Morrison's case — a tea leaf, from the lips through the mouthpiece to generate the vibrating column, which emerges as sound at the business end of the instrument.

He recalled how he practised the technique on brother John's trumpet when John was out, and was in a strong position come audition day. 'The bandmaster was stunned when I played the entire C major scale,' laughed Morrison, 'and the legend was born!'

'Okay,' he then said, 'We'll do more questions later. Let's have a run-through with the stage band.'

He dropped in a quick jazz history lesson about the classic instrumentation of this new ensemble — saxes, trumpets, trombones and rhythm section — and briefly discussed the big bands of the forties and fifties, and the concept of 'pop music'. He pointed out that Duke Ellington ('Not a member of the British Royal family!') had written what in the forties would have been considered pop music, just as Mozart wrote the pop music of his day.

'Pop music is popular because people can relate to it through the tune. For that reason, techno music will never be pop music,' he suggested. 'We'll play "Sophisticated Lady" and you'll learn the melody quickly. That's the essence of the thing.'

Morrison got the group to repeat the last four bars a couple of times to tidy the ending, and suggested dragging the tempo back a bit. Then he was happy.

More questions. 'What's your favourite instrument?' he was asked.

'It's funny,' he responded, 'in Australia, I'm a trumpet player; in the States, a trombonist. In Europe they call me a multi-instrumentalist.' Then he added a rider, leaving the students undecided about whether their legs were being pulled or not. 'When I was at school,' he said, 'I wanted to play the tuba. At the end of the day, they always let the tuba player up the front of the bus queue with his huge case.'

'Can you play the trumpet upside-down?' Now the questions were becoming silly, but James was unfazed. He inverted his horn and riffed away, prodding two fingers upwards onto the valves. Then, just for good measure, he rotated the trumpet in complete circles on his lips while playing — degree of difficulty about ten point five!

One smart young lady raised her hand. 'I haven't got a question,' she said, 'just a comment. You're really good!'

'Do you still get nervous?' another asked.

'I never did,' the man replied. 'When I was eight I played a solo on the trombone and the slide came right off.' He demonstrated. 'Everybody clapped and smiled. I thought, *If people will clap that, I'm going to spend my life onstage!* Your audience has come to enjoy themselves, so they don't want it to be bad.'

'I do!' chirped some smarty-pants, probably the same boy who reckoned he could play *The Godfather* tune. James grinned, but the teacher's gaze burned threateningly into the boy's brain.

'You know that feeling,' the guest continued, 'when you've got a great new joke to tell your mates; that's how I feel before I play. "Wait'll you hear this!" If you're going to enjoy it, so will the audience.'

Someone asked about improvisation.

'Everyone can improvise,' said James. 'We all create things in our head. It's like language — once we couldn't talk, but we practised until now we just do it. We don't rehearse it, we just do it!'

He got a lad to play a note on his clarinet. He said, 'Now play "Waltzing Matilda", starting on that note.'

The boy did, with an occasional wrong note, which he quickly corrected by ear.

'There you are, that's improvising. Just keep doing it, and you'll get better and better. You used to start all your stories with, "Once upon a time …" but now you might say, "It was a sultry and overcast night." It's just practice and familiarity.'

The school bell sounded; it was time to go. There was one last question.

'Can you play two instruments at once?' It seemed a sensible ending — he'd done everything else.

'Of course,' he said and sat at the piano, playing chords with his left hand and a melody on the trumpet in his right.

The rehearsal, sketchy as it was, was over. One run through each piece, a few tops and tails: beginnings and endings, a bit of discussion, and that was it. How could it possibly be 'right on the night' when tonight *was* the night?

Kids crowded round to get mobile phone pictures and signed instrument cases before eventually allowing Morrison and Emma Pask to slip away for a meal and a rest before the evening concert.

At a similar event at the Penrith Anglican College in western Sydney, Nicola 'Nikki' Poore, one of the school's young music teachers, confessed to feeling a little underwhelmed. She said,

> We hoped he would run a workshop, but it was less a workshop and more a rehearsal. He didn't give any real instruction or lessons like, 'This is how you improvise.' I think our program for the night was too ambitious; there were too many ensembles. There wasn't time for much else.
>
> However, his rapport with our clarinet player, one of our most promising students, was exceptional. So while there was no formal Q and A session, the little informal tête-à-têtes he had with some of the kids were just brilliant. He was so affirming. He would say, 'Why don't you try this?' He pulled aside one of our junior soloists and gave her some tips. That's what he tended to do. Sometimes he'd address them all — students and the staff we had sitting in. 'Stop, stop!' he'd say. 'My music says "piano".' He'd bring it right down, so he wasn't afraid to instruct.

James knows the impact he can have on a student's musical life.

> Some of them do contact you and let you know, sometimes years later, 'I'm doing this now and I wouldn't be doing this if you hadn't.' On the day, they were maybe just one of the kids there that you took a moment to talk to. At the time you don't think, *This will change your life*, but I'm aware that that can happen. Being aware of it is a two-edged sword. On the one hand, it's lovely that you get a chance to have that effect. On the other, you have to bear in

mind every offhand comment, everything, could be having that effect. You can't control whether that effect is for the better or the worse. You might say something well-meaning about music that makes them go, 'Okay then, it's not for me.' You might think that's a bad effect, but nonetheless as long as your intent is to pass on whatever you can, the results are up to them. I'm aware now you have to be honest in what you do; I wasn't always, but over the years you hear the stories and you go, 'Wow, every little thing.' You can't know which thing is not little to them and so you start to go, 'Okay, I can't start to watch my words; I can't know what's important and what's not. I'll just make sure that whenever I'm addressing them, it's what I really think and what I really believe.' That's all you can do.

In the interval between rehearsal and the gig in Penrith's brand new College Hall, the kids went home, and the school music staff and James went backstage for a snack and a rest. James didn't hang around long. 'We had finger food and sandwiches and fruit we'd prepared, but James hardly touched any. He might as well have been a "breatharian" as a "fruitarian" for all he ate,' said Nikki, referring to James' onetime, well-publicised fruit-only diet.

It was a couple of hours before the gig so James, as Nikki put it, 'plonked himself down at the piano and sat there with his headphones on, working at something on Sibelius'.

The staff were a little disappointed not to make more of a connection with him. 'He wasn't dreadfully keen to … but then, I suppose, you're not going to want to sit down and chat. Even when we said, "There's stuff out here," he was happy enough. I suppose he was busy, but I did find that' — she searched for a word — 'interesting.' She added,

> He switches it on onstage, though. His group played six or seven songs, each with lengthy chorus sections. He was very amusing, as usual. His gags were funny and he talked up some of the kids big-time. He was very gracious; he'd shake their hands after solos,

> that kind of thing. When Emma Pask, his vocalist, came out, they worked 'Mack the Knife' really hard, bearing in mind how he discovered Emma. James told the audience the story. 'It was a high school setting, just like this. Up she came and we talked through what songs she could do, etc. She knew 'Mack the Knife', so we finished off with that. Emma and James have a great rapport and she certainly holds her own in the onstage banter.

After the gig, James stayed back to sign autographs and have his photograph taken on a hundred mobile phones, while the music staff sold his autobiography and CDs.

The night was very successful for Penrith College. It was expensive to put on. James and his group cost about $12,000 and, by the time printing and photography costs were added in, the profit would have been marginal.

> We might even have been a little out-of-pocket, but that's the price you pay to raise the profile of the school and to have his calibre of musicians — James brought old friend and fellow international star Dale Barlow with him — mixing with the kids. That's really the benefit.

Financially, Camberwell High fared much better. Gary Chan, one of the parents on the music tour fundraising committee, claimed that by selling out their 500-seater venue they made a very healthy $13,000 profit.

Both schools got pretty much what they wanted from James and his sidemen, and achieved a fine and lasting result. He has been, at various times, a virtuoso, an inspiration, a comedian, a teacher, a celebrity, an encourager and a fundraiser. He does it over and over again, in schools from central Sydney to Oodnadatta, and beyond. Mostly he goes where the students are, but once a year hundreds of jazz-playing school kids make their way, like a pilgrimage to Mecca, to work with him at Mount Gambier in South Australia.

Chapter 29

Generations in Jazz

As if being the youngest lecturer ever appointed to the Sydney Conservatorium wasn't enough, in the May semester break of 1983, James ran the Pan-Pacific Jazz Camp in Sydney, funded by the University of Sydney, the New South Wales Government and the Australia Council. James was musical director, and the camp was almost a 'Morrison jazz family' affair: it was administered by Ken Laing and staffed by regular Morrison sidekicks, including Steve Elphick (bass), Kevin Hunt (piano), Jason Morphett (reeds), Steve Brien (guitar), Dick Montz and Ralph Pyl (trumpets), along with his faithful drumming companion and Assistant Musical Director, brother John.

Sixty-four students turned up from New South Wales private and public schools in Sydney, and as far afield as Broken Hill and Wagga Wagga. The curriculum included playing in various combos, musicianship and some choral training with vocalist Nina Solomon. Almost inevitably, and as a reward for the students' labours, Don Burrows arrived to entertain them one night, with the Morrison boys and Dave Pudney on bass and vibes.

Many of the campers were relative newcomers to improvising. 'Yet,' Eric Myers was able to write of the final concert in *Jazz* magazine, 'they played spirited jazz. The level reached by the big band under James' direction was a credit to the enthusiasm of the various students and the skill of the teachers.'

That was James' blooding into jazz camps, but he got a taste for it that he never lost. Working alongside dozens of enthusiastic kids keen to grow in the genre under hothouse conditions suited his philosophies and aspirations for the betterment, promotion and future of jazz. When he got a call from Generations in Jazz (GIJ) just four years later, he was more than ready to go, especially since he and John could nip down to South Australia and back in the new Commodore Turbo he'd just bought.

Generations in Jazz started in 1982 as a one-off jazz festival put on, as James put it, 'by this mob down in Mount Gambier. There were these old blokes, who were in their seventies playing, and their sons in their forties.' One of the sons just into his forties at the time was Dale Cleves, businessman, onetime jazz pianist and occasional vibes player. Cleves said,

> It was the brainchild of my old friend, Leigh O'Connor, and it was to be a testimonial to three senior gentlemen here that had been involved in music for many years. One was my father, Frank Cleves, one was Leigh's father Tom, a pianist, and the third was Joe Hannigan, who had been in the RAAF Band in World War II and was a fine clarinet and sax player.

A small committee was formed with Malcolm Bradley, a Mount Gambier piano player originally from Adelaide, Ian Giles, the local manager for the ABC, Libby Ahrendt, a music enthusiast, and Dale himself. They chose a weekend for their event when Leigh's daughter, who was studying music in Adelaide, would be home with a group of her university friends and, consequently and logically, the title Generations in Jazz was born.

Dale Cleves invited some old mates — drummer Ron Sandilands, trumpeter Bob Venier and Peter Salt, who brought his big band — from Melbourne to share the festivities. Sandilands, whose drumming CV includes just about every popular musical event, live or on television in the city in the last thirty years, had known Dale Cleves for some time:

He was the jazz bloke from Mount Gambier and I was the jazz bloke from Warrnambool. Whenever Dale wanted a band put together, he'd give me a ring and I'd organise some players for him. Sometimes we'd go to Mount Gambier for single night jobs — balls and corporate functions — but Generations in Jazz stretched over the weekend; a Saturday night concert and a big barbeque on Sunday.

It was held at the Barn Palais, which was on a property owned by the Cleves family. The Barn, a landmark in the area, was a farm outhouse but had become a 'Palais' in 1937, when it was transformed into a dance hall. Over a thousand people had flocked to its opening night. Fifty years later, when the Morrison brothers turned up in a fast car, the Barn Palais was being used for a variety of functions, including jazz concerts, and claimed its restaurant offered 'the finest steaks in South Australia'.

The first Generations in Jazz event was a very congenial and enjoyable weekend; fathers were honoured, tributes were paid, good jazz was played, great beef was eaten, beer was drunk, old adventures were recalled and a musical feast was had by all — and that, thought Dale Cleves, was that. Generations in Jazz was done and dusted, till he got a phone call out of the blue some years later from the SA Great!, an organisation promoting tourism to and within South Australia.

SA Great!'s representative was none other than Bruce 'Dizzy' Raymond, entrepreneur, brass band conductor, educator and firm friend of James Morrison. He asked if Dale would be interested in a concert visit from James. Of course he would, was the swift reply. Cleves organised another weekend using the Generations in Jazz tag again, as well as his Melbourne associates, Sandilands, Venier and the Peter Salt Big Band.

Between 1982 and 1986 there was no Generations in Jazz, but when James' attendance was mooted and confirmed 'it was sort of resurrected', said Dale. 'We thought there was a chance here — and it was mainly Leigh's dream again — to approach James and ask if we could form this scholarship in his honour.' Sandilands added, 'I recall sitting around the steakhouse after the gig in 1987 at which James was the guest artist. He put on a little show for us and that's where it all started. That's when they started talking about running a scholarship.'

Morrison recalled, 'I said to John as we were driving away, "Well, this is going to be interesting: a scholarship and a competition. Let's see what happens."' He couldn't have envisaged then how big it was all going to become.

The following year the James Morrison Instrumental Scholarship was announced, and by 1989 the first cassettes from young entrants had been received, heard and assessed. Morrison himself listened to them all. Six young jazz players were invited to play-off live. The ABC recorded the finalists for Jim McLeod's *Jazztrack* radio program. The chosen half-dozen were saxophone players Kellie Santin and Andrew Robertson, tubist Dan Gordon, guitarist Craig Fermanis, pianist John Foreman and vocalist Darren Paul. Kellie Santin was the inaugural winner. James, soon after, started to use Darren Paul as his group vocalist, and most of the others have gone on to professional musical careers. The bar for the finalists, let alone the winners, was set very high from the outset. It has remained there ever since.

The scholarship grew rapidly. In 1990, the 120 audition tapes were pruned down to thirty semi-finalists, before seven were chosen and flown in from all over the country for the live play-offs at the Barn.

The generosity of that soon became a problem and a financial burden. Dale said,

> The difficulty was that the prize money for this great event was $10,000 to the winner, and that took a bit of raising. We had some sponsorships in the early days, but nothing lasted for terribly long. It was really unsustainable and the only income we had was from a cabaret once a year.

Just when it was needed, and because he doubtless spent a lot of time thinking about it, Cleves had an epiphany:

> I was always interested in the stage band movement. As a sixteen-year-old back in the 1950s, I used to subscribe to *DownBeat*, and all the American magazines. And I remember many, many years ago, maybe the late 1960s or early 1970s, North Texas State University Band came out here — a bunch of school kids, university kids basically. They wowed everybody across the country — they were so young, they were so good.
>
> I remembered reading that there were about 5000 high school stage bands across America. I always used to think, *Wouldn't it be wonderful if we had that situation in Australia.*
>
> We got our local council here to come up with some backing for us, and in 1993 our stage band awards were inaugurated. We had six bands come here. One of them was a local, a couple from Adelaide and three from Victoria.

The booklet 'All That Jazz: celebrating 20 years of Generations in Jazz' claims eight bands turned up for that first battle of the stage bands. The numerical discrepancy with Cleves' memory of it is small beer — either way, six or eight bands, it's a far cry from the almost 150 groups across five sections in 2014. The event attracted tourism awards from region and state almost annually over the years, as more and more school ensembles and their supporting parents and friends were drawn to it.

When the GIJ Vocal Scholarship was introduced in 2004, giving singers a section separate from instrumentalists, an unknown Megan Washington became the winner. By 2012, she had added two ARIA Music Awards, including Best Female Artist, to her trophy cabinet. She become a nationally known name and a familiar face through her mentorship of Keith Urban's team on the incredibly popular television program *The Voice*.

In 2009, James announced his first all-star band, selected from the players in the senior section of the stage band competition. In later years, the other adjudicators in the junior sections have chosen their best players to form Superbands.

The event is impressive even if judged by numbers alone; it may be the largest of its kind in the world, as the organisers have sometimes claimed. In 2014, almost one hundred schools brought over 140 bands and the vocal ensemble section, only introduced in 2012, attracted fifty-four groups and more spectators than the smaller venue could hold. Morrison promised a larger space in future. The James Morrison Scholarship, worth $10,000, attracted sixty applicants and the GIJ Vocal Scholarship, worth $5000, attracted thirty-four.

About 3200 student performers turned up, an increase of 500 on the previous year. The marquee used for the plenary sessions was bulging at the seams with wall-to-wall teenagers. When he first saw it, TV personality Daryl Somers, a drummer/vocalist and patron of the event, declared himself 'flabbergasted' at the size of the tent. 'I walked into it and thought the supporting act must be Cirque du Soleil, and that there must be a trapeze section because it was so big.'

On top of the student attendance, 1200 tickets for the Saturday night concert featuring the Gordon Goodwin Big Phat Band from America, one of the world's leading contemporary big bands, were also sold to the general public and to visitors, who had to find accommodation as far away as Millicent, Beachport, Cape Bridgewater, Port MacDonnell and Naracoorte. Karyn Roberts, GIJ's Executive Officer, estimated the event brings $800,000 or more into the local economy. It's no wonder Dale Franklin Cleves, businessman, restaurateur, beef breeder, entrepreneur, jazz muso, GIJ co-founder and still hands-on prime mover in the event, was awarded an OAM in the 2012 Queen's Birthday honours list for 'his service to the tourism and hospitality industry, and to music'.

In recent years, the event has outgrown its original Hocker tent, which at the time was the largest available supported by a single pole.

Some serious thought and planning went into the possibility of building a permanent structure capable of holding audiences approaching 4000. Cleves said,

> We put a plan up to the local council, but it was a bit of a dream to do it. The risk of it was that whatever we did in the way of a permanent building may only be good for three or four years, then we run up against the problem again. This year we got a real stroke of luck. We met Tony Gasser, who runs a company based in Melbourne called Unique Attractions. Gasser has a big top background — his father owns Silvers Circus — and he's designed an expandable, modular tent. We used this magnificent structure this year. It's phenomenal, the engineering side, how it all works, and acoustically it was wonderful, too.
>
> We can grow with that because we can actually expand it; it can be three times bigger than what we had so it's taken the pressure off us. If we had put a permanent building up, I'd got James' permission to call it the James Morrison Pavilion, but since he's now representing the Schagerl Instrument Company in Austria, we called the new tent the Schagerl-James Morrison Pavilion.

Chapter 30

'Oh what a circus! Oh what a show!'

However big the Schagerl-James Morrison Pavilion is, it's not immediately apparent as you take the Nelson Road out of Mount Gambier, looking for Generations in Jazz on the strangely named OB Flat. The unsealed road quickly runs out of street lighting as it heads towards the coast. Just as you think that the given directions must be wrong, in the distance the countryside lights up like Luna Park.

Suddenly, you're slowing down and approaching a circus set up out of town. Signs indicate it's the venue for Generations in Jazz. *Beware Changed Traffic Conditions* they add, and you wonder how many school band competitions change traffic conditions.

This musical circus has several big tops, including the Schagerl-James Morrison Pavilion, housing the main events of the competitions that run through the weekend, as well as doubling as dining rooms for young campers, their teachers and chaperones, who have already booked out all the motel accommodation in town. Late arrivals can find themselves staying as far out as Penola, an hour's drive away and St Mary McKillop's birthplace, as well as other country centres.

The hectic three-day event opens with an introductory session and dinner. There are hundreds of overexcited teenage participants packed into the main marquee to be welcomed by James Morrison and the crew, then serenaded by last year's winners in the instrumental and vocal sections, both immediately impressing as young people of immense talent.

When the session is over, the school groups disappear into the night, following their school name on a stick like a tour group at the Coliseum. Finalists for the current year's individual scholarships have other obligations. They stay to perform the first half of their program, ballad or up-tempo number, for the judges in the Barn Palais, the venue's permanent building, which is complete with bar and cabaret tables.

It's always a tough contest; there's a lot of ability on show for the adjudicators, who over the years have included Australia's premier big band leaders Tommy Tycho, Graeme Lyall and Ed Wilson, half of the celebrated eponymous Daly-Wilson Big Band. Recently, the faculty has added two Americans with impressive film composition credentials: Bill Broughton, now resident in Adelaide, and Grammy Award-winning Californian Gordon Goodwin, leader of the Big Phat Band, a pace-setter for modern stage bands.

The compere for the first round is Ross Irwin, a first-call Melbourne studio trumpet player and composer, who can empathise totally with the competitors having himself been a finalist for four years without actually winning. His consistency and talent did gain him a permanent spot on the staff, though, and an opportunity to write an annual set piece for competing bands.

Ross can smile now about his efforts to take off the main prize, though at the time it must have been extremely frustrating:

> I was in the finals four times, but never quite managed it. I was the only person to have been in the finals that many times and not won. No-one else had done it three times in a row and not won!
>
> Every year, you send in an application and a recording of yourself playing two songs, a ballad and a blues. James wades through the hundreds of entries and picks the top six from around the country. It's open to any instrument; it's a jazz improvisation award. Usually you get a fair mix of instruments — every so often you'll get three pianos, two basses and a drummer. But most of the time, it's a fairly mixed bag of instrumentalists.

I'm not sure where I came in the six each year. James did tell me I got close in my third year — he said he was really torn between me and the winner. But it worked well anyway because after the fourth year he invited me to join the staff of GIJ, so I'm back there every year adjudicating the junior sections.

The stage band events occur on the Saturday. The groups are split into four divisions, with Section 3 entries so numerous they're broken into two halves of about twenty each. The standard of Section 1, which James adjudicates, is sensational. The leading bands are fit to perform professionally anywhere, maybe even Monterey, where James himself made such a splash all those years ago, when he was a similar age to many of the senior band members here in Mount Gambier.

In the late afternoon, the scholarship contenders perform the second halves of their program and finish in time to be present with everyone else at the grand public concert. It's always a night of high excitement. Mexican waves roll across the tent arena as the hyped-up students, high on adrenaline and self-inflicted sleep deprivation, fill in time before the start.

By the time the winning band of the previous year has played a pre-concert set, the joint, as they say, is jumpin'. James announces some awards. The best players in the top three divisions are nominated by the adjudicators to play in a sectional Superband, and the Future Finalists are announced — players whose improvising skills within their own school groups have caught the judges' ears and who have been nominated as possibilities, and encouraged to apply for, next year's James Morrison Instrumental Scholarship.

Every name is greeted with the sort of enthusiastic response only students can bring to an occasion. They cheer, they chant, they whistle in boisterous delight that someone they rate has been recognised as a very promising player.

The concert itself is a big band bonanza with bonuses. One highlight followed another in the Generations in Jazz event of 2014.

The very special Tenison Woods College Big Band from Mount Gambier itself was presented early. The Generations in Jazz Academy at that College — a direct spin-off of Generations in Jazz and initiated by James Morrison and Graeme Lyall, AM, saxophonist, composer/arranger and the former musical director at Channel Nine in Melbourne — offers a one-year post-year-12 music course. It concentrates on big band and is a bridging course to music study at university level. The standard is increasingly high and the audition rigorous. Only the best need apply and there's one chair per big band part. If twenty-five pianists apply, only one is chosen each year.

Idea of North, the a cappella jazz vocal quartet with whom Morrison shared an ARIA Award in 2010, brought their own classy, close harmonies before being joined by Rai Thistlethwayte, known to most of the younger audience members as the vocalist with pop rock band Thirsty Merc, but a fine jazz singer and pianist in his own right.

It may have been enough for an ordinary night's music, but ordinary wasn't part of the vocabulary here. James played a quartet set with the wonderful Romanian pianist Marian Petrescu before introducing the Gordon Goodwin Big Phat Band, returning to Generations in Jazz for a second successive year. This was big band jazz featuring driving, contemporary arrangements played by LA's finest studio and recording musicians, such as Wayne Bergeron, who has played on more Hollywood film scores than there are semiquavers in 'The Flight of the Bumblebee'!

Morrison soloed in front of the band, but claimed his ambition was to be a bona fide member. Could he audition, please?

The five trumpeters — Morrison and four Phat men — took centre stage and launched into a pyrotechnic brass showdown. It was pure showbiz, but high-pitched, dynamic, powerful and virtuosic. Morrison more than passed his audition and 3000 students wandered out of the tent declaring it 'awesome' and determined to practise harder.

It was a celebration of all things jazz, and it wasn't over yet. The newly formed Superbands rehearsed on Sunday morning, with their adjudicators now becoming their bandleaders. The finale concert in early afternoon was another public concert, which featured their work, and more performances from James and his guests. Finally, James announced the winners of the three major awards: Stage Band of the Year, the James Morrison Instrumental Scholarship and the Generations in Jazz Vocal Scholarship.

The honours board since 1987 reads like a who's who in youthful Australian jazz. Well-known jazz names of today are among the GIJ nominations of the past. In addition to Ross Irwin, there is John Foreman, a well-known TV pianist who was nominated twice for the James Morrison Instrumental Scholarship and runner-up to the first winner, and Kellie Santin, a saxophonist now based overseas. Early nominees Jordan Murray (trombone), Anton Delecca (sax), Jamie Oehlers (sax), Matthew Jodrell (trumpet), James Annesley (sax) and Sam Anning (bass) are familiar names on current jazz club billings. Phil Stack, who features regularly as a member of James' current bands, was himself a winner back in 1997.

In 1989 and 1991, the name Darren Paul appears in the list of finalists, the only vocalist in two fields of jazz instrumentalists. Darren was good; he didn't win, but James invited him to become part of his groups on his regular gigs and tours. Darren worked with James for eight years. He described himself as being 'the Harry Connick Jr of Australia' for a while, before he drifted away from the jazz genre. In May 2012, after languishing somewhat for several years doing his own one-man gigs 'to forty people in a 200-seat venue', he resurfaced as Darren Percival in *The Voice*, where his velvet sound and total immersion in the lyrics won him a huge following, and opened doors to a recording contract and a mainstream music career. He got his start and wonderful stage experience at least in part from James Morrison and the Generations in Jazz.

Sarah McKenzie, who won the jazz ARIA in 2012 for her second CD *Close Your Eyes*, pipping James' nomination for *Snappy Too*, is a young lady whose ability to play piano and sing were evident very early in her secondary school days at Balwyn High. Her GIJ record is unique and makes even the tenacious Ross Irwin look like a dilettante! She was nominated first in 2004 as a jazz pianist. In 2005, 2007 and 2008 she was a finalist in the Vocal Scholarship. Remarkably, in 2006 she was in both categories, before finally winning the Vocal Scholarship in 2009. Sarah acknowledged that the $5000 she eventually won was 'lovely', but said,

> The real prize was actually being in it for six years. The opportunity to play with James and all the other young musicians was the highlight.
>
> At the big dinner for finalists every year at the Executive Officer Karyn Roberts' house, James would sit down with every person and talk to them — every finalist, about thirteen of us — for thirty to forty-five minutes about our careers and aspirations. I looked forward to that fabulous talk with him every year. It was the highlight of my year — the talk, the food, the laughter, with all the people involved with Generations. All of us finalists had an absolute ball.
>
> Until I went to GIJ I had no idea you could be a jazz musician. I don't come from a musical family and my friends didn't like jazz much either. I loved the feel of it, but never thought of taking it as a career till I heard James and Dale Barlow, and all the other finalists at Generations in Jazz.

In another interview, she said that 'there's a whole new generation coming who are passionate about jazz'. When she was asked what was driving it, she said,

> More than anything it's Generations in Jazz. Every year you have 2500 kids going; workshops and seminars, and people like Ross

Irwin from the *Cat Empire*. When you put jazz on the main stage with rock-star lighting, suddenly it's not just an old man's thing.

Cleves, Morrison and their crew have turned a one-off country jazz gig into Generations in Jazz, a remarkable and inspirational educational program. Cleves is still a little amazed by it all:

> There's huge interest in the whole program. The thing is so alive and well in the schools system. I sometimes have to pinch myself, and I think, *It's alright for people of my age who grew up in the swing era, but James gets kids playing in big bands and playing swing music and enjoying it.*

James undoubtedly loves it — why else would he have done it for twenty-five years without, as Dale Cleves points out, ever taking a fee? — the students love it and the tutors have a fine old time, socially and musically. Graeme Lyall, Sammy Davis Jr's preferred horn section leader on Australian tours, has moved to Mount Gambier to run the GIJ Academy at Tenison College. He acknowledges that GIJ provides the best opportunity for students to listen to their peers and to leading professional players, but other aspects of the weekend make it *de rigueur* for him:

> The thing I've enjoyed most is getting to know James and John, sitting at a table with them, watching James devour half a cow — before he became a vegetarian — and listening to the most incredible stories about music. It's the funniest night of the year; it's hysterical. I look forward to just sitting down, getting to know James. And the more you know him, the scarier he is! He's probably one of the few geniuses I know, and to have someone of that calibre involved in this festival, is just …

And he ran out of words.

Amidst the fun and camaraderie, it was a very rewarding weekend that enabled James to do one of the things he believes most passionately in. Together with Dale Cleves, Leigh O'Connor and the visionaries who first thought of Generations in Jazz he is, as Rory McEwen put it, 'celebrating the past by making an investment in the future'. Morrison says nothing makes him happier.

Chapter 31

'Then who's the real James Morrison?'

No-one in music in Australia can doubt James Morrison's ongoing commitment as a jazz educator, fostering the genre through his work in schools and Generations in Jazz. But of his own playing there is still, in some minds, a doubt as to whether he's an entertainer or a musician — as if the two were incompatible.

Gail Brennan of the 'performing seal' quote expressed it colourfully; John Shand more carefully: 'Question marks may hover over his emotional sincerity when playing.' Even his old tutor from the Con, Judy Bailey, suggested,

> What has happened over the years is that he's been pigeon-holed into the sort of role-play it's thought the public expect. There are so many entertainers — musicians, actors — who get painted into a corner. They feel under an obligation to the paying public to deliver the goods, and they know what is expected of them. If you placed James in front of a knowledgeable, discerning audience it'd be a different story.

Ms Bailey is probably right. 'Sometimes when I'm seen to be lacking in certain areas,' James thinks, 'I feel if only the critics knew what I do overseas.'

He told Peter Thompson on ABC TV,

> On a gig in Australia, you can do a couple of originals, new songs we've just created that they don't know. As long as you do plenty of good standards, then you can throw one or two originals in. If I was playing to the general public in Germany, they'd want

to hear 'Take the "A" Train', too. I think that I play to a different crowd. Not that different, but I have a much broader appeal in Australia; I play to mums and dads, and the kids. In Germany, I play to the hardcore jazz fans.

That sort of statement, rather than mollifying the critics, adds fuel to the fire. They want to know which is the 'real James'. Adrian Jackson, the jazz writer for *The Age*, asked,

> When is James simply being himself? Is it when he plays the entertainer before Australian audiences? (I believe so — it seems to come so naturally to him.) Or is it when he performs overseas, or even at home with international jazz stars like the Ray Brown Trio, and essentially lets his instrument do the entertaining. Why isn't he such an extroverted entertainer on the international stage? Is it because the *music* suffers? If it's fair enough to put the music first overseas, why not do the same here? Is it because Australian audiences are not sophisticated enough to appreciate good music on its own merits?

To Morrison, it's partly a numbers thing:

> It's not that Europeans are better musically educated or Australians aren't so literate, it's simply that while there's a sprinkling of jazz aficionados in audiences here, in Europe there are more. The population is ten times ours and they fill the clubs. I've got a much greater cross-section of people in my Australian audiences.

In 1990, he said,

> On my last tour [overseas], the audience was listening with educated ears that had heard Charlie Parker and Oscar Peterson, and they wanted to know what I could come up with. Here, the audience mainly wants to be entertained. I could play a Charlie Parker quote and in Europe they'll think, *Oh yes, very good*, but here they just think I'm playing a lot of notes.

This ability to suit the repertoire to the expectations of his audiences has misled fellow musicians on occasion, too. Some have admitted after a first gig together that they'd seen him purely as some sort of floor show act, and that playing with him would be easy and not a serious jazz workout.

He remembers taking the fine jazz pianist Paul Grabowsky to Europe in a quartet in 1993. The two had played together intermittently over the years, going back to gigs at the Limerick Arms in South Melbourne — once the city's favourite jazz pub — even before the Australian Jazz Orchestra's Bicentennial tours of 1988, when Grabowsky and his bass player mate Gary Costello were building their reputations in their hometown, and James and John Morrison were guest stars from Sydney.

> I think Paul saw me as a good instrumentalist, but from the cabaret end of jazz. He agreed to tour Europe with me, and we played what we do over there. He said, 'How do you do this?'
>
> I said, 'This is what I do all the time here.'
>
> 'But no-one back home would have a clue you play like this and do this sort of thing.'
>
> 'They don't need to; they're not interested in it.'
>
> 'Some people are,' said Grabowsky.
>
> 'Yeah, four of you! There would be no-one to play to. I wouldn't have a crowd in a venue in Australia. I play what they respond to and want to hear from me.'
>
> 'But why are you putting that on?'
>
> 'I'm not putting that on. I love "St James Infirmary". I love free improvisation; I love some funk.'

Then came the inevitable question: 'Then who is the real James Morrison?'

James remembers going into detail with Paul about what he felt. He explained that although he admires musicians who specialise in a certain sound, style or era, he can't be categorised like that. 'I'm so glad those musicians exist,' he said, 'because through them, I can hear a real Dixieland musician, or whatever. But that's too small for me. I don't want to appear to be critical of or above other guys. I'm not. I'm just different.'

He pointed out that there is sometimes little difference between music and noise. Musicians can just make noise if they are playing and thinking, *When does this gig finish and when do we get paid?* James said,

> I just want to communicate something. The real James Morrison is concerned only about real communication. If I play something and you don't 'get it', it's not the 'real me' no matter what style it is. The 'real me' wants you to 'get it'. When I play music I'm not really interested in the sounds, I'm interested in the effects.

James recounted to Paul the feeling he got when he first heard a band. He was moved by it the way others might be moved by a Mozart Requiem or a Metallica song. He knew then that he wanted to create that feeling. To do that he had to be, as he put it, 'into every style, depending on who you're talking to and trying to communicate with'.

> When you hear me playing, I'm not putting on something for the audience; I'm not thinking, *Oh I'd better play down to this audience.* There's no such thing. In effect, by definition you can't play down to an audience if you've got my reason for playing music. Playing to the audience is up; the only way you can play down is to disregard them, to actually not play to them. 'You want "Take the 'A' Train"? No, I'm not going to play down to you.' That doesn't make sense given my reason for making music. The real James Morrison is whatever sound, whatever style, whatever band is required to have this communication, this experience with the audience.

Paul started to get it. 'So if you played an avant-garde festival somewhere, you could play free, pull the mouthpiece out and throw things around?'

'Absolutely!' said James. 'That would be the most appropriate way to get to that audience. I can admire players who specialise in one small corner of jazz and zoom in on it. I love it, but it's not what I'm about.'

James knows that he isn't selling out to the audience. In fact, it's just the opposite:

> If I played just, say, a particular part of the jazz of the 1930s, the only audience I can speak to is the audience who are into that particular part of the 1930s or people who are pretty open — but they won't want to hear it every night. Once you say, 'No, I'm into giving people a really wonderful musical experience,' your audience is every human being on earth. It means I can play an avant-garde festival in Germany or a gig at the Dapto Workers' Club — and I'll fill them both.

Paul Grabowsky, looking back now, doesn't remember the conversation in anything like the detail James recalled, but did see the trumpeter moving away a little even then from his typical Australian fare:

> We played a more stretching-out sort of jazz, and James cut me a lot of rope. I don't think there was a huge difference between what he would do in Australia and what he would do in Europe. But he would construct his sets as if there was the inner need to be the entertainer that he was in Australia, and in Europe more a musician. Musically, it was probably the same message, but he had to sell it in a much more showbiz kind of way in Australia. He knew how to do that successfully; he could do it without even thinking about it.

James was quick to discover what best suited his overseas audiences, and has been filling jazz clubs and concert halls in Europe and America for a long time now. He went to the latter first as the last-minute replacement in the Cab Calloway Band — the 'added extra' to his second visit to the US back in 1987. He played Ronnie Scott's Club in London and several European festivals, but initially in other people's groups. In 1988, he featured again at Montreux, this time with pianist Adam Makowicz as two of Edith Kiggen's young 'nurture artists'.

By 1990, he was ready and had a big enough profile to take his own groups. His manager at the time, Peter Brendle, had the contacts and Morrison now had the confidence to make it work. James invited his brother John on drums, his mates Jonathan Zwartz on bass and Steve Brien on guitar, and was delighted that his mentor, Don Burrows, declared himself available. 'Inviting Don along as my guest,' said James 'was a big thing. It was me under my own steam doing my own thing; it was a big tour.'

His face still registers disbelief when he remembers that the sixth touring musician was Glenn Henrich — not that Glenn was incompetent or a misfit, just that his instrument, the vibraphone, was about the least convenient imaginable for a three-month tour in a band bus!

Before the tour got underway, Brendle was contacted by a European agent, Burkhard Hopper. His actual name was Hoppe but he added the final 'r' to make the correct pronunciation more obvious. Hopper, who had heard James on the Superband tours, told Brendle that some of the clubs James was booked for appeared unsuitable. 'I can book him into better ones,' he said, 'would you like me to help out on this?'

Brendle, to his credit, saw the wisdom of using the man on the spot. Hopper, who now lives in London, was in Munich at that time. He agreed and Hopper has been instrumental in Morrison's Euro-ventures ever since, even linking James to Ray Brown and drummer Grady Tate in a band he was putting together for Lalo Schifrin. This later led to the whole *Jazz Meets the Symphony* series of recordings and worldwide concerts.

It also led to the 1992 collaboration between Ray Brown and Morrison in making a recording, *Two the Max*, and the tour that publicised it. This recording was nominated for an Australian ARIA Award for the Best Jazz Album in 1993.

Adrian Jackson acknowledged in his *Age* review that

> jazz police types may complain about the depth of the music James sometimes plays for local fans, but he enjoys a solid reputation on the international jazz circuit and this album shows why. If ever Morrison was going to knuckle down and play to the best of his ability, it was when he had the chance to record with Ray Brown and his trio. Brown, pianist Benny Green and drummer Jeff Hamilton lay down a swinging groove, and Morrison fits right in with them, whether playing excited trumpet on 'Max', relaxed flugelhorn on 'Honeysuckle Rose' or warm-toned, remarkably articulate trombone on 'Moten Swing' or 'Imagination'.

Jackson, who over the years has seen fit to both praise and criticise Morrison's performances, has never doubted his intrinsic ability: 'You don't muck around when you're playing with [the late, great] Ray Brown. He [James] played beautifully and I'm sure that's the sort of playing that, to a large extent, his international reputation is based on.'

Hopper, in Munich, was in no doubt as to James' standing and virtuosity. He told Eric Myers in *JazzChord* magazine,

> Contrary to some comments I hear about James' reputation in Australia, he is regarded as a very serious musician over here, and stays in direct competition with trumpet greats like Wynton Marsalis, Jon Faddis and Roy Hargrove. If money is any indication, he received fees in 1995 that were in the category of Wynton Marsalis, and he not only played but headlined some prestigious festivals last year.

By March 1996, Morrison could top the bill in his own right and the calls for his services, through Hopper, were plentiful and diverse. One minute he could be leading his own band, and the next, soloing in front of European big bands and orchestras.

In 2000, for example, it was Morrison who was invited by the

Westdeutscher Rundfunk in Cologne to write and perform music for the celebration of the hundredth birthday anniversary of Louis Armstrong. He conducted it, too, describing himself as being 'busy as a one-armed paperhanger'. He left work on the assignment till the last two weeks, and finished it on his computer on the plane en route to Germany. 'It's amazing how much work you can fit in instead of sleep,' he quipped.

He downloaded the parts in Cologne and handed them around the orchestra almost before the print had dried. It worked out so well he was immediately asked to arrange 'Der Treue Husar (The Faithful Soldier)', a German tune Armstrong had become attached to in Europe in the 1950s, for another concert in three days time. It caused more sleepless nights, but was completed on schedule.

James had now been chosen to represent three of the great trumpet masters — he'd already performed Schifrin's tributes to Beiderbecke and Gillespie — and he made it a double hat-trick when, in late 2000 in Birmingham, England, he performed the famous Miles Davis solo part of the original Gil Evans/Miles Davis suite, *Porgy and Bess*, with the BBC Big Band.

James saw it, he told Eric Myers in the *JazzChord* interview in 1996, as 'a huge honour and a challenge. I love the music of Gil Evans and Miles Davis, but it is not my normal stylistic approach. Gil knows Miles so well that [while] much of the music we hear is actually written out, it sounds like Miles improvising.'

Those years listening to the brass-playing jazz masters of previous generations, like Bix, Louis and Miles, stood James in good stead. While he made no attempt to imitate their sounds and mannerisms, he was well-equipped to pay a modern musician's respects to them. He said of *Porgy and Bess*, 'Playing this music, music that I've heard many times, was a sublime experience — the writing is gorgeous. To stand in amongst the band and hear it live was like a dream.'

But at the same time James was honouring the heroes of the past, he was also putting together some of his own more innovative groups, particularly for the European jazz market, which he felt was more prepared to accept a less mainstream James Morrison. Eric Myers reported that

> James believes he has established himself internationally in the same way as other leading jazz artists have gained a foothold — by showing that he has mastered the playing of standards, i.e. the classic repertoire of American jazz music. But beyond a certain point, he says, sophisticated audiences overseas want to hear a musician presenting his own music.

And, by the mid-1990s, James Morrison was ready to do just that.

Chapter 32

Hot Horn Happenings

In 1994, James Morrison formed the seven-piece group Hot Horn Happening. The name wasn't his choice. Burkhard Hopper coined it, James reckons, because he thought it was a great joke to be able to pick up the office phone and say, 'Hot Horn Happening, Hopper here. How can I help you?' In his German accent it sounds even better than it reads! The cool American sax players James had recruited, Jeff Clayton and Rickey Woodard, raised their eyebrows, so Burkhard explained further: 'Quite frankly, I know in America you wouldn't call the band Hot Horn Happening, but in France, in Germany and in Italy, this English works. It gives them "hot", "horn", it's "happening", so it will get the message over.' He was right; 'No-one blinks an eyelid over there,' said James.

The group was a departure for James from quartets playing standards and a vehicle for his own compositions, which were increasing in number. The band's first tour took in Berlin, Mülheim, Stuttgart, Vienna, Salzburg, Geneva, Lucerne, Baden, Graz, Paris and London in a four-week period. James put together a cosmopolitan crew featuring the two American saxophonists, Woodard on tenor and Clayton on alto, both from Los Angeles; a trombonist from London, Mark Nightingale; a German bass player, Martin Wind; a Scottish pianist, Brian Kellock; and the two Morrison brothers from Sydney, Australia.

Hopper recommended Mark Nightingale, the young trombone player, to James. He said 'he's the hot trombonist around'. Wind had played a couple of gigs with the Morrison brothers during the 1993 'Grabowsky' tour. Somehow his drummer friend, Thilo Berg, had an arrangement to sit in for John, and requested that Martin play bass at the Q4 Club in Rheinfelden, Switzerland. In the event, Berg couldn't do the gig, but Wind still sat in for a couple of memorable nights.

James was evidently impressed with the young musician, and remembered him a year later when he was putting the Hot Horns together. It was an honour for Wind:

> I got recognition in Germany because I was touring with an international band. James could have asked anybody to play in that group. Later, he told the biggest German jazz magazine that I played like he envisioned Ray Brown would have played at my age. That was a fantastic thing for someone to say. It really put me on the map.

Morrison used the principles of putting a band together that he had learned from Burrows — promoting virtually unknown musicians alongside established names. Wind continues,

> The tour was where I grew up musically. I'd finished studying classical music in Cologne and it was like going back to school again. We had four horn players, so the songs lasted for a long time. We would play straight fours in the same groove for sometimes twenty minutes. I still think that a lot of my foundation, my time-keeping, my groove-playing, comes from my experiences with that group.

The extended soloing of four frontline players and the pianist, particularly in Rickey Woodard's fast blues 'Tokyo Express', which went like the bullet train, took a toll on Wind's flying fingers and wrist. In a brief break in the middle of the tour, he needed a cortisone injection to gain relief from the pain caused by the nightly musical workout and to carry him through the rest of the tour. When it was over, he visited his physiotherapist: 'I had tendonitis or something, from playing those fast tempos for twenty minutes every night. It was the most physically challenging playing I've ever done in my life.'

It was demanding, but great fun. The band travelled and roomed together. It was as harmonious offstage as it was on. James remembers one reporter trying to find an angle for his story, looking for a bit of friction in the team.

'You're a League of Nations,' he said. 'Are there ever any tensions within the band?'

'Absolutely,' said James, and the hack gripped his pencil in excitement. 'Between the Englishman and the Scotsman. Every time they talk about football, there's arguing and yelling over accusations of cheating going back to 1966!'

James added, 'I thought it was funny that we started this band from all over the world, and the only problem was between the Englishman and the Scotsman!'

James enjoyed sponsorship from BMW, which generally supplied a car of his choice and a van. 'We'd travel by car from Paris to Austria and play the same night,' recalls Wind. 'We had some of the greatest concerts after being in the car all day, taking a ferry somewhere and waiting around. Then we'd get onstage totally exhausted and play the roof off!' Trombonist Mark Nightingale added,

> What was helpful was that there was never any post-mortem about how a person played on a gig. If anyone had any figures that had gone a little bit wrong, there was no finger-pointing or recriminations. James trusted people to sort it out for the next time. He understood people could make slips.

Morrison was no touring prima donna — he operated more on the easygoing B. B. King style than the fault-finding Ray Charles model. There was one particular journey that impressed Mark:

> We did a gig in Linkoping in the south of Sweden. We travelled down and back from Stockholm in a hired minibus. There

weren't enough seats in the van and James insisted on being the person sitting on a little stool made out of his trumpet case, or something. He wouldn't hear of anybody else doing that.

Morrison was generous about the repertoire, too. It was made up of several of James' originals — it was his group after all! — but the others were invited to bring along their own charts. The arrangements had to be written in some detail for a band with four 'frontline' players. That necessitated a day of rehearsal at the beginning of each four-week tour.

Mark said,

> We'd run through the new music literally just a couple of times, but it did need a quick look. The band could have played anything from early swing, through bebop, to avant-garde had it wanted to — the musicians were certainly capable of it. The path we ended up on was more bebop/modern mainstream — if there is such a thing! We played our original compositions: some bebop, some more swing-orientated. Nothing sounded dated, but it wasn't exactly 'cutting-edge' — just good tunes with good sequences.

One of Mark Nightingale's original numbers for the group was entitled 'Thwing!' He taught James to announce it with the preposterous lisp of a politically incorrect English comedian of the time, Freddie 'Parrotface' Davies. You'd have to ask how such gags might work in a European context, but Morrison, as always, was adept at getting the audience onside, sprinkling a few words of the local language into his intros.

The tour's final gig of 1994 at the New Morning Club in Paris was recorded by Hopper, co-produced by John Morrison and released by East-West Records as, prosaically, *Live in Paris: James Morrison and the Hot Horn Happening*. The eight tracks are all originals: straight, swinging jazz — lengthy pieces played by superb jazz players — without a 'St James Infirmary' or 'The Old Rugged Cross' in sight. It was a different recording for a different audience; James doesn't even play trombone on it, although on tour dates he generally did, revelling in 'trombone battles' with Mark Nightingale.

The Englishman had expected that Morrison would play more trombone: 'I knew he was a multi-instrumentalist and, to be honest, I was surprised he stuck to the trumpet as much as he did. We only did a couple of numbers on trombone together. It was exciting — a bit of showmanship. We'd improvise and play off each other. The crowd loved it.'

So James was entertaining even in this serious environment? Mark said, 'I think his attitude was, "Why be po-faced about it? We're up there having fun, why not share it?"'

He added that he'd heard the accusation in England, as in Australia, that James might not be a 'real' jazz musician: 'I saw him play the same set night after night for a whole month and not repeat himself. He's an improvising jazz musician who creates something new every night. I can vouch for that because I've watched it first-hand.'

Mark also found James' stamina and resilience remarkable:

> On one of the trips, there was a nasty bug going around; it really knocked you sideways. I remember when I had it, I could hardly get out of bed in the morning, let alone play the trombone on a gig!
>
> James got it in his turn. He was completely wiped out for the day — very quiet, unable to do anything just like everyone else had been. When we got to the gig, though, it was like somebody put a thousand volts of electricity up his arse! Suddenly, he turned into the guy who was putting on the show and trying to please the audience — full of life and energy. I had no idea how he did it. At the end of the gig he was as white as all the rest of us, a really tired guy. But he'd managed to turn it on for the audience; he made it happen. It was quite amazing.

The 'League of Nations' line-up continued to tour Europe for several years, and toured Australia once with home-grown players, in September 1994. James said at the time that getting a band like this together to play original music has been a long-term plan. This is a band I can see myself working with for many years to come. I want to write music for this band, and grow and expand as a musician with it. Much as I enjoy it, I don't want to keep playing standards with the quartet forever. There's a lot more scope with a band like this, where you've got four horns in the frontline. There are enough colours there for you to make some interesting voicings for the different soloists to play against — and, of course, there are a lot more different soloists there, too, to keep you on your toes.

I'd like it to be something like Art Blakey's Jazz Messengers, which of course went for something like forty years, with many changes in personnel. But it was always the Jazz Messengers; you knew what sort of music you were going to hear. I'd like to develop a personality for this band, so that even if the personnel changes down the road, we'll have the same instrumentation, playing the same sort of music.

Adrian Jackson's *Age* review after the Melbourne Hot Horn Happening gig was generally positive, after first outlining his critical reservations about Morrison's normal Australian jazz output. The review demonstrates again Australian critics' continued ambivalence towards James' musical presentations.

Jackson noted that Morrison's usual Australian fare would be expected to be standards, with 'jokes, yarns and running gags between the numbers'. He looked forward to 'hearing Morrison in a context where he had to extend, or even discipline, himself'.

He found Hot Horn Happening the 'welcome change' he was looking for, with Morrison playing his own compositions alongside outstanding local players who 'provided plenty of competition' and took the roles of the cosmopolitan assemblage with which Morrison had toured Europe.

Jackson added, though, that Morrison 'tended to home in on the upper register, where his tone takes on an unattractive shrillness. Some of his solos built to a convincing climax, while his flugelhorn on the ballad, "My Beautiful" was elegant in both tone and phrasing.'

The review also commended the three frontmen, Dale Barlow on tenor sax, Blaine Whittaker on alto and James Greening on trombone, and the solos from the rhythm section members, bassist Jonathan Zwartz and pianist Bobby Gebert, but reflected that John's drum solo set piece drew bigger applause. Jackson concluded,

> the leader made all sorts of jokes about the tastelessness of drum solos; I can only wonder whether the irony was intended. Of course, the Morrison brothers' refusal to take themselves too seriously partly explains their appeal beyond the core jazz audience. It also explains the reservations some jazz fans hold, even when they deliver a generally rewarding performance.

The record made by the European Hot Horn Happening was well-received both at home and overseas, where the septet was indeed compared to the Art Blakey Jazz Messengers in its prime, and with groups led by luminaries like Frank Wess and Frank Foster.

Jim MacLeod, presenter of the ABC radio program *Jazztrack*, observed in *24 Hours* that

> in a sense, it might be regarded as James' first real jazz album, completely away from attempts to entertain above all, and to appeal to as wide an audience as possible. That's not to say that it isn't entertaining, but that it should be free of accusations of 'circus tricks'.

The band toured for three years, which is very creditable for a band of its size. James said,

> It's hard to tour a band that big and that expensive. Some of those players had their own bands in their own right and weren't

available cheaply, yet it lasted for three years. It was very successful, and I put that down to the fact that it was just by chance, or if you don't believe in chance, it was the right mix.

There's talk, among the members, of a reunion. James thinks it'll happen at some stage. It would be good if it did, if only so Burkhard could rehearse his aspirates: 'Hot Horn Re-Happening, Hopper here. How can I help you?'

Chapter 33

Living on the Edge

Undoubtedly, Hot Horn Happening, with or without 'circus tricks', increased James' stature as a live performer. By mid-1996, the group, still approaching the high point of the European jazz festival season, had already given more than seventy concerts. Hot Horn Happening never did achieve the longevity of the enduring Jazz Messengers, which Morrison had aspired to. But, typically, he was off and running with new ideas for another adventurous jazz enterprise — one that, surprisingly, he hadn't had a crack at before.

James had never hidden his enjoyment of hearing and playing the trumpet in its highest register. He discovered his ability to do it early in his teenage years, and the thrill of the 'squeal' has never lost its edge. He says,

> It's funny, you don't get groups of clarinettists going, 'Let's scream up high!' but trumpet players have got to do that. A musician came up to me one night at a gig as the crowd was roaring, 'More! More!' and said, 'Don't you get sick of playing all that high, fast stuff for the crowd?' I looked at him — he was a guy who was into this real, cool, introverted jazz — and I said, 'Did it ever occur to you that I like that, too?'

Even when he's sitting in the audience and hears a trumpet playing the right sort of song, something inside him says, 'Yeah, baby, take it up! Do it!' All his earlier heroes 'did it' — Gillespie, Armstrong, 'Cat' Anderson, Maynard Ferguson. He finds it powerful and exciting, and the buzz it draws from a crowd is enormous.

The *Scream Machine* recording in late 2001 seemed a natural consequence of his stratospheric range addiction. The working title had been *Trumpet Mayhem*, but *Scream Machine*, suggested in an online competition, seemed to James to aptly capture the essence and effervescence of the enterprise. It was, in part, a tribute to another explosive, but sadly short-lived, trumpeter. Bill Chase, a lead player with the Woody Herman Thundering Herd throughout the 1960s, had done something like it before. His band, Chase, recorded one particularly successful eponymous album, which sold 400,000 copies. It used like never before a section of high note specialists in 'complex, cascading lines, a literal waterfall of trumpet timbre and technique'.

The description, apart from the misuse of 'literal', suits the first track of *Scream Machine* to a tee, announcing itself unmistakably with the sound of five trumpets roaring out a sustained high G before gushing down. It made a belter of a concert opener.

The comparison between the two extreme register groups fades soon enough, as Chase was driven by a jazz-rock rhythm backing and featured several rock-style vocalists from the band. *Scream Machine* stuck to jazz instrumentals: originals from James, including the title track, and classics from Hancock, Ellington and 'the man himself', Dizzy Gillespie, ever James' greatest trumpet influence.

The other stand-out difference from Chase was that while the American used three other established big band lead players, James over-dubbed all the trumpet tracks himself. He couldn't do that when the band hit the road briefly in Australia or when he toured it around the major European festivals in the summer of 2002. 'If I'm going to perform this live,' he decided, 'I'm going to need four other trumpeters who are stupid enough to do this and don't have any regard for their own personal safety!'

In Australia, he lined up three Sydney friends from way back, Ralph Pyl, Paul Panichi and Paul Thorne, plus Dave 'DJ' Newdick from

Melbourne. Outgoing DJ laughs when he's asked how he was invited to participate. 'Tell James that Dave Newdick realises now he got the gig because he needed a token Melbourne player for national balance.' The reason is more likely that DJ was recognised as a fine player with a great range that James had heard in the house band backing him on his frequent appearances on *Hey Hey It's Saturday*.

'I could play high notes when I was a teenager, but,' Dave added modestly, 'lots of players play extreme range these days.' He was rapt at the chance to play in the unique-sounding band and to fly to Sydney for gigs at The Basement, then home to Melbourne to play the Athenaeum. The concerts were full of energy and adrenaline, starting with the super G opener, through 'Chameleon' and 'Caravan' (with a metal-jazz guitar middle eight) to James' own 'Fugue II' (he'd recorded 'Fugue I' on a previous CD), with James on piccolo trumpet leading the others in classical contrapuntal lines.

James gave his new digital trumpet an airing — befitting for a concert billed as part of the Electric Jazz Festival. The novel instrument was 'a striking, almost two-dimensional synthesised horn with glowing, neon panels and bubbling wah-wah sound that maximised the tune's vigorous groove.' Reactions to *Scream Machine* ranged from 'exhilarating' to 'exhausting', and 'staggering' to 'shrill'. The skirl of five jet-trajectory trumpets is not everyone's cup of hot cocoa, but it was impossible, Jessica Nicholas wrote in *The Age*, 'not to be won over by the unbridled delight that Morrison displays as he plays, which helps mould this intriguing, but potentially limited line-up, into a genuinely exciting ensemble'.

Morrison himself knew full well that such a group had a short life expectancy. 'It was just an iconic thing to do. It was something inevitable for trumpet players, but it was never going to be a long-lived thing. It was just that one album; I don't have any desire to do it again in my career.'

Ironically, for all the excitement of the rocket-fuelled gigs, Dave Newdick recalled the ballads best. 'I know what James can do range-wise, but what impressed me was the beauty of his long notes and phrases in the restful 'Con Alma'. When he plays a ballad, it's gorgeous.'

The *Scream Machine* European summer tour of 2002 had used local trumpeters, Australian David Jones, one of James' most compatible drummers, and Simon Stockhausen, the son of the avant-garde composer Karlheinz, on keyboards and soprano sax. Morrison, Jones and Stockhausen had been collaborating a few months earlier during a two-week tour with sold-out concerts in Cologne, Dortmund and Leipzig. James was there as conductor/composer/arranger. James was able to use Stockhausen and Jones as guest artists, as well as Australian guitarist Peter 'Zog' Zografakis.

James told *JazzChord* that the program was interesting as it

> included two compositions of Peter Zog's, which I arranged for the band, and the piece I wrote (Fugue 1) as a tribute to Bach. This was an interesting choice, given the concert in Leipzig and we wondered how it would go down. The composition began with a very 'legit' sound — baroque trumpet and pipe organ (myself and Simon) and went through a few metamorphoses until arriving at one stage at Simon playing examples of Afghan preachers chanting. The idea was to take Bach and see where it went, given the much broader canvas of sounds available to the modern keyboard player than Bach had. It was received with a standing ovation, due mainly to the amazing creativity of Simon Stockhausen.

> Elsewhere, Peter Zog blew them away with the phenomenal playing of both bebop and fusion. Peter is a complete guitar player if ever there was one. David Jones once again demonstrated that he was a master percussionist and stunned audiences with his virtuosity. The reputation of Australian jazz musicians overseas continues to grow.

James first met Stockhausen on one of his Schifrin excursions. For his album, *Esperanto,* the master arranger wrote a 'Concerto Grosso for Big Band and Six Soloists', and chose players from around the world on diverse and unlikely instruments to speak an international language: jazz. He used Jean-Luc Ponty from France on the violin; he had Nestor Marconi on bandoneon from Argentina; Trilok Gurtu from India and Sydney Thiam on percussion; the dreadlocked American Don Byron on clarinet; and German-born Simon Stockhausen on electronic keyboards.

'Lalo had written this incredible thing that used them as only he could — bandoneon, violin and Stockhausen together. He had bebop happening on the bandoneon! It was this incredible project — bigger than Ben Hur — we spent ten days together in the studio.'

James sat fascinated by Marconi and his bandoneon, more a relative of the concertina than the accordion. The instrument has buttons on both sides, which can play different notes depending on whether the player is pulling the bellows in or out, giving it, in effect, four keyboards in two hands. Morrison attempted to play it, but for once was defeated. 'It's the most complicated instrument you've ever seen. It's fantastic, but it's diabolical!'

Nestor Marconi just laughed. He told James, 'We have a saying in Argentina: "If you haven't taken up the bandoneon by the time you're ten, you won't live long enough to learn it"!'

Stockhausen, as you would expect of the son of an iconoclastic figure in the classical musical world, was no common or garden keyboardist. While his father introduced him to Beethoven and Stravinsky, he discovered John Coltrane himself.

He got his first synthesiser, a mini-moog, at nine years of age and rapidly explored its capabilities. He collected environmental sounds, processing them and taking them out of context:

> I always feel like Alice in Wonderland. It's a never-ending fascination to detect a cool rhythmical structure in a bombastic

factory sound, for instance, or understand the code of a singing bird after transposing it down eight octaves or time-stretching it so that one can actually hear all the notes it sings.

In retrospect, James sees his pairing up with Stockhausen as 'most unlikely. He wasn't someone I would have sought out prior to the Schifrin recording. I was aware of Karlheinz Stockhausen's music and, brilliant as it may be, it wasn't for me.' And of all the people after the *Esperanto* event who might have continued to collaborate,

> the one you wouldn't have picked would have been Simon Stockhausen and James Morrison, but we just hit it off. We got together because we discovered that where he lived musically wasn't any good for me; where I lived musically wasn't any good for him, but where we met was exciting for both of us.

In the *Esperanto* project, Lalo hadn't written anything that had the two trading off each other. They didn't jam together to make a connection; it was purely cerebral: 'We just got this feeling when we got together and talked; "we could do something". It was weird because most things come out of a musical event together — something happens when you trade fours. This came out of us just talking.'

In the back of his mind, Morrison saw Stockhausen as an ideal colleague for one of his European bands. James talked about it before it materialised. It would feature, he told John Shand, Stockhausen, Jones, bassist Evripides Evripidou and himself.

> That would be a really exciting quartet. Certainly you'd have to stand well back. There'd be a lot of energy coming off that one. Now, I have no idea how you'd begin to promote that and say to everyone, 'I've got a new quartet — here's who's in it.' And if they're people who're into mainstream and don't know those guys, I guess they're going to find out!

Nothing happened for a year and a half, and when it did neither Jones nor Evripidou were part of it. Morrison waited for the moment and found it in Perth, Western Australia, where he was scheduled to play a *Showcase* concert with the West Australian Youth Jazz Orchestra. Someone pointed out that four young West Australians had each won the James Morrison Instrumental Scholarship at Generations in Jazz in recent years; not only that, their instrumentation would form a great combo line-up. There was trumpeter Mat Jodrell (winner in 1998), Troy Roberts on sax (2001), Dave Alderson on electric bass (2002) and Andrew Fisenden on drums (2003). All it lacked was a keyboard player!

'We played together,' said James, 'and it went off!' That night he was on the phone to Stockhausen. 'I've found the band. They're all young guys but we're right to go.' The keyboard player was enthusiastic and James invited experienced percussionist Sunil de Silva, another 'old man', James said, to help address the age imbalance.

On the Edge seemed like an appropriate name because 'that's how it felt,' James said. 'This is going to be dangerous,' he continued. 'It may be fantastic or it may be a disaster; it's "on the edge".'

They recorded a live album in the Studio at the Sydney Opera House, and then toured Europe in 2004 and 2006.

> It was difficult for me to start in Australia because it was so far removed from what I normally do. I wasn't game to say 'James Morrison in Concert' and then play originals from me and Simon. The audience would say, 'Where's "The 'A' Train?"' So we billed it as a special event, 'On the Edge'. The people who came loved it. It's funny though, that the recording and the DVD was done here but most of the work of the band was in Europe.

The concerts certainly weren't standard jazz quartet fare, featuring, as they did, the extraordinary sounds Stockhausen coaxed from his synthesisers. The most unusual work may have been 'da Speech', which

Simon created from speeches and sound bites after the 9/11 tragedy, as he tried to express his reaction to the event.

There was also tight, aggressive 'big band' lines from the four frontmen, creative percussion, vivid trumpet duets, and mellow flugelhorn and bass trumpet sequences. It was music a little left of centre and well-suited to jazz buffs, which may have led to James, at long last, getting an invitation to the Wangaratta Festival of Jazz, widely considered to be Australia's foremost jazz event. Remarkably, James had never before played at that festival. This was partly due to James' touring schedules, but also due to the fact his fans in Australia were not the aficionados who attend Wangaratta, or so the festival organisers thought. 'His audience,' the festival's artistic director Adrian Jackson explained, 'probably doesn't go and hear jazz, and knows James because they've seen him on TV.'

James knows the score:

> This was the first time I'd had a band Wangaratta would have. I'm not right for Wangaratta because I'm too straight-ahead. They have a philosophy on what the festival is all about. What it's not about is firstly having someone on you can hear around Australia anytime and, secondly, it's got to be something worth putting on. On the Edge, a collaboration with Simon Stockhausen, has 'Wangaratta' written all over it.

James was right. 'The festival,' John Shand reported, 'ended on a high note — literally — with James Morrison, who brought On the Edge, his lethal collaboration with Simon Stockhausen. This was to music what a Lamborghini is to cars, but faster, louder, slicker, and very entertaining.' The petrolhead part of Morrison would have loved the analogy!

The group appealed to European audiences too, finishing, as it often did, with a cheering and stamping reception after a 'Caravan' so authentic you could almost smell the camel dung, followed by James alone at the piano, accompanying his own blizzard-of-notes finale to 'Basin Street Blues', and proving once again that audiences, the cognoscenti just as much as the 'musically illiterate', love his singular right hand/left hand dexterity.

Some years ago Eric Myers, a man better acquainted with the Australian jazz scene than most, when writing in the magazine *JazzChord* declared himself 'flabbergasted' to find out what James was doing overseas. He compared James' success in international jazz to the status of Dame Joan Sutherland on the world opera stage and the crop of Australian actors, like Geoffrey Rush and Cate Blanchett, picking up Oscars in Los Angeles. But whereas their successes were deservedly plastered all over the Press, James' exploits were largely unreported in jazz circles, let alone the daily papers.

James admitted he felt liked, even loved, at home but the lack of recognition for the pinnacles he'd reached frustrated him more than he was generally inclined to admit. It reawakened within him the 'if only they knew' sentiment.

At home, there was awareness of the occasional Jazz Meets the Symphony project, and brief visits from Morrison's ensembles. But there was little acknowledgement of the ongoing strength of the collaboration between Schifrin and James in recordings and at concerts all over the world, let alone Morrison's Grammy Award-nominated Lalo-scored track, or the number of times James was the instrumentalist chosen to play tributes to the great trumpeters of the past.

There was scant appreciation of James' tours with the aging, but enormously respected, greats of the jazz world, virtually no recognition of his output of original music for the unique ensembles he set up, or the originality of the groups themselves. The fact is that James was increasingly able to command international festival fees equal to the best in the jazz world. But this substantial achievement was not widely known to his critics in Australia. Those critics tended to remain unconvinced that he was much more than a jazz-oriented one-man band and, moreover, they were uncertain about who the 'real' James Morrison was.

Morrison recalls, with some significance, Paul Grabowsky posing that question back in 1993; Grabowsky now, for his part, can't remember that he did specifically. He does remember many long drives across Europe and many long conversations about aspects of music. He said,

> I think James has always had a very clear view about his own musical mission. I think he arrived at his musical gestalt or his musical persona very early and has been very comfortable in that role for a very long time. I think there is a real consistency between all he does but, as I see it, it's simply the context in which he does it that informs his modus operandi.

It's nicely put — 'the context informs his modus operandi'. He chooses the right ensemble for the tour, the right repertoire for the audience, the right music for the mood, the right instrument for the setting and *le mot juste* for the occasion.

He satisfies the festival audiences of Europe and America, and thrills Australian mainstream audiences equally with diverse groups and playlists. If his overseas ventures remain virtually unknown or overlooked and unheralded by local critics, 'How can I complain?' he says philosophically. 'I get to perform more or less what I want, where I want. And when I'm not performing, I'm out messing about in boats on Pittwater!'

Chapter 34

The Others

'What really interests me,' said Paul Grabowsky, reflecting on shared European tours and gigs with James, 'is what we've done in more recent times. We've done an album called *The Others* that has shown a side of James I've never seen before that really did cause me to reconsider what sort of musician he is.'

The Others is a recording of completely free jazz put down in James' studio in August 2010 by Grabowsky, Morrison and a young drummer called Mark Maher. A fairly typical set-up in some ways, the two older heads encouraging an up-and-coming percussionist. But Mark Maher is better known to the world as Kram, the loud and long-haired 'Black Betty'-blasting drummer from the chart-topping rock'n'roll band Spiderbait — certainly not the first name that would recommend itself for an improvised jazz collaboration.

Yet it was Kram's idea and it happened at Kram's instigation. 'It's weird,' he said, 'people know you because you're a rock star and sell a lot of records and play festivals, but it doesn't always tell the true picture of what you're passionate about.' Kram has loved jazz for a long time and was heavily into it in his university years, long before pop stardom.

In early 2010, his old friend and fellow music student Sean Baxter —'we used to drink a lot and play video games together' — invited him to be part of the Melbourne International Jazz Festival. Sean, a well-known avant-garde jazz drummer, was setting up a big band, one whose repertoire would be completely improvised.

> I went to do this gig with Sean. It was great to play with him again, and to be involved in that world again. I used to play a lot of jazz shows and I always loved improvising. It was so inspiring to play that night. It brought back such energy and excitement for this music, the interactions between musicians to spontaneously create something.
>
> In pop music there's spontaneity in writing songs, but jazz is different in that you create it on the spot. It's ethereal. It's unique in that way; all the communication going on in that band was incredible. I was on a real high at the end.

He was still up there when later the same night he bumped into Grabowsky after Paul and Baxter had played a set. The paths of Grabowsky, Morrison and Kram had crossed on numerous occasions over the years while doing the peripheral activities musicians have to do to publicise their events and recordings. Kram and Paul had even been two of those chosen to represent the arts at the 2020 Summit in Canberra 2008, the talkfest designed to help shape a national future. They'd gotten on well.

James laughs about his first contacts with Kram: 'He and Paul hang out at the Prime Minister's national conference; I meet him in the Green Room at the ABC before *Spicks and Specks*!'

Kram never missed the opportunity to tell James and Paul how keen he was to jam with them. After the inspiration of his big band night at the Melbourne International Jazz Festival, he was fired up to talk to Paul again.

> I'd always had incredible respect for those two musicians who were similar to me in that people know them, not just for their music, but for a lot of other things. We gelled as personalities and decided to do it. The idea was that we wanted to be a bit dangerous, not to be cautious in any way; just plunge in and see what would happen.

James, too, was struck by the unlikeliness of the collaboration which, without Kram's perseverance, would never have eventuated. 'Paul and I would never have thought to get together and do a free thing, let alone with Kram.' Later, James reflected on Erroll Garner's preparation for his great 1955 album *Concert by the Sea*, and how the pianist wrote about not the music, but of the drive from San Francisco along the coast to Carmel in a limo with his trio, Eddie Calhoun and Denzil Best. It set the ambience for the recording. James thought to try and replicate the feeling in his own way.

He offered to pick Kram up from Burrawang, near Bateman's Bay in New South Wales, where Kram was taking a break with his wife and kids at his father-in-law's property. 'I was expecting James to drive down, but no, he flies his own plane down and picks me up from the tiny Moruya airport. He's cruising in in what essentially looks like a sports car with wings. It's a killer!'

Len Hegh, Kram's father-in-law, offered James a horn he'd created out of a conch shell and some old whalebone; 'James immediately grabbed it and produced a beautiful tone.' He later blended it into the recording session. The flight to Sydney, according to Kram, was 'really cool; so trippy, bizarre and awesome'. James remembered it, too. 'We didn't know each other well, but we flew on a sunny afternoon just becoming evening through the clouds over the Harbour. This great scene; nothing to do with the music, but everything to do with the music.'

There was welcoming wine and cheese and conversation at the studio. 'We discussed something totally unrelated — something artistic, it could easily have been Matisse.' Eventually, in a very comfortable and relaxed headspace, the musicians ventured downstairs to James' meticulously prepared studio. There was a grand piano and variety of synthesisers for Paul, a huge drum kit and assorted percussive instruments for Kram, and James' menagerie of horns, including a vocoder and his newly acquired South Coast conch horn.

Without discussion or preparation, the three started playing. Nothing was written, no riffs were preconceived, no figures worked out beforehand. At one stage, Kram said, 'I've got this idea for a groove.' James stopped him. 'Do you want to go down that path? Don't say another word because we'll hear you. It'll be like saying to a jury, "Disregard that last remark." Once you've heard it, you can't disregard it. Do you actually want to do that? Let's just set no parameters; nothing at all.'

The trio played for six hours straight. Whoever wanted to, started; whatever developed, developed. Kram wisely insisted on recording everything from the first note of the first piece, which ran for about twelve minutes and became 'First Contact'. Kram declared,

> It turned out the piece had great heights, got quite crazy, then really chilled out. Everyone seemed to know when to stop. That was how it worked, and we did piece after piece. I think we recorded eight or ten pieces, some of which were really superb, like really awesome and, honestly, releasable. It was like creating the soundtrack for a film which didn't exist, like you're creating a film in your mind. Eventually we'd made what I think is a record.

All three of the players knew they had created something significant and original, and realised it was their dissimilarities, their point of musical difference, that had enabled it to happen. James said,

> Kram is, in the most complimentary way, a cavemen — everything that's good about a caveman; he's unconcerned. He's going to beat that drum; he's going to do his snare. Paul is the Renaissance man, very civilised, should be wearing cravats, and me, I'm just whatever you want to classify me as. So you've got a rock drummer, a classical pianist and a jazz trumpeter. It's very hard for me to do a free jazz performance because I've always been with musicians who weren't free, as in, 'we had history'. My usual groups are quite comfortable playing free, but because we play a lot together it will end up doing certain things. With Kram,

that was never going to happen. That doesn't mean it was atonal. It wasn't, and when it became tonal it was more classical, while Kram played rock'n'roll drums — and it worked. We thought it would, but it exceeded our expectations.

Paul added,

> What we discovered playing that day was, coming from three different directions, there was a willingness, in fact an absolute passion, to communicate, to make sure we were trying to make music which was reflective of our own musicianship and interests, but desirous of a communal and collective outcome which was greater than the sum of its parts. I came away from that day very, very inspired.

The elated trio celebrated at a local restaurant near the beach. 'We were like three kids,' said Kram, 'we were so excited.' James decided the group needed a name straight away in order to capture the moment and consummate the relationship. James suggested 'The Others' and it felt right. 'I liked how the name seemed to indicate you were outside everything that was going on,' said Kram.

The drummer rented a car to drive home. 'I put on the rough mix the engineer gave me and I cranked it! I played it so loud; I just blazed it all the way through Sydney and down the coast road. It was awesome driving by myself with this music playing, music that I was immediately so proud of.'

Finding time in three busy and disconnected diaries to set aside a recording day was hard enough, but that proved easier than finding ways to release the edited and completed tapes to the world. The problems were multiple and almost insurmountable. After four years, the congested schedules, the difficulty of finding the right venue and publicising the unusual combination of artists playing free jazz had still not been overcome. Yet the excitement and passion of the recording was not diminished by the time lapse, and the willingness and enthusiasm to put it out remains.

The trio discussed festival appearances; Kram thought it might make a TV special, while the other two considered that a smaller, dedicated jazz venue like Sydney's 505 Club might be the go. Paul said,

> Even if nothing happens, it certainly revealed to me that James is capable of all kinds of things. His musical intelligence is not predicated in a particular place and time. He is very open to inputs from all over the place and that's the point he's at now, that having established himself in a particular musical genre, he is very interested in taking that wherever he can. In that sense, he reminds me of his great inspiration, Dizzy Gillespie. Dizzy was obviously a bebop trumpet player, but he was a guy who took that language and, for example, fused it with Afro-Cuban music and created a whole new sound by bringing those two things together. I think James, one could say, is in a similar stage, where he's got this language which he's mastered but he's really interested in putting it into all kinds of different contexts.
>
> The thing about it is when you improvise with him, he's got such good ears and he can hear what's going on and can find things to play. And he's a very lyrical player, a natural player, and that side of his playing is as good as anything.
>
> There are obviously trumpet players and trombonists who are doing different things melodically, rhythmically and harmonically, and pushing the boundaries in different directions. James is not necessarily one of those people, but his musicality in a way transcends that.

James remembers with some pride Paul's comment as they listened to the rough mix on recording day: "'I can't wait for this to come out. I can't wait to play this to some people — the naysayers will have to change their tune now,' Paul was a little surprised himself. I don't know if he was prepared for where we could go together.'

Paul affirmed,

> The cat's out of the bag as far as I'm concerned. I might be a little more critical of James in the future if he doesn't show evidence of what he's revealed to me and Kram, because we know what we did together and we know how good it is. If that stuff doesn't see the light of day and we don't follow up on it then I will feel that a golden opportunity was lost.

Kram was blunter. He wanted to play a free jazz set at a national music awards ceremony in order to, as James remembers him saying, 'stick it up 'em!' and show what the incongruous musical group — erroneously pigeonholed rock star, pianist/academic and multi-instrumentalist — could produce.

'Whatever!' said James philosophically. 'They still won't get the point that whatever I play is appropriate to who I'm with, whether it's free jazz or "St James Infirmary".' James did admit, though, that when Grabowsky had declared, 'I can't wait to play this to some people,' he'd thought, *I wasn't aware I was speaking!* It was as if Paul had voiced his very own thoughts. James isn't mean-spirited or spiteful, but you suspect there was some residual desire to prove a point to the critics at home — might even 'stick it up 'em', as Kram colourfully put it.

Chapter 35

'Very lazy ...'

James strolled insouciantly past his fiftieth birthday in 2012. Schagerl, the Austrian instrument maker he's represented since 2010, threw him a party in the magnificent historic Melk Abbey overlooking the Danube, with the manic Mnozil Brass, and a surprise visit from Judi, his wife of almost twenty-five years. It was a night to remember, with the master instrumentalist surrounded by a big band and the brilliant Mnozil, Monty Pythons of the musical world.

If he'd had a moment to reflect, he might have marvelled at how far he'd come; how the nervous little boy wailing loudly as he approached the primary school gates holding his mother's hand had metamorphosed into a supremely confident musician comfortable demonstrating his talent anywhere in the world.

He'd conquered a wide variety of musical stages, playing a bewildering array of non-complementary instruments, each to an arguably world-class standard. He'd even created a couple of his own. In 2007, he and Steve Marshall, an electronics designer and robotics expert, produced the Morrison Digital Trumpet. It was an instrument with a huge range, on which James could produce all kinds of sounds, from flute to horn to bass, much like an electronic synthesiser. James described it as resembling a space-age instrument suitable for the creatures in the *Star Wars* cantina band. 'And if you turn it backwards, it looks something like a ray gun, which makes it very difficult to carry on aeroplanes these days,' he joked.

Less threatening was the bass trumpet he unveiled at Melbourne's

Stonnington Jazz Festival in 2010. James designed that at the Schagerl factory, he said, 'mostly by just standing there and talking to them, and pointing to bits and saying, "What if you put one of those there, and if you made that bigger and put that there, how would that be?"' James loves the new baby, with its mellow tone and depth; he plays it frequently on gigs.

So James added another to his ever-lengthening list of achievements. Instrument design sat alongside the other manifold facets of his career: his performances, his compositions and arrangements of dozens of original pieces, and the boutique sound studio the Morrison brothers opened in July 2002, where James and John released five albums at the studio launch, and have since produced both their own recordings and numerous others for artists, mainly in the jazz genre. James' first CD on his new label was, appropriately, *So Far So Good*.

Away from the concert stages, James had found success and pleasure as a petrolhead (or 'motoring enthusiast', as he puts it), a yachtsman, a triathlete, a pilot, an abseiler, an author, a scriptwriter, a TV presenter and personality, and an educationalist. It's a remarkably impressive curriculum vitae accomplished with wry humour and a 'Simon the Likeable' persona.

Journalists have struggled for years to find words to sum up his talent. Genius, prodigy, freak, phenomenon have all been used. Is he blessed or just lucky? James claims he's lucky and lazy. He laughs and says, 'Put a "very" in front of both of those!' By his own definition that laziness is not doing anything you don't want to do, he says he's extremely lazy. 'It's very hard to get me to do anything that doesn't interest me. I'll never get around to it.' It echoes to a large extent Mark Twain's theory that 'work consists of whatever a body is *obliged* to do and that play consists of whatever a body is not obliged to do'.

But given that James' life is crammed with things he does want to do, there's little opportunity to be indolent. David Green, his manager for seventeen years until April 2014, said, 'James works extremely hard. He often works till three or four in the morning, then gets up at six and keeps working. If something's got to be done, he gets it done.'

Like his old friend Dizzy Raymond, James doesn't overdose on sleep. 'I've got this theory,' he says — James has theories about most things — 'If you went to sleep, as long as you got a bit of sleep, and someone changed the clocks and told you you'd had six hours when you'd only had four, how would you know? I just steal time out of sleep so I don't know.'

He'd put the theory into practice the previous night by going to bed at midnight and getting up just after 3am, to prepare the *Cirrus* for an early interstate flight. For James, as Tom Jones said, 'it's not unusual'.

It's hard, in view of the evidence and seeing the remarkable and tiring workload Morrison gets through, to contend that he's lazy. He may be too tired to mow the lawn, but stick the trumpet in his hand and an audience in front of him, and the inertia vanishes. Morrison has always worked hard at his musicianship, perhaps harder than even he recognises.

In his book, *Outliers*, Malcolm Gladwell simplified and popularised the theories of the Swedish psychologist Anders Ericsson, who contended that expert performers in any field need ten years or 10,000 hours of deliberate practice to achieve elite performance levels.

Mozart may have done his hours by the age of seven or eight, and most symphony players achieve theirs by the age of twenty. Morrison, of course, denies that he ever practised much at all — and his mother confirms he was seldom heard around the house. Ericsson's 'deliberate practice' is defined as goal-setting, quick feedback and countless drills. In that sense, Morrison could be right, as he never worked on scales, arpeggios and exercises.

But there's more than one way of skinning a musical cat. Ken Smith, the exceptional New Zealand cornet player, rated in the top ten of all time, spent long hours perfecting his immaculate technique, with

Arban's propped on his music stand. At his prime, he recorded many of the book's exercises on a classic album, called *The Voice of the Cornet*. He turned basic etudes into perfect musical miniatures. His compatriot, Gordon Webb, a fine symphonic trumpeter, eschewed the textbook method, studying only the musical literature required for his craft.

Daniel Barenboim, the great pianist and conductor, was of the latter school. His father told him that all the exercises are in the repertoire, so there's no need to practise studies and etudes. It's a sentiment Morrison echoed: 'How about I just learn the solos, then I'll be able to play the exercises.'

And learn the form of the solos he did. It's not that he didn't practise. In fact, from the time he picked up an instrument, he did little else but practise. He just didn't practise in the 'deliberate' way. He worked to acquire the styles, sounds and techniques of the master trumpeters, particularly Gillespie, that he heard on his recordings.

He would have done the 10,000 hours to achieve his mastery by his early teens but may not, even now, totally recognise the time he put in. As young Tom Sawyer might have seen it, it was play; something 'a body was not required to do'. It's hard to get Morrison to do anything he doesn't want to — just ask his old high school teachers — but playing music was never a chore because it was what he wanted, was intrinsically driven, to do.

Ben Hogan, one of the world's greatest golfers, was once asked whether his hands ever ached from hitting all those golf balls. 'Never!' said Hogan. 'Your hands don't ache from doing what you love.' Exactly. Morrison, one suspects, felt no pain from his long hours of practise, whether it was on the trumpet, the trombone — his inspiration, Pastor Neil Gough, once said, 'He was obsessed with playing that instrument and has been all his life. Once he got it, he never took it out of his mouth' — or figuring out the mysteries of Erroll Garner's piano sequences. In fact, much of the time he didn't even realise he was practising.

Professor Gary McPherson is the Ormond Chair of Music and Director of the Conservatorium of Music at the University of Melbourne, Australia's foremost researcher into musical giftedness, and himself a former champion cornet player. He said, in considering the talent of Morrison, but speaking of prodigies in general,

> They say they haven't practised but, when you look at it, they've probably practised five or six hours a day. They just enjoy it and they reflect back on it, 'Oh no, I never used to do much practice,' because it was never effortful in the sense that they were sitting down being forced to do it or thinking they had to do it. They just did it because they loved it.

This ability to overlook the hard yakka involved may partly explain the remarkable ways in which Morrison learned the saxophone and, later, the double bass.

James played the alto on a gig within six days of first picking up the instrument partly because he already understood the principles of breathing, phrasing and tonguing. He just had to learn the fingering, which he claimed was quite easy as the 'buttons are all in line.'

'How would he know where the fingers had to go?' asks McPherson. 'Watching people? That's vicarious observation. That's a really strong way of learning — just observing someone and concentrating intensely.' The Professor suggests vicarious observation might explain the circumstances under which James learned the bass, which to the layman seems even more extraordinary than the ability to play a saxophone professionally within a matter of days.

Morrison thinks it's probably a combination of vicarious learning and sleep learning, which he believes has some validity for him:

> I was watching Darcy Wright play the bass at the Paradise Jazz Cellar in Kings Cross. You watch people playing guitar or bass or piano and sometimes their hands look like it sounds. They

look right and beautiful. He had those kinds of hands, the way he plays. You can see just how the bass is played.

'That's vicarious learning!' cries the educationalist, but Morrison goes further. It was approaching 3am and he was very tired and a bit out of it. He watched the bass player, staring intently, and imagined that the hands were his hands. As Darcy drove him home, James could still feel it. As he slept, in the car and later in bed, he kept visualising it. 'I was playing the bass all night,' James says. He thinks it was a combination of sleep learning and vicarious learning. He watched Darcy intently to start with, then practised non-stop for eight hours while he slept.

> If you're in a fully conscious state, you ask a lot of questions and make judgments, and waste a lot of time. If you're asleep and learning something, your subconscious goes, 'Where do you put it? There? Okay. What do I do now?' So when I woke up I was aware the song had finished and I thought, *I've been playing for hours*. I knew right away. It was like a knowing; like 'I can play the bass, I know I can.'

He rode his bike to old primary school mate Russell Carter's place.

'I grabbed his bass and played a walking bass line. It was just like I thought it was,' Morrison remembers.

Carter was stunned. He asked 'When did you learn bass?'

'Last night! Darcy Wright taught me but he doesn't know it yet!'

It didn't seem all that remarkable to James, however mystical it might seem to the rest of us. 'I was quite aware of what happened. I know I'd been playing for eight hours and in a sleep state, where you can really go for chips.'

The clincher was the blisters on his two plucking fingers when he woke that morning. 'That's what convinced me. I looked at them and went, "I've actually been playing the bass."' Mentally he had, so his body showed the physical evidence. It confirmed for him what he already believed about the theory of sleep learning.

> I've watched documentaries. I heard about it. What's disappointing is it's totally random. You can't go, 'Okay, what shall I learn next?' It either happens or it doesn't. All you can do is set the conditions. I've been helped along with the instruments I play, and even with flying and driving. But that's the most graphic example; one day I couldn't play the bass at all, the next I could.

James concludes that his ability to play instruments is not in proportion to the amount of practice time he's put in.

> Some I haven't spent any time on; some a little and some a lot. But what I can do on the instrument is out of proportion to how much time I've spent practising. I put it down to the same thing, I think. I've spent a lot of hours working on it while I haven't had it in my hands.

It may have helped, but James' talent for playing musical instruments hasn't come about solely by him practising while he sleeps. If dreaming it was doing it, we'd all be Test cricketers or pop divas. His virtuosity has come through a ton of hard work, acknowledged or not, and a modicum of good fortune in terms of his genes and his environment. We must head all the way back to Boorowa to examine them.

Chapter 36

'… and very lucky!'

We've disproved to a large extent the first half of Morrison's claim to be 'very lazy and very lucky'. You'd have to acknowledge, however, a deal of truth in the second part; in some areas of his life he has been very lucky.

Had Mozart been born to a different family, or five or ten years later or earlier, it's likely he might never have become what we know him to be. His father, Leopold Mozart, was an ambitious court composer and one of the finest teachers in Europe. Wolfgang grew up hearing his father at the organ and his sister, Nannerl, on the harpsichord. The seeds of music were sown in fertile soil, and a musician's ear developed early. Leopold home-schooled the boy with the advanced teaching techniques he'd constructed and drove him relentlessly to practise. By the age of six, the prodigy was ready to tour the palaces and great cities of Europe.

There are muted parallels with James Morrison, who sat on the organ stool in Boorowa alongside his musical mother both in utero and for several years after. Not only that, but physically he had the right characteristics to be a brass musician. He had the strength, the reflexes, the agility and the coordination for the career, and was also gifted the physiognomy that allowed him to play extremely high on the instruments of the brass family, a facet of playing not natural to everyone.

Morrison says simply, 'That came in fairly early. Some people can play high on the trumpet; some people can't. You can teach them to play higher, but those people who can naturally play high can just do it.' James is apparently one of those people.

The fact that James was born with a high IQ is no hindrance either, though James himself is somewhat dismissive of it. 'It doesn't measure creativity,' he says. Professor Gary McPherson agrees: 'It means he has intellectual awareness; it means he can process things quicker. It might facilitate things but it's not a determiner (of musical success). But it obviously helps if everything else is coming into shape.' And for James, it was.

According to science journalist David Shenk, 'some people are simply born with certain gifts while others are not; that talent and high intelligence are somewhat scarce gems, scattered through the human gene pool; that the best we can do is locate and polish these gems and accept the limitations built in the rest of us.'

This assumption gives rise to the feelings I had when I first heard Morrison all those years ago at that brass band concert. However long I worked, however much I practised, I could never come near his achievements. I wasn't 'gifted' that way; I didn't have 'the genes'.

But as well as the genes, the prodigy's environment, parents, teachers, intrinsic motivation and other factors play a large part. When the genes and these environmental factors all come together in the right place, at the right time and under the right conditions, a talented artist is able to flourish.

This happened for Morrison. He was born in a country town, hearing music at close range from conception. He moved to Sydney and attended a primary school where the head teacher was keen on banding and who permitted him to take home every instrument in the cupboard. His family worshipped at what was probably the only church in the suburbs that had a live jazz band that not only played in services but ran concerts for the general public. He acknowledges the unlikelihood of it all. 'We came to Sydney, we came to that suburb, we went to that church, the only one with a band — what are the chances?' he asked interviewer John Cleary one night on ABC radio.

McPherson found in his studies that there are three key psychological drivers related to the development of the gifted: pleasure in their own competence, a connectedness with others of similar views and a need for autonomy. Morrison had all three in spades.

He found immediate satisfaction from public performances in school, church, busking outside Coles and in concerts. In the latter he even garnered supportive applause when his slide fell off mid trombone solo. Playing music had to be the best thing in the world!

He readily found others with similar views in the same locations, though the fact that sometimes their dedication didn't match his at Mona Vale Primary frustrated him. The Kerugma church band, particularly its talented leaders Neil Gough, and later Chris Marshall, fostered his talent till eventually he found his way to the Young Northside Big Band, a group of kindred spirits if ever there was one.

McPherson emphasises the need for autonomy — the need for personal choice and self-motivation. Morrison certainly had that; he did what he did because he wanted to, not because he was told to. In fact, at high school he had people — his careers advisor and his physical education teacher in particular — telling him not to do it!

Even at the Sydney Conservatorium, which he entered much younger than he should have done due solely to his own determination, he virtually planned his own course and got his experienced teacher, Dick Montz, to agree to it.

Generally parents, like Mozart's father Leopold, are the primary drivers of musically gifted children. James' folks, while supporting their children, never pushed them in any direction, but gave them freedom to pursue whatever they wanted.

He took his mother at her word when she said he could do whatever he liked, and used that to justify many early decisions he made. For example, if a teacher advised him not to play multiple instruments lest he ruin his embouchure, he could say to himself, 'I can do whatever I like; Mum said I could.'

> Autonomy means I'm not subject to the rules. I'm autonomous; I have your adult rules. I don't have to comply with how it's normally done; the done thing; how someone thinks it should be done; what's acceptable — none of these things apply. The only criterion I'm judging it by was whether I want to do it. 'Mum says I can do anything I want to.'

So James, gifted with the right physique, physiognomy and intelligence, quickly had all the psychological needs — competence, connectedness with others and autonomy — of a young, especially gifted musician met.

When the three come together, rapid progress ensues. In some aspects James was born lucky; in others, he worked damned hard, without realising it, to become a highly skilled practitioner at an early age and, as is usual, the more he achieved, the more he played and the harder he worked.

The influence of James' family and their Christian environment should not be underestimated. Morrison, who did a lay preacher's course and considered becoming a minister, thinks his upbringing 'sets the tone' for who he is. It gave him a 'mode of decorum' he says, laughing. 'I don't think I've got an image as a religious person, or even as a Christian, that people are aware of.' It is arguable that he still has and there are several websites that claim him as a 'Christian jazz entertainer'. He was certainly prepared to testify in July 2005, when his first gospel album came out.

He talked then of having made a commitment to Christ: 'It was a gradual awakening. The pennies dropped over time. I didn't have a Paul on the road to Damascus conversion, where a light came down and everything was different. It was an awakening; growing into a life I already had in me.'

The Salvos' On Fire Big Band took Morrison on tour with them twice, to the North Coast of New South Wales in Easter of 2003, and later to Victoria. Gavin Staines, the leader of this band, remembers

James back then both testifying and leading prayer before the group went onstage to perform what were exciting evangelical concerts. Nowadays, James is more likely to endorse the power of the music and its effect on him and his listeners. He describes himself as 'spiritual' rather than religious, though his ethics are Christian.

At Easter in particular he seems to be drawn back to his roots, touring with On Fire, participating in the full gamut of services at the apostolic The Edge church in South Australia or, as he did in 2013, performing with Edge musicians at the annual Easterfest of Christian music in Toowoomba. It's an environment that's still second nature to him.

> I'm quite comfortable sitting there while someone's preaching a sermon. In my early days, when I studied lay preaching, I'd sometimes give the sermon. In more recent times, in some gigs I've done, I've been asked to speak in the service. It's not as though I read a passage of scripture and give a sermon, but I certainly speak and I'm quite comfortable doing that.

He spoke at the Easter Saturday concert at Edge and said that he couldn't think of anywhere else on Earth he would rather be. He said that the songs at the Cross he was about to play 'are the ones closest to my heart'.

> What happens on a gospel program is it gives another context to the music. It adds to the experience. It makes the experience more vibrant. Rather than the music saying 'I'm happy' it's saying 'I'm happy for a reason', and that's the extra context that it puts it in. I've got that. I grew up with it. I get inspired when I play in a jazz festival and I'm inspired when I'm playing gospel music. You put the two together, it's a pretty powerful thing.

While he's not an active Christian these days, there's no doubt his upbringing and environment has influenced who he is immensely — and hearing his father in the pulpit, and doing a lay preacher's course, almost certainly benefitted his stage presentation, and his confidence and timing at the microphone.

Sports scientists have identified four stages that gifted youngsters pass through on their way to reaching their full potential: sampling, specialising, investment and maintenance. Morrison passed quickly through all four stages. He sampled every instrument in the primary school cupboard. He specialised in high school, spending little time on any other activity. His parents moved back to the city almost fortuitously and enabled him to intensify his learning at church, at university and with Sydney's leading players. He's maintained his career over forty years, with no sign of any deterioration in his abilities.

Morrison's ability is undoubtedly far beyond ordinary. I wrote in the Prelude of this book of my feelings when I first heard him in concert many years ago: 'he was on a different plane to the rest of us — I felt I was in the presence of musical genius.'

'Genius' is a word bandied about too easily these days and I was probably too liberal with the hyperbole, though not by any means the first to fall into that trap where Morrison is concerned. Steve Marshall, the robotics expert with whom James created a digital trumpet, described him as a genius. 'He's a real visionary,' he added, 'not just in music but across so many subjects.' Graeme Lyall, a fine saxophonist and a co-educator at *Generations in Jazz*, used the same word when speaking of James' contribution to jazz education: 'He's one of the few geniuses I know.' Greg Spence, in the vanguard of Melbourne's trumpeters, echoed the sentiment in an online response to Dan Quigley's complimentary James Morrison blog: 'Hey Dan,' he wrote, 'Thanks for promoting one of the two geniuses I have ever met in my life.' (The other was songwriter comedian Tim Minchin.)

It's an understandable description to hang on Morrison when every footballer who kicks a remarkable goal and every TV talent quest winner is called a genius in the popular media. As far back as

1993, Eric Myers, writing in his 'DisChords' column of *JazzChord* magazine, had urged more circumspection. 'By the way, all you entertainment writers in the tabloid press, James Morrison is not a "jazz genius", as you insist on describing him. But he is a "jazz freak" by virtue of his extraordinary ability to adapt to so many different wind instruments.'

McPherson, better qualified than most to assess the nature of Morrison's giftedness, agrees with Myers. He defines a genius as someone who's 'transformative — doing something others couldn't have thought about doing', like a mathematician who comes up with a new formula. Of Morrison he says, 'You might call James a genius in the commercial sense. We celebrate the uniqueness; we celebrate the talent. He's certainly an expert at what he does. He's incredibly gifted, he's talented, he's probably a prodigy, but a genius? I don't know; I'd have to think about that.'

In the end, finding the right label for him — prodigy, phenomenon, genius, freak — is meaningless. All I know is after hearing him play in dozens of differing situations over the years, he still has the ability to make me — and countless others — grin from ear to ear. I can't do it, I can't explain it (though, God knows, I've written a book trying!); I can only appreciate and enjoy it.

James himself isn't much fussed about it. He never claimed to be a genius, or anything of the like. He just laughs and says he's lazy and lucky. In the meantime, his career surges on. In a recent year, for example, he flew overseas at least once a month for events at music festivals, symphony concerts, brass band celebrations and jazz clubs. Idaho, Singapore, London, Vienna, Rheingau, Tennessee and even Wigan were all on the itinerary. He played in every state in Australia, from hometown gigs in Sydney's familiar Basement, to outback Yarrabah in Queensland, to Torres Island to work with Indigenous community musicians.

He keeps excellent health despite the giddying schedule and the physical demands. He does no physical jerks these days; certainly doesn't run triathlons for which the training was too time-consuming. 'You have occasions when you're fitter than others,' he admits. 'Usain Bolt has days when he runs a second faster than others. It's just ebb and flow. What you want is for the range of the ebb and flow to be between really fantastic and even more fantastic. That way, you never have a bad day — you have a day when it's only great.'

At fifty-two, he has no plans other than seeing where his career takes him. He wants to keep playing as long as he can, like his mentor Don Burrows, who played at his own eightieth birthday celebration despite his increasingly arthritic fingers. 'I can't see myself stopping performing because making music is too much a part of who you are, not what you do,' James repeats.

He'd like more time with his family, but that's beginning to happen anyway. His sons, William, who plays bass, and Harry, who plays guitar, perform at gigs with him. Their group, Inheritance, played a night at the Stonnington Jazz Festival in 2014, they all play together in a soul band and Harry and James have done some duo gigs at corporate events. At Carols by Candlelight in Melbourne, Harry came onstage, followed by James lugging his small bass amp. To some, James is the eighth wonder of the world; to his sons, he's just Dad —'Can you carry that guitar amp on, please?'

The other thing he'd like to do, granted the time, is explore further the idea of sleep learning. 'I have this vague idea that I have a method. I haven't quantified it; I just know it works. At some stage, I should think through all those parameters and quantify them in some way; crystallise it and see if it's possible to pass it on as a method of learning. It's not just music; it's a way to learn anything.'

But mostly what James wants to do is what he was born to do — make music and pass on the joy of making music to the next generation.

Coda

In May 2013, at the eleventh annual Billy Hyde Graeme Bell Awards, James Morrison was inducted into the Jazz Awards Hall of Fame. James quipped that Don Burrows had once told him that you're only as good as the company you keep — which made James pretty good, as he was in outstanding company alongside Bernie McGann, Brian Brown, Tony Gould, Bob Barnard, as well as the old mentor himself.

It was a very meaningful accolade in a still incomplete career — acceptance by his pure jazz-playing peers, taking him beyond the criticisms he received for being too commercial in his earlier years. The criticisms are virtually unheard these days, Morrison being acknowledged for who he is and admired for doing what he does in his own way.

His acceptance speech was brief and mostly referred to his twenty-year stint with *Generations in Jazz* — 3500 kids in Mount Gambier, 116 big bands and forty choirs all performing jazz, he said, to a huge round of applause — and to the setting up of jazz bands in the remote communities of Queensland, where six months ago the students had barely heard of jazz, but now turn up regularly at school to be part of the program. Such is the transformative power of music.

James said if the award was an acknowledgement of that work, then he'd humbly accept it. Perhaps it was in some part, but it was also recognition of James' pre-eminent position and worldwide standing as Australia's foremost and most popular jazz instrumentalist.

Only two months later, in his role as director, Morrison unveiled his first Queensland Music Festival with a bonanza of musical events not merely centred on the capital of Brisbane, but spread all over the vast state, from the suburbs to the Indigenous communities. There were over 200 scheduled events and Morrison was better situated than most directors to attend many of them:

> The engine of my aeroplane will not go cold for seventeen days. We can hit three towns a day and get right around the state. I'll be finishing seeing a concert, or being in one, leaping in the plane and flying to the next town, ready for the next thing. Whatever's going on, I want to be right in the middle doing it.

And so he was, playing a new jazz-inspired double concerto with the Queensland Symphony Orchestra and fronting the Morrison Creative Generation Big Band, made up of Brisbane's best young players. This was among numerous other events, where Morrison was, predictably, unable to resist getting his trumpet out.

Festival events popped up all over the state — remote Birdsville, Stradbroke Island, Charleville, Cunnamulla included — and the Yarrabah Band Festival appeared at Aurukun, Coen and Hope Vale. Yarrabah Band was formed on an Indigenous mission in 1901, lapsed in 1911, but was re-formed in 1950. It made another re-emergence in recent years, with students from the Cape York Aboriginal Australian Academy, supported by James, marking a return of Indigenous bands to North Queensland. This was the sort of promotion of music to Indigenous communities James took pride in at the Bell Awards ceremony.

The kick-off for the Queensland Music Festival was two conjoined events of the publicity-grabbing style for which critics had once heaped coals on Morrison's head, but which promoted music to thousands. He organised attempts to break two Guinness World Records in one day.

On Saturday 13 July 2013, he assembled, through the Queensland Music Festival, the world's largest trumpet ensemble of 1200 in Brisbane's King George Square. It marched through the streets to link up at Suncorps football stadium with the other members of a 7224-member orchestra.

It was typical Morrison; he puttered into the stadium on a Segway to front his musical host. The sound the orchestra made was enormous and featured in news bulletins around the world. In mid-December 2013, the Guinness Book of Records confirmed that it was indeed the world's largest, clearly beating the 6452-member ensemble the Vancouver Symphony Orchestra had assembled in 2000. Morrison's event also produced the world's largest brass ensemble, the largest woodwind ensemble and the world's largest clarinet ensemble. The record book planned to include the new records in its 2015 edition, published in late 2014.

Morrison acquired one more notch on his multifaceted career belt — Guinness World Record holder — but that wasn't what it was all about. It was about involving people in music, promoting what he loves and sees as worthwhile and, as always, encouraging the next generation.

James was, of course, out front, leading the monstrous ensemble, cutting through and above as he did at the opening of the Sydney Olympics, with his soaring improvisations over his own all-embracing arrangements of 'Waltzing Matilda', 'Song of Joy' and 'We Will Rock You' for every instrument, from strings to triangle.

After thirty years of listening to James Morrison in a variety of situations, I recently sat in his audience again. Unlike that first occasion in the school hall with a brass band, this time I knew what to expect. I knew he would play a variety of instruments brilliantly; I knew he would do jazz improvisations in high registers and mellow melodies that the listeners knew; I knew the program would be tailored to the audience; I knew it wouldn't be cutting-edge contemporary jazz, but I did know it would be entertaining.

I understood a good deal better now who he was, his background and how he developed his innate talents even as his fellow artist,

Grammy and Emmy Award winning big band composer Gordon Goodwin, expressed his surprise at the skills residing in the man when he first heard him four years ago. I understood in my own way where he was coming from.

James Morrison is a unique Australian jazz instrumentalist, born with many and varied gifts. He never became the jazz innovator like Armstrong or Davis that some felt he should. It's more in his nature to play the jazz he loves on whatever instrument he chooses and to entertain a very wide audience. If James had done no more with his life than that, it would have been enough to mark him out as a very special and gifted Australian.

But Morrison has chosen — been driven — to become the most effective promoter of jazz among young people the country has ever had. Among all his myriad achievements, this may one day prove to be his finest legacy.

Professor Gary McPherson noted once that Morrison has 'had a blessed career; he's had a blessed life'. So he has, and the best thing is that he's shared its riches, not only for the nation's entertainment, but for the nation's heritage.

Acknowledgements

This book has been several years in the making and numerous people have helped along the way.

My first thanks must go to James Morrison himself who, somewhat modestly and perhaps a little reluctantly, gave me permission to write it. James was generous in finding time in his hectic schedule to fit in interviews at my request.

Many others, including James' parents George and Jessie Morrison, and his brother John, were happy to talk to me at some length. A full list is appended below, and I am grateful to every person on it for their memories and opinions. Thanks, too, to those who gave me permission to use photographs from their private collections. The book is the better for their generosity.

I'd like to especially thank Eric Myers, who was Australia's National Jazz Development Officer from 1983 to 2001. In that capacity, he was editor of *JazzChord* magazine from 1993 to 2001. Previously, he was publisher and editor of *Australian Jazz* magazine from 1981 to 1986. Eric supplied photographs for this book and volunteered to read the manuscript with a critical eye. His corrections and insights have been invaluable.

Sheila Hollingworth wouldn't claim to know much about jazz, but she knows a lot about writing and publication; she has co-written a couple of books on it. Her guidance, enthusiasm and faith in my writing encouraged me to believe I could produce this book.

Thanks to the volunteers at the Victorian Jazz Archive, who offered up their well-maintained resources to me. Also thanks to David Tenenbaum at Melbourne Books, who believed the book was worth putting into the public domain, and to his editor, Chloe Brien, for piloting it through.

And thanks to my old friends, Mike and Margaret Poore, in Sydney. Mike is a mean jazz trombonist himself, who entertained me in every sense of the word, and transported me around an unfamiliar city to assist with interviews.

Finally, to my wife Chris, whose capacity for work and love of family never ceases to amaze me. The longer we're together, the more I admire her tenacity in the face of all difficulties and for her support of us all.

Interviews were conducted with:

- James Morrison
- John Morrison
- Jacki Morrison (nee Cooper)
- George Morrison
- Jessie Morrison
- Dale Barlow
- Don Burrows
- John Clare
- Dale Cleves
- Ruth Cunningham
- Reynold Gilson
- Paul Grabowsky
- Ross Irwin
- Kram (Mark Maher)
- Sue Cappy McDonald
- Sarah McKenzie
- Gary McPherson
- Eric Myers
- Dave Newdick
- Mark Nightingale
- Nicola Poore
- Ralph Pyl
- Bruce Raymond
- Tim Rollinson
- Ron Sandilands
- Gavin Staines
- Martin Wind

Bibliography

Books

Abbott A. and Collins D. 'Eliminating the dichotomy between theory and practice in talent identification and development', *Journal of Sports Science*, vol. 2, no. 5, 2004.

Anderson, Sheila E. *The Quotable Musician*. New York: Allworth Press, 2003.

Andrews, Paul Pax. *Without a Song*. www.smashwords.com/books, 2010.

Ball, Kenny. *Blowing My Own Trumpet*. London: John Blake Publishing, 2004.

Barnard, Len. *Jottings of a Jazzman: Selected Writings of Len Barnard*. Loretta Barnard (ed.). Self-published, 2000.

Brash, Geoff with Tarling, Lowell. *Brash Business: Ten Business Commandments*. Melbourne: Information Australia Pub., 2000.

Chambers Dictionary. Edinburgh: Chambers Harrap Publishing Ltd., 1998.

Clare, John. *Bodgie Dada and the Cult of Cool*. Sydney: UNSW, 1995.

Feinstein, John. *A Good Walk Spoiled*. Boston, US: Little, Brown and Company, 1995.

Harris, Janey with Evancho, Bob. *Elegant Soul: the life and music of Gene Harris*. Caldwell, Idaho: Caxton Press, 2005.

Hatterstone, Simon. *The Best of Times*. London: Guardian Books, 2006.

Jenkins, Alan and Stirzaker, John. *A Decade Beating Time*. UK: SP&S, 2010.

McPherson, G. E. and Welch, G. F. *The Oxford Handbook of Music Education Volume 2*. US: Oxford University Press, 2012.

Morrison, James. *Blowing My Own Trumpet*. Sydney, Australia: Murdoch Books, 2006.

Scholes, P. *The Concise Oxford Dictionary of Music*. London: Oxford University Press, 1973.

Shenk, David. *The Genius in All of Us*. London: Icon Books, 2010.

Stokes, W. Royal. *Living the Jazz Life*. New York: Oxford University Press.

Terkel, Studs. *Giants of Jazz*. New York: The New Press, 2002.

Tycho, Tommy. *The Tommy Tycho Story*. Ringwood, Australia: Brolga Publishing, 1995.

Newspapers and magazines

24 Hours magazine
    Shand, John. 'Hornblower'. November 2002.

2MBS-FM Stereo FM Radio magazine
    Wahlquist, Gil. 'One player, four instruments'. April 2006.

Adelaide Advertiser
    'Brass at its brilliant best'. 15 December 1986. Author unknown.

'All That Jazz: celebrating 20 years of Generations in Jazz' booklet in *All That Jazz: a moving celebration* CD.

Beat Magazine
    Pertout, Alex. 'So far, so good'. Issue #836, 27 November 2002.

Brisbane Courier Mail
    Dean, Peter. 'Living for the music'. 18 March 1989.
    Stacey, Helene. 'Next the world'. Sunday Magazine, 26 November 1989.
    Stacey, Helene. 'True love 'n' the jazzman'. Sunday Magazine, 26 November 1989.

Brisbane Times
    Bochenski, Natalie. 'Morrison flying high for music festival'. 13 May 2013.

DownBeat magazine
    Milkowski, Bill. 'Riffs: James Morrison'. Vol. 56, Nov 1989.
    Szantnor, Jim. *Chase* band record review. 3 February 1972.
    Whitehead, Kevin. Record and CD reviews. Vol. 58, May 1991.

Extempore magazine (Editor: Miriam Zolin)
    Webster, Belinda. 'Conversations with Judy Bailey'. Vol. 2, 2009.

Herald Sun
    Ife, Holly. '"I blew it" says trumpet star'. 29 November 2003.
    Nicholas, Jessica. 'In the driver's seat'. 9 May 1996.
    Phillips, Shaun and Brown, Terry. 'Wrong anthem sparks outrage'. 29 November 2003.

Inpress magazine
    Watt, Andrew. 'They say I use too much levity'. Issue #21, 1990.

Jazz: Australian Contemporary Music Magazine, (Editors: Dick Scott and Eric Myers, 1981–1985. Publishers: Peter Brendle and Audrey De Graff)
    Jenson, Joya. 'A swinging journey to Monterey'. March/April 1981.
    Myers, Eric. 'Jazz jottings'. July/Aug 1993.
    Myers, Eric. 'Morrison Bros. Big Bad Band'. Vol 3, #5, Spring 1983.
    'The Young Lions'. May/June 1981. Author unknown.
    Williams, Mike. 'Northside One'. March/April 1981.

JazzChord magazine (Editor: Eric Myers, 1995–2002)
    Jackson, Adrian. 'When is James simply being himself?' Correspondence page. July/August 1996.

'James Morrison receives the AAM'. June/July 1997. Author unknown.

Millar, Sam. 'Concert review'. June/July 2000.

Myers, Eric. 'DisChords'. September/October 1993.

Myers, Eric. 'James Morrison in Iowa'. February/March 1997.

Myers, Eric. 'James Morrison's international success'. March/April 1996.

Myers, Eric. 'James Morrison's overseas success'. April/May 2002.

Myers, Eric. 'Jazz on television'. October/November 1997.

Turner, J. Neville. 'Walking straight ahead'. Summer 1998–9.

LA Times

Feather, Leonard. 'Creativity, careful planning work in concert'. 7 August 1984.

Feather, Leonard. 'Down Under's Upbeat New Australian Jazz Orchestra'. 19 April 1988.

Stewart, Zan. 'Australian Jazz Orchestra at Catalina Bar and Grill'. Jazz review. 21 April 1988.

LA Weekly

Foundas, Scott. Film reviews. 20 April 2006.

New York Times

Wilson, John S. 'Review: Jazz All-Stars from Australia'. 14 April 1988.

Quad City Times

Davis, Shirley. 'James Morrison in Iowa'. 13 October 1996.

Sydney Morning Herald

Batties, Rebecca. 'Off the asteroid to take great jazz to the Big Apple'. 11 December 1985.

Brennan, Gail. 'Beyond The Basement'. 13 May 1993.

Brennan, Gail. 'Morrison gets it all together'. 9 October 1991.

Brennan, Gail. 'When brass is short of class'. 30 August 1988.

Covell, Roger. 'A poor beginning to a refreshing event'. 28 October 1991.

Cunningham, Harriet. 'World premiere: Lalo Schifrin and Ambre Hammond'. 20 July 2007.

'Feud, glorious feud', 29 October 1991. Author unknown.

Hinds, Richard. 'Not to blow our own trumpet but Lleyton still won'. 29 November 2003.

'It's all go at Batchy's Cheviot; All over after lunch'. 13 October 2004. Author unknown.

Jenson, Joya. '1988 Bicentennial Tour, Australian Jazz Orchestra'. 11 December 1987.

Jenson, Joya. 'Farewell Jim at long last'. 27 April 1987.

Kennedy, Alan. 'Adelaide Grand Prix stars earn their licence to thrill'. 13 November 1987.

Khoo, Valerie. 'Man with the golden touch'. Career section. 20 January 2007.

Meacham, Steve. 'The talented Mr Morrison'. The (Sydney) Magazine insert. 26 May 2004.

McCullum, Peter 'Fearless hitter of high notes'. Obituary for Dick Montz. 28 January 2006.

Myers, Eric. 'Fiery swing to bebop roots'. 23 June 1981, p. 8.

Myers, Neville. 'Jazz comes to Tinsel Town'. 11 July 1990.

Shand, John. 'A baton aimed at musical prejudice'. 11 February 2005.

Shand, John. 'Horns of plenty in Festival mix'. Metropolitan section. 3 November 2002.

Shand, John. 'The modest man behind the music – and all that joyful jazz'. Obituary for John Speight. 2 June 2007.

The Age

Daly, Mike. 'Life at top speed'. 19 October 1990.

Jackson, Andra. 'Got brass in the pocket'. 30 June 2010.

Jackson, Adrian. 'A happening thing for a hot horn player'. 12 September 1994.

Jackson, Adrian. 'High quality, variety and quantity should assure Montsalvat's future'. 7 February 1991.

Jackson, Adrian. 'Morrison makes himself popular'. 20 December 1983.

Jackson, Adrian. Record reviews. 4 November 2003.

Jackson, Adrian. 'Seriously but with humour'. Arts and Entertainment section. 18 September 1994.

Lallo, Michael. 'Sound the trumpets'. Sunday *M Magazine*. 27 May 2012.

McDonald, Cindy. 'Upfront column'. *Good Weekend*. 1 September 2007.

Murfett, Andrew. 'Now he's calling the tunes'. Green Guide. 14 June 2012.

Nicholas, Jessica. 'In your face excitement'. Electric Jazz Festival review. 4 December 2002.

O'Connell, Clive. 'Boston Pops conductor gets into the swing of things'. 8 September 2009.

Webb, Carolyn. 'Virtuoso keynote for next wave'. 10 September 2007.

Wilkie, Meredith. 'Milestones'. *Agenda* magazine. 15 February 2004.

The Australian

Ball, Martin. 'Uncertainty rules in jazz-classical dialogue'. 25 August 2003.

Jones, Kevin. 'New lions take pride of place'. 12 September 1991.

Myers, Eric. 'A hero's welcome for local stars'. 2 November 1987.

Wyndham, Susan. 'Top Brass'. *Australian magazine*. 18 November 1989.

The Border Watch
   Morello, Sandra. 'Jazz city'. 4 May 2012.
The British Trombone Society newsletter
   Tracy, Sheila. 22 June 2008.
The Bulletin
   Dancer, Helen. 'For James, what a wonderful whirl'. 5 August 2000.
   Hall, James. 'Horn of Plenty'. 7 April 1987.
The Canberra Times
   Foster, Michael. 'Burrows upstaged by pupil'. 10 September 1986.
   Foster, Michael. 'Fine musicians'. Record review of *Burrows at the Winery*. ABC Records (Festival). 14 May 1984.
   Foster, Michael. 'High Spirits for Jazz'. 16 October 1986.
The Hobart Mercury
   Thow, Penny. 'Jazz master goes digital'. 4 January 2007.
The National Times
   Myers, Eric. 'Young Lions of Australian Jazz'. 6–12 February 1983.
The Times on Sunday
   Guilliatt, Richard. 'Fanfare for an Uncommon Jazzman'. 6 October 1987.
Time magazine
   Button, James. 'On the run from the jazz police'. 20 January 1992.

Radio and TV interviews
Interview with John Cleary. *Sunday Night Live*. ABC Radio, 3 July 2005.
Interview with Peter Thompson. *Talking Heads*. ABC TV transcript, screened 23 November 2009.

Websites
Boothman, Peter. 'The Story of Jazz in Sydney'.www.blogs.myspace.com/index.
Collins, Merv. 'Black Dyke: Above and beyond'. www.brasshub.com.au.
Fox, Iwan. www.4barsrest.com/reviews/concerts/con405.asp website. 22 May 2007.
Payne, Doug. 'Lalo Schifrin'. Review. www.dougpayne.com/ls_rev.htm.
Payne, Doug. Record reviews. www.dougpayne.com.
Quigley, Dan. www.dqjazz.com. Blog. 30 April 2004.
Rotten Tomatoes. www.rottentomatoes.com.
Scott Yanow. *AllMusic*. www.allmusic.com.
Smith, Joseph. 'What I know about all that jazz'. www.sydneyanglicans.com.au. 4 July 2005.
Stockhausen, Simon. 'Head to head'. www.applied.acoustics.com.
Swanson, Bill. 'An Upper from Down Under'. CD review. www.allaboutjazz.com, 1 March 1997.

Other
Morrison, George. 'Being a Father'. Unpublished article. Date unknown.

James Morrison's Honours and Awards

1980	Associate Diploma in Jazz Studies from Sydney Conservatorium
1986	Jazz Musician of the Year at NSW Music Week*
1987	Australian Centennial Musician of the Year
1988	13th Mo Awards: Ricky May Jazz Performer of the Year
1989	Variety Club Award for Showman of the Year
	14th Mo Awards: Ricky May Jazz Performer of the Year
1990	Jazz Trombonist of the Year at the Gold Coast International Hotel Jazz and Blues Festival
	15th Mo Awards: Australian Performer of the Year; Best Male Jazz Performer; Ricky May Award for Best Jazz Performer
1991	Gold Award in recognition of sales of *Snappy Doo* from Warner Music
	16th Mo Awards: Ricky May Jazz Performer of the Year; Male Jazz Performer
1992	ARIA Award nomination for Best Jazz Album (*Manner Dangerous*)
1993	ARIA Award nomination for Best Jazz Album (*Two the Max*)
1997	Member of the Order of Australia
1998	23rd Mo Awards: Jazz Instrumental Performer of the Year
2000	Honorary Doctorate from Griffith University
	25th Mo Awards: Jazz Instrumental Performer of the Year
2002	ARIA Award nomination for Best Jazz Album (*Scream Machine*)
2003	28th Mo Awards: Jim Beam Black Label Jazz Instrumental Performer of the Year
2006	31st Mo Awards: Ricky May Jazz Performer of the Year**
2008	ARIA Award nomination for Best Jazz Album (*The Other Woman*, with Deni Hines)
2010	ARIA Award winner for Best Jazz Album (*Feels Like Spring*, with Idea of North)
2012	ARIA Award nomination for Best Jazz Album (*Snappy Too*)
2013	Inducted into the Graeme Bell Hall of Fame at the 11th Annual Australian Jazz Bell Awards

* Don Burrows, James' mentor, was 'Outstanding Reed Player'.

** Up until 2006, the Mo Awards were the premier awards for all showbiz genres, such as opera, ballet, drama, pop, rock, musical theatre and jazz. From 2007 onwards, they focused on club performers, and the theatrical, classical and jazz categories were dropped.

Discography

1984	*A Night in Tunisia*		2001	*Scream Machine*
	with The Morrison Brothers Big Bad Band		2002	*So Far So Good*
			2003	*On the Edge*
1984	*Live at the Winery*			with Simon Stockhausen
	with The Morrison Brothers Big Bad Band		2005	*Gospel Collection*
			2006	*2x2*
1988	*Postcards from Down Under*			with Joe Chindamo
1989	*Swiss Encounter*		2006	*Gospel Collection Volume II*
	with Adam Makowicz		2007	*Christmas*
1990	*Snappy Doo*		2007	*The Other Woman*
1991	*Manner Dangerous*			with Deni Hines
1992	*Two the Max*		2010	*Feels Like Spring*
1993	*This is Christmas*			with The Idea of North
1994	*Live in Paris*		2010	*Three's Company*
	with The Hot Horn Happening			with Phil Stack and James Muller
1996	*Live at the Sydney Opera House*		2011	*Snappy Too*
	with his Big Band			with Jeff Hamilton
1998	*Quartet*		2012	*Live at Edge*
1998	*Three Minds*		2014	*Chermoula*
1999	*European Sessions*			

With Lalo Schifrin in the *Jazz Meets the Symphony* series

1992	*Jazz Meets the Symphony*
1993	*More Jazz Meets the Symphony*
1995	*Jazz Meets the Symphony 3: Firebird*
1998	*Jazz Meets the Symphony 4: Metamorphosis*
1999	*Jazz Meets the Symphony* boxed set, CDs 1–4
2000	*Jazz Meets the Symphony 5: Intersections*
2005	*Jazz Meets the Symphony 6: Kaleidoscope*
2011	*Jazz Meets the Symphony 7: Invocations*

Index

24 Hours, magazine 261
42nd Street, musical 165
60 Minutes, TV show 182
505 Club, Sydney, NSW 278

A

ABC (Australian Broadcasting Corporation) 15, 46, 49, 64, 79, 91, 93, 96, 129, 134, 136, 137, 182, 183, 193, 234, 246, 261, 274, 288
ABC Studio Orchestra 52
Abney Cemetery, London 57
Abominable, film 185, 186, 197
Adelaide Advertiser, The 215
Adelaide Festival of Arts, SA 214
Adelaide Oval, SA 214
Adelaide Rams Rugby League Club, SA 216
Advent Brass, Melbourne, VIC 218
Adventures of Barry McKenzie, The, film 93
Akhurst, Jack 16, 17, 18, 19, 20, 28, 225
Age, The, Melbourne, VIC 128, 165, 185, 206, 212, 224, 252, 260, 265
Ahrendt, Libby 232
Albert Hall, The, London 167
Alder, Warwick 90, 91, 95, 132
Alderson, Dave 269
All About Jazz website 13, 158
AllMusic website 136
All That Jazz, booklet 235
Alonso, HRH, King of Spain 174
America's Cup, The
Anderson, William 'Cat' 10, 263
André, Maurice 199, 205
Andrews, Paul Pax 69, 72, 90, 91, 93, 95
Anne, HRH Princess 167
Annesley, James 242
Anning, Sam 242
Ansell, Tony 79
Arban Trumpet (Cornet) Method, The, book 20, 31, 33
ARIA Awards 169, 235, 241, 243, 251
Armstrong, Louis 29, 31, 92, 98, 192, 198, 203, 204, 222, 253, 263, 298
Arnhem Land Dancers 93
Arsenio Hall Tonight Show, TV show 168
Art Blakey's Jazz Messengers 40, 260, 261, 263

Art Gallery of New South Wales 165
Arturo's Restaurant, New York 105–107, 123
Asian Festival of Arts, Hong Kong 85
Athenaeum, The, Melbourne, VIC 265
Atkinson, Rowan 126
Atlantic Records, Los Angeles 122–124, 136
Australia 2020 Summit 274
Australian, The 124, 165, 206
Australian Bicentennial Authority 131
Australia Council for the Arts (formerly Australia Council) 167, 231
Australian Grand Prix 125, 126, 217
Australian Jazz Bell Awards 76
Australian Jazz Orchestra 131, 132, 134, 248
Australian Jazz Quartet 49, 78
Australian Mo Awards 159
Australian Opera Orchestra 96
Avalon Cinema, Sydney, NSW 165

B

Bach, Johann Sebastian 198, 200, 266
Bailey, Judy 51, 52, 206, 207, 246
Baker, Chet 107
Baker, Tom 70, 90, 93, 94, 223
Ball, Kenny 17, 18
Ball, Martin 206
Balwyn High School, Melbourne, VIC 243
Barbarella, strip club, Rio de Janeiro 118
Barenboim, Daniel 196, 283
Barenboim, Enrique 196
Barlow, Bill 41
Barlow, Dale 40, 42, 43, 44, 45, 68, 69, 132, 165, 210, 230, 231, 243, 261
Barnard, Bob 98, 295
Barnard, Len 71, 82, 83, 156
Barn Palais, Mount Gambier, SA 233–234, 239
Barry Harris Big Band 162
Barton, Mr 12
Basden, David 91
Basement, The, Sydney, NSW jazz club 34, 132, 265, 293
Basie, William James 'Count' 41, 75, 122, 136, 148, 149, 154
Baxter, Sean 273, 274
BBC Big Band 253

Index   309

B. B. King and the Superband live at the Apollo, recording 154
Beaconsfield Hotel, Melbourne, VIC 86
Beckenbauer, Franz 138
Beethoven, Ludwig van 267
Behind the Wheel, TV show 182, 184
Beiderbecke, Bix 98, 197, 203, 204, 253
Beiderbecke Memorial Society 203
Bei Wei Hotel, Beijing 84
Belleclaire Hotel, The, NY 119, 156
Bennett, Cary 40
Benny Carter Quintet 121
Benson, George 106
Berg, Thilo 255
Bergeron, Wayne 241
Bern Jazz Festival, Switzerland 147
Berrigan, Bunny 104
Bertles, Bob 132
Best, Denzil 275
Bevy's Place, nightclub, Sydney, NSW 112
Biddell, Kerrie 117
Big Band Soul, recording 154
Billy Hyde Graeme Bell Jazz Awards 295, 296
Black Dyke Band (formerly Black Dyke Mills Band) 9, 181, 215, 219–221
Black Slacks Band, The 72
Blakey, Art 42, 69
Blanchett, Cate 271
Bleecker St, New York 104, 106, 123, 155, 163
Blowing my own Trumpet, book 185
Bluenote, nightclub, Tokyo 95
Bluenote, nightclub, New York 105
Blues Brothers, The, film 119
Bolt, Usain 294
Boothman, Peter 68, 75
Boston Pops Orchestra 208, 213
Botelo Telo, nightclub, Rio de Janeiro 117
Bradley, Malcolm 232
Bradley's, nightclub, New York 106
Bradman, Sir Donald 140
Brash Business: Ten Business Commandments, book 82
Brash, Geoff 81, 82, 84
Brashs Music 81
Brendle, Peter 108, 110, 113, 114, 124, 132, 160–162, 194, 251
Brennan, Gail (see also Clare, John) 137, 158, 188–190, 192, 194, 203, 246
Bridgewater Hall, Manchester 220
Brien, Steve 72, 90, 91, 167, 173, 174, 231, 251
Brisbane City Hall, QLD 166
British Bandsman, The, magazine 221

British Trombone Society 74
Broadstock, Dr Brenton 205, 207–213
Broadstock, Harvey 208
Broadstock, Lyndon 208
Broughton, Bill 239
Brown, Brian 295
Brown, Cecilia 166
Brown, Clifford 135
Brown, Ray 13, 14, 147, 148, 152, 156, 158, 166, 167, 198, 202, 251, 252, 256
Brown, Warren 184
Bud and Bird, recording 35
Buddy Rich Big Band 39
Bulletin, The 119, 124
'Bung' New York boatie 103, 105
Burke, Johnny 45
Burrell, Kenny 14, 152, 154
Burrows at the Winery, recording 136
Burrows, Don 46–54, 60, 66, 71, 73, 75–88, 90, 95, 97, 99, 104, 105, 108, 112, 114, 125, 138 132, 134, 164, 176, 193, 194, 251, 256, 294, 295
Burton, Gary 50
Bush, George Sr 168
Byron, Don 267

C
Cachibache, film 196
Cadogan Hall, London 220
Calhoun, Eddie 275
California All-Star Youth Band 43
Calloway, Cab 119–121, 123, 193, 250
Camberwell High School, Melbourne, VIC 223, 230
Canberra Times, The 67, 80
Cape York Aboriginal Australian Academy, Cairns QLD 296
Capicchiano, Felix (Cappy) 113–118, 130, 141–146
Capicchiano, Sue (Cappy) 114–117, 130, 141, 143, 144, 146
Carden, Joan 166
Carnegie Hall, New York 49
Carney, Harry 153
Carols by Candlelight, Melbourne, VIC 294
Carter, Benny 39, 121
Carter, Ron 106
Carter, Russell 23, 285
Cascades Jazz Festival, Portugal 121
Castle, Roy 12
Castlemaine State Fair, VIC 114
Cat Empire, rock band 244
Catalina Bar and Grill, Los Angeles 133
Ceberano, Kate 106
Chan, Jackie 197

Chan, Gary 230
Channel Nine (see also Nine Network) 241
Chappell, Ian 126, 127
Charles, Prince of Wales 132, 168
Charlie Parker Quintet 108, 109
Charles, Ray 22, 152, 153, 154, 165, 257
Chase, Bill 264
Cheers, TV show 105
Childs, Nicholas 219, 221
Childs Brothers, Nicholas and Robert 12, 215, 219
Chudnick, Robert (see also Red Rodney) 108
Cincinatti Kid, The, film 196
Cirque du Soleil 236
Clare, John (see also Brennan, Gail) 137
Clayton, Jeff 255
Clayton, John 157
Cleary, John 288
Cleo, magazine 173
Cleves, Dale 217, 232–237, 244, 245
Cleves, Frank 232
Clinton, Bill 168
Close your Eyes, recording 243
Clothier, Larry 107, 110, 119–123
Club One, nightclub, Rio de Janeiro 117
Coles New World Supermarket, Mona Vale, NSW 24, 26, 193, 289
Coltrane, John 105, 267
Concert by the Sea, recording 275
Connick, Harry Jr 242
Conservatorium of Music, University of Melbourne, VIC 284
Cool Hand Luke, film 202
Coombs, Jeffrey 186
Cooper, Jacki 89
Cooper, Kathryn 223, 224
Copland, Aaron 198, 202
Cory Band, Wales 219
Costello, Gary 248
Count Basie Orchestra/Big Band 14, 153
Covell, Roger 165
Cox, Charlie 184
Crocker, Barry 94
Cross, Peter 90, 91
Cummins, Arnold 105, 123
Cunningham, Bradley 106
Cunningham, Ruth 16, 17, 27
Curson, Ted 105

D

Dallas Brooks Hall, Melbourne, VIC 90
Daly-Wilson Big Band 40, 44, 173, 239
Dancer, Robert 23
Dave Brubeck Quartet 39, 106
Dave Martin Quintet 68, 72
Davies, Freddie 'Parrotface' 258
Davis Cup 174
Davis, Miles 29, 98, 105, 108, 188, 191, 197, 198, 208, 209, 212, 253, 298
Davis, Lisa 161
Davis, Sammy Jr 244
Davis, Shirley 204
DeFranco, Buddy 39, 119, 120
Delecca, Anton 242
Denis, Kerugma Fellowship member 29
de Silva, Sunil 269
Desmond, Paul 106
Dial, Gary 136
Diana, Princess of Wales 132
Dick Gibson Jazz Party, Denver 110, 148
Dirty Harry, film 197
Dizzy Gillespie Quintet 146
Dodgion, Jerry 148
Don Burrows Collection, The, TV series 79
Don Burrows Supper Club 49, 98, 111–113, 190
Done, Ken 130, 136, 165, 172
Doris Porter School of Dancing 57
Dorsey, Tommy 98
DownBeat, magazine 136, 158, 235
Dr Seussberger 186
Drummond, Ray 106
Drums, Drums, Drums, recording 29
Dudley Moore Trio 35
Duffy, Paul 221
Duke Ellington Orchestra 10, 153

E

Easterfest, Toowoomba, QLD 291
East-West Records 136, 258
Eastwood, Clint 197
Edge, The, church, SA 291
Edison, Harry 'Sweets' 14, 148, 152, 154
Egger, Bob 75
Elder Hall, Adelaide, SA 112, 215
Eldridge, Roy 222
Electric Jazz Festival 265
Elizabeth II, HRH The Queen 131, 167, 181
Ellis, Herb 13, 156
Ellington, Duke 149, 200, 202, 212, 226, 264
Elphick, Steve 90, 231
El Rocco, jazz club, Sydney, NSW 49
Emmanuel, Tommy 166
Emmy Awards 298
Enter the Dragon, film 197
Ericsson, Anders 282
Ertegun, Ahmet 122, 138
Ertegun, Nesuhi 122, 124, 134–136, 138
Esperanto (part of the Jazz Meets the Symphony concert series) 268

Estensorro, Victor Paz, President of Bolivia 144
Evans, Gil 35, 253
Evripidou, Evripides 268, 269
Exorcist, The, film 196

F

Faddis, Jon 111, 139, 198, 252
Farnham, John 159
Fauré, Gabriel 202
Feather, Leonard 97, 134, 136, 147, 171, 192
Featherstone, Benny 12
Ferguson, Maynard 10, 11, 13, 32, 189, 192, 262
Ferin, Roy 162–164
Fermanis, Craig 234
Festival of Asian Arts, Hong Kong 85
Fisenden, Andrew 269
Flanagan, Tommy 106
Foden's Band 13
Ford Theatre, Los Angeles 97
Foreman, John 234, 242
Foster, Al 135
Foster, Frank 261
Foster, Michael 67, 79
Four Kinsmen, The 94
Fox, Iwan 220, 221
Fox, Lindsay 179
Frampton, Roger 45, 46, 50, 112
Freeman, Cathy 172

G

Gander, Andrew 43
Garner, Erroll 34, 35, 87, 192, 275, 283
Garside, Derek 9, 11
Gasser, Tony 237
Gaston, Ed 49, 50, 53
Gaston, Di 50
Gebert, Bobby 261
Generations in Jazz 164, 217, 232–238, 240, 241, 243, 244–246, 269, 292, 295
Generations in Jazz Academy, Mount Gambier, SA 241, 244
Generations in Jazz Superbands 241, 242
Generations in Jazz Vocal Scholarship 235, 236, 242, 243
Gershwin, George 135, 202
Gesualdo, Carlo 197
Gettler, Leon 185
Getz, Stan 43, 196
Giles, Ian 232
Gillespie, John 'Dizzy' 15, 29, 30, 32, 39, 42, 49, 73, 98, 108, 111, 138–140, 151, 155, 283160, 172, 173, 192, 193, 196, 198, 199, 203, 262, 264, 278

Gilson, Reynold 218
Gladwell, Malcolm 282
Golla, George 49, 50, 53, 78, 79, 86
Gómez-Angulo, Juan Antonio, Minister of Sport, Spain 174, 175
Goodwin, Gordon 239, 298
Gordon, Dan 234
Gordon, Dexter 107
Gordon Goodwin Big Phat Band 236, 239, 241
Gough, Neil, Reverend 21, 22, 23, 25, 29, 31, 32, 57, 283, 289
Gould, Tony 295
Grabowsky, Paul 132, 133, 248–250, 255, 272–279
Graham, Peter 218
Grammy Awards 203, 271, 298
Grappelli, Stéphane 49
Green, Benny 252
Green, David 176, 281
Green, Judith; Miss Australia (see also Morrison, Judi) 126-7, 129–130, 135
Green, Trevor 199, 201
Green, Urbie 14, 98, 110, 134, 148, 152
Greening, James 189, 261
Greenwich Village Jazz Festival, New York 35
Griffith University, NSW 170
Guilliatt, Richard 110
Guinness Book of Records 297
Guinness World Records 296, 297
Gulpilil, David 93
Gurtu, Trilok 267

H

Hall, James 119, 124
Hamilton, Bob 27
Hamilton, Jeff 13, 148, 149, 156, 158, 252
Hammerschlag, David 146
Hammond, Ambre 199
Hampton, Locksley Wellington 'Slide' 110
Hancock, Herbie 122, 135, 264
Hanley, James F. 135
Harbord Public School, Sydney, NSW 39
Hardy, Oliver 53
Hargrove, Roy 121, 252
Harris, Gene 14, 147, 148, 151, 152, 154
Harris, James, Reverend 57
Harris, Janie 148, 149, 151
Harris, Rolf 93
Harry James Orchestra 39
Hawkins, Coleman 196
Hawthorn Town Hall, Melbourne, VIC 223
Haydn, Joseph 164
Hegh, Len 275
Herald Sun 174

Henrich, Glenn 167, 251
Hey Hey It's Saturday, TV show 159, 178, 265
Hippopotamus, disco, Rio de Janeiro 118
Hirt, Al 196, 199, 205
Hobcroft, Rex 50
Hocker tent 236
Hodges, Johnny 196
Hoffman, John 44
Hogan, Ben 283
Holiday, Billie 39
Hopper, Burkhard (Hoppe) 251, 252, 255, 262
Hooton, Shane 212
Hot Horn Happening 167, 168, 255, 260, 263
Hubbard, Freddie 69, 110
Humphries, Barry 94
Humphreys, Huw 208
Hunt, Kevin 9 1, 231
Hunter Symphony Orchestra, NSW 206
Hutton, Timothy 106
Hyatt Hotel, Adelaide, SA 216

I
Idea of North, vocal group 169, 241
I'm Talking, rock band 106
Inheritance, jazz group 294
Inpress, magazine 187
Interlace, costume shop, Dee Why, NSW 85
International Trumpet Guild 205
Irwin, Ross 239, 242, 244
Isaacs, Mark 205–207

J
Jackson, Adrian 86, 87, 247, 252, 260, 270
Jacobson, Shane 184
James, Clive 126
James Morrison Instrumental Scholarship 234, 236, 240, 242, 243, 269
James Morrison-Schagerl Pavilion 237, 238
James Morrison Quintet 72, 73, 112
James Morrison Quartet 125
JazzChord, magazine 159, 166, 252, 253, 266, 271, 293
Jazz, magazine 40, 108, 231
Jazz Action Society of NSW 112
Jazz at the Opera House, recording 136
Jazz Centre 44, Melbourne, VIC 34
Jazz Cultural Theatre, New York 106
Jazz Forum, magazine 135
Jazz Meets the Symphony, recordings 198, 199, 203, 204
Jazz Meets the Symphony, concert series 164, 198–201, 251, 271
Jazztrack, radio program 234, 261

Jenson, Joya 45, 112, 131
Jimmy the pianist, Arturo's, New York 106
Jodrell, Matthew 242, 269
John Thompson Piano Method 35
Johnny Carson Show, The 10
Johnson, Bob 90, 91, 112
Johnson, J. J. 32
Jones, David 266, 268, 269
Jones, Hank 106
Jones, Harold 152
Jones, Ignatius 171, 172, 183
Jones, Quincy 196
Jones, Tom 282
Jottings of a Jazzman, book 82
Juan Carlos, HRH King of Spain 174
Just the Beginning, recording 76

K
Kardash, Scott 44
Kakehashi, Taro 81, 82
Kellock, Brian 255
Kensington and Norwood Band, SA 215
Kenton, Stan 75
Kerugma Fellowship 2, 3, 25, 29, 30, 72, 289
Kiggen, Edith 110, 111, 119–122, 251
Kind of Blue, recording 208, 209
King, Riley B. (B. B.) 152–154, 165, 257
Kirribilli Ex-Services Club, Sydney, NSW 112
'Koala Bear', NY, Owens cabin cruiser 103, 105
Kohler, Richard Wildblood 12
Kram (see also Maher, Mark) 273–279
Krupa, Gene 189
Kupsch, Tim 182

L
LA Weekly, newspaper 186
Lalla Meryem, HRH Princess of Morocco 149, 150
Lane, Joe 92
Laing, Ken 95–99, 105, 108, 120, 121, 164, 193, 194
Langden, Chris 224
Laser and Jazz Spectacular 166
Lee, Bruce 197
Leigh Theological College, Enfield, NSW 56
Leonard, NY, boat seller 102
Liberace 96, 97, 99, 100
Liepolt, Horst 34, 41, 42, 45, 68, 104
Lightsey, Kirk 106
Limerick Arms, Melbourne, VIC 248
Lisner musical instruments 82
Live at the Town Hall, NYC, recording 154
Live in Paris; James Morrison and the Hot Horn Happening, recording 258

Index   313

Lockhart, Keith 208, 209, 211–213
London Missionary Society 56
London Philharmonic Orchestra 198
London Symphony Orchestra 85
Los Angeles Times, The 133, 134
Lovano, Joe 168
Lush Life, New York jazz club 35
Lusher, Don 74
Lyall, Graeme 239, 241, 244, 292
Lyons, Jimmy 41

M
MacLaine, Shirley 96
MacNee, Bobby 114
MacNee, Christopher 116, 141–143, 146
MacNee, Ian 113, 114, 116–118, 141, 144, 146
Magnum Force, film 197
Maher, Mark (see also Kram) 273
Makowicz, Adam 121, 122, 134, 135, 136, 154, 251
Man from U.N.C.L.E., The, film 196
Manchester CWS Band 9
Mangelsdorff, Albert 99
Manhattan Transfer 121
Manly Boys High School, Sydney, NSW 40
Manly Daily, The 39
Manly Jazz Festival, NSW 34, 40, 45, 90
Manly to Monterey, recording 45
Mann, Herbie 187
Manne, Shelly 98, 171
Manner Dangerous, recording 157
Marconi, Nestor 267
Marsalis, Wynton 121, 137, 252
Marshall, Chris 22, 25, 26, 289
Marshall, Donna 22
Marshall, Steve 280, 292
Martin, Dave 68, 69, 71
Martin, Norma 69
Matisse, Henri 275
May, Ricky 125, 169, 178
McCoy, Matt 186
McDowell, Malcolm 186
McEwen, Rory 245
McGann, Bernie 132, 133, 295
McKenzie, Sarah 243
McKillop, St Mary 238
McLachlan, Craig 159
McLeod, Jim 193, 234, 261
McPherson, Professor Gary 284, 285, 288, 289, 293, 298
McRae, Carmen 107, 121, 139
Media Music, Sydney, NSW 95
Meggs, Ginger 53
Melba, Dame Nellie 112
Melbourne Concert Hall, VIC 92, 209

Melbourne Cricket Ground, VIC 178
Melbourne International Jazz Festival 273, 274
Melbourne Staff Band of the Salvation Army 219
Melbourne Symphony Orchestra 200, 207
Melbourne Town Hall, VIC 200
Melk Abbey, Austria 280
Méndez, Rafael 9, 11, 205
Mental as Anything, rock band 72
Mersey Valley Music Festival, Tasmania 214
Merzi, Gus 26
Messiaen, Olivier 196
Methodist Church Conference Stationing Committee 57, 59
Metallica, rock band 192, 249
Meyers, Neville 165
Midsummer Jazz Festival, Sydney, NSW 94
Mighty Zulu Nation Theatre Company 220
Milkowski, Bill 136, 137
Millar, Sam 207
Miller, Glenn 29, 178
Minchin, Tim 292
Minogue, Kylie 159
Miss Australia Quest 128
Mission: Impossible, TV series and recording 197, 202
Miss NSW Quest 129
Mitterrand, François 168
Mnozil Brass 280
Mo Awards 169
Modern Jazz Quartet 29
Mombassa, Reg (see also O'Doherty, Chris) 72
Mona Vale Methodist Church, NSW 21, 22, 23, 56
Mona Vale Primary School, NSW 15, 16, 19, 23, 28, 38, 104, 171, 175, 215, 225, 289
Moncrieff, Gladys 112
Monterey Jazz Festival, California 39, 41, 42, 43, 44, 45, 69, 72, 81, 98, 136, 240
Montgomery, Wes 72
Montreux Jazz Festival, Switzerland 15, 49, 111, 121, 123, 138, 251
Montsalvat Jazz Festival, Melbourne, VIC 165
Montz, Dick 46, 47, 231, 289
Moody, James 148, 149
Moore, Dudley 35
Morphett, Jason 90, 91, 231
Morrison, Andrew, great-grandfather 55
Morrison Brothers Big Bad Band 79, 88, 89, 94, 95, 112, 125, 163, 165, 178
Morrison Creative Generations Big Band, QLD 296
Morrison Digital Trumpet 280

Morrison, Eva (nee Jones), grandmother 55
Morrison, Fred, uncle 55, 56
Morrison, George, father 30, 55, 56, 59–61, 63–64, 71
Morrison, Harry, son 167, 294
Morrison, Jessie (nee Williams), mother 30, 36, 38, 55–58, 60–61, 63–66, 71
Morrison, James, grandfather 55
Morrison, John, brother 15–17, 21, 24, 26–27, 29, 30, 35–37, 53, 55, 58, 60–61, 64–67, 71–72, 79, 89, 90–93, 96, 97, 99, 101, 104, 105, 107, 108, 112, 115, 119–121, 125, 127, 135, 136, 145, 155, 167, 172, 173, 174, 187, 225, 226, 231, 233, 234, 244, 251, 255, 256, 258, 261, 281
Morrison, Judi (nee Green) 146, 150, 160–162, 164, 167, 179, 180
Morrison, Kathryn, sister 21, 55, 63, 71, 115, 165
Morrison, Mary (nee French), great-grandmother 55
Morrison/Pudney Duo 87
Morrison, Ray, uncle 55
Morrison, Sam, son 167
Morrison, William, son 167, 294
Mossman, Mike 149
Mozart, Leopold 287, 289
Mozart, Nannerl 287
Mozart, Wolfgang Amadeus 192, 198, 203, 226, 249, 282, 287
Mulligan, Gerry 39
Munro, Mike 166
Murcott, Jim 126, 127
Murdoch Books, Sydney, NSW 185
Murray, Jordan 242
Music is an Open Sky, jazz concert series 34
Musica Viva 97
Myers, Eric 73, 78, 90, 91, 97, 98, 124, 125, 166, 231, 252–254, 271, 293

N

Narrative of Missionary Enterprises in the South Sea Islands (1837), book 56
National Band of New Zealand 218
National Times, The 77
Neesby, Peter 42
Neighbours, TV show 159
Nelson, Sandy 29
Nesuhi, recording 138
Network Ten 182
Newdick, Dave 'DJ' 264, 265, 266
New Morning Club, Paris 168, 258
Newport Jazz Festival, California 49, 50
New South Wales Conservatorium of Music 50
New York Cosmos 138

New York Post, The 155
New York Times, The 101, 133, 134
Nice Jazz Festival, France 121
Nicholson, Jack 91
Nicholas, Jessica 265
Nightingale, Mark 255, 257–259
Night in Tunisia, A, recording 94
Nine Network (see also Channel Nine) 166, 184
Nobel Peace Prize 169
Nobs, Claude 122, 138
Nock, Mike 50
Norman, Greg 126
North Sea Festival, Holland 111, 121, 195, 202
Northside Jazz Club, Sydney, NSW 40
North Texas State University Band 235
NSW Premier's Gala Concert 95
NSW Water Police, The 65

O

O'Boyle, Sean 205, 207
O'Connell, Clive 206, 212
O'Connor, Leigh 232, 234, 245
O'Connor, Tom 232
O'Doherty, Chris (see also Mombassa, Reg) 72
O'Doherty, Peter 72
Oehlers, Jamie 242
Oliver, Joe 'King' 222
Olympic Jazz Festival, Los Angeles 97
Olympic Games, Los Angeles, 1984 97, 99, 171
Olympic Games, Sydney, NSW, 2000 74, 89, 171, 173, 183, 297
One Flew over the Cuckoo's Nest, film 91
On Fire Big Band 290, 291
On the Edge, concert and recording series 269, 270
Order of Australia 38, 45, 49, 170
Others, The, recording 273, 277
Outliers, book 282
Oz Bop, big band 112

P

Palm Beach Golf Club, Sydney, NSW 37
Panachi, Dave 133
Panachi, Paul 264
Pan Pacific Jazz Camps, Sydney, NSW 164, 231
Paradise Jazz Cellar, Kings Cross, Sydney, NSW 68–74, 76, 96, 284
Parker, Charlie 'Bird' 92, 109, 247
Parliament House, Canberra ACT 166
Pask, Emma 223, 228–230
Paul, Darren (see also Percival, Darren) 234, 242

Pavarotti, Luciano 189
Payne, Doug 198, 201
Payne, Geoffrey 205
Paynesville Brass Band 48
Penrith Anglican College, Sydney, NSW 228–230
Peoples, nightclub, Rio de Janeiro 117
Pepper, Art 69, 70
Percival, Darren (see also Paul, Darren) 242
Peterson, Oscar 32, 35, 122, 136, 247
Petrescu, Marian 241
Philharmonic Orchestra of Buenos Aires 196
Philip Morris Corporation 147
Philip Morris Superband 14, 147, 149, 150, 153, 156, 158, 160, 161, 165, 189, 222, 251
Phillip, Arthur, Governor of NSW 131
Pittwater High School, NSW 16, 26, 34, 38, 74, 87
Pittwater High School Big Band 27, 28
Pittwater Regional Mission, NSW 21
Pizzati, Steve 184
Philip, HRH Prince 168
Planet of the Apes, The, film 196
Play School, TV show 183
Pollard, Geoff 175
Polished Brass, Adelaide, SA 111, 215
Ponty, Jean-Luc 267
Poore, Nicola 228, 229
Pori Jazz Festival, Finland 121
Porter, Cole 204
Porter, John 134
Postcards from Downunder, recording 136, 137, 138, 159
Prince, rock singer 159
Pudney, Dave 25, 36, 37, 53, 67, 72, 79, 82, 86, 87, 90, 231
Pyl, Ralph 44, 231, 264

Q
Q4 Club, Geneva, Switzerland 256
Qantas 185
Quad City Symphony Orchestra, Iowa 203
Quad City Times, Iowa 204
Queen's Birthday Honours List 170, 236
Queensland Music Festival 295, 296
Queensland Symphony Orchestra 296
Quigley, Dan 292
Quiet Breaker, recording 41

R
Ragtime, nightclub, Rio de Janeiro 117
Ray Brown Trio 247
Ray Martin Show, The, TV show 96

Raymond, Bruce 'Dizzy' 111, 112, 214–217, 219, 233
Record Breakers, TV show 12
Red Ale Café, Sydney, NSW 165
Red Rodney, (see also Chudnick, Robert) 108, 109, 110, 111, 124
Red Rodney Quintet 136
Reeves, 'Splinter' 189
Regent Hotel, The, Sydney, NSW 49, 80, 98, 111, 178
Regina, Fatima 117
Republic of China Symphony Orchestra 83
Rhinoceros Studios, Sydney, NSW 156
Rich, Buddy 43
Roberts, Karyn 236, 243
Roberts, Troy 269
Robertson, Andrew 234
Roger Frampton Trio 112
Roland Corporation of Japan 81
Rolling Stone, magazine 68
Rollins, Theodore 'Sonny' 135
Rollinson, Tim 41, 43, 44, 72, 73
Romberg, Sigmund 135
Romero, Angel 106, 107
Ronnie Scott's Jazz Club, London 146, 250
Rosolino, Frank 99, 107
Ross, Ross 43, 72
Rotten Tomatoes, film review website 186
Royal Command Performance 95, 167, 178
Royal Variety Performance 41
Royal Motor Yacht Club, Sydney, NSW 37
Royal Opera House, London 167
Royal Shakespeare Company, Stratford-upon-Avon 85
Rush, Geoffrey 225, 271
Rush Hour, film 197
Rytmeister, Gordon 200

S
Saffron, Abe 68
SA Great! State promotional campaign 216, 233
Salt, Peter 232, 233
Salvation Army, The ('Salvos') 10, 214, 217, 290
Sandilands, Ron 232–234
Sandoval, Arturo 139
Sangster, John 53
Santin, Kellie 234
Sawyer, Tom 283
SBS, broadcasting service 184, 207
SBS Youth Symphony Orchestra 207
Scales, Prunella 85
Schagerl Instrument Company 237, 280, 281

Schifrin, Boris Claudio 'Lalo' 164, 186, 195–203, 251, 253, 267, 268, 271
Schifrin, Luis 196
Schifrin, Ryan 185, 186, 197
Scott, Craig 79, 112
Scott, Ronnie 146
Scream Machine, recording 264–266
Sedergreen, Bob 190
Severinsen, Carl 'Doc' 9, 199
Seventh-day Adventist Church 218
Seymour Centre, Sydney, NSW 90 92
Shand, John 40, 41, 246, 268, 270
Shanghai, tugboat 49
Shaw, Woody 121
Sidi Mohammed, HRH Crown Prince of Morocco 149
Silver, Horace 69
Silvers Circus 237
Sinatra, Frank 22, 49
Shenk, David 288
Shu, Eddie 189
Sky Lounge, The, nightclub, Sydney, NSW 49
Smith, Bessie 92
Smith, Howie 50, 51, 75
Smith, Ken 282
Snappy Doo, recording 13, 156, 157, 158, 159, 169, 190
Snappy Too, recording 14, 157, 169, 243
So Far, So Good, recording 281
Solomon, Nina 231
Somers, Daryl 130, 236
Soup Plus, nightclub 112
Sousa, John Philip 19
Speight, Johnny 39, 40, 41, 42, 43, 45, 52
Spence, Greg 292
Spicks and Specks, TV show 274
Spiderbait, rock band 273
Stack, Philip 200, 242
Staines, Gavin 290
Stan Getz Quartet 39
Stanhope, David 205
Star Wars, film 280
Steve Vizard Show, The, TV show 160
Stewart, Zan 134
Stirling, Keith 98
Stitt, Sonny 69, 107
Stockhausen, Karlheinz 165, 266, 268
Stockhausen, Simon 266–270
Stonnington Jazz Festival, Melbourne, VIC 281, 294
Story of Jazz in Sydney, online book 68
St. Patrick's Catholic Church, Boorowa, NSW 60
Strangeways Prison, Manchester 221

Stravinsky, Igor 267
Sturt Football Club, SA 214
St Vincent de Paul's Op Shop, Mona Vale, NSW 53, 85
Sullivan, Peter 209, 210
Sunbury Rock Festival, VIC 207
Suncorps Stadium, Brisbane, QLD 297
Sunday Mail, Brisbane, QLD 127
Superbone 9
Sutherland, Dame Joan 159, 271
Swanson, Bill 13, 158
Sweet Basil, New York jazz club 35
Swing City, big band 89, 172
Swiss Encounter, recording 134, 137, 138, 155, 158
Sydney Conservatorium of Music 37, 45, 50, 57, 67, 74, 75, 80, 89, 116, 181, 206, 231, 289
Sydney Conservatorium Big Band 65
Sydney Conservatorium Secondary School 38
Sydney Eisteddfod, City of 17, 27
Sydney Entertainment Centre 95
Sydney Morning Herald, The 46, 73, 112, 126, 137, 146, 158, 161, 165, 170, 185
Sydney Opera House 34, 41, 90, 93, 95, 166, 167, 172, 179, 221, 269
Sydney Spring Festival 165
Sydney Symphony Orchestra 96, 198
Sydney Town Hall 34, 92, 125, 155

T

Talking Heads, TV show 15, 182
Taree Methodist Church, NSW 58
Tate, Grady 147, 198, 251
Teagarden, Jack 98, 134
Tennis Australia 175
Tenison Woods College Band, SA 241, 244
Terkel, Studs 39
Terry, Clark 111
Thiam, Sydney 267
Thirsty Merc, rock band 241
This is Your Life, TV show 166
Thistlethwayte, Rai 241
Thompson, Peter 15, 182, 246
Thorne, Paul 264
Tijuana Brass 17
Tiki, boat 93, 115
Times on Sunday, The 110
Top Gear, Australia, TV show 184, 213
Tracey, Sheila 74
Trapaga, Monica 183
Tribute to the Giants of Jazz, concert 98
Trotta, Peter 90, 91
Turnbull, Alan 49, 53, 68, 69, 79, 112, 132, 133

Turner, J. Neville, Professor 193
Turre, Steve 139
Twain, Mark 281
Two the Max, recording 251
Tycho, Tommy 96, 104, 120, 194, 239

U

Umbria Jazz Festival, Perugia, Italy 111, 121
Under the Jasmin Tree, recording 29
Unique Attractions Pty Ltd 237
University of Melbourne 207
University of Sydney 38, 50, 76, 231
Urban, Keith 235

V

Vancouver Symphony Orchestra 297
Van Heusen, Jimmy 45
Venier, Bob 132, 232, 233
Vierteljahrrespreis der Deutschen Schallplattenkritik (quarterly award of German record critics) 169
Vig, Tommy 97
Village Vanguard, nightclub, New York 110, 124
Villa-Lobos, Heitor 200, 202
Voice, The, TV show 235, 242
Voice of the Cornet, The, recording 283

W

Waldron, Mal 69
Waller, Thomas 'Fats' 134
Wangaratta Festival of Jazz, VIC 87
Warana Festival, Brisbane, QLD 90
Warner Bros Records, California 122, 159, 161
Wangaratta Festival of Jazz, VIC 270
Warringah Stage Band, Sydney, NSW 40
Warwick, Dionne 96
Washington, Megan 235
Watrous, Bill 98, 110
Watt, Andrew 187
WDR Orchestra, Cologne, Germany 198,
WEA Records 122, 136, 138
Webb, Gordon 283
Wen, Warren 135
Wentworth Hotel, The, Sydney, NSW 49, 50
Wess, Frank 148, 261
West Australian Symphony Orchestra 207
West Australian Youth Jazz Orchestra 269
Westdeutsher Rundfunk (WDR) Germany 253
West, Timothy 85
Whist, Andrew 147, 148
Whitehead, Kevin 158
Whittaker, Blaine 261

Wilby, Philip 220
Wilesmith, Greg 77
Williams, Charles 'Buster' 135
Williams, Glyn 13
Williams, Doris (nee Seller), Nan, maternal grandmother 57, 63, 64
Williams, Jack, Pop, maternal grandfather 57, 63–654
Williams, John (Reverend), forebear 56, 57
Williams, Mike 40
Willis, Craig 175
Wilson, Ed 239
Wind, Martin 255–257
Wizard of Id, The, comic strip 103
Woodard, Rickey 255, 256
Woods, Phil 42
Woodward, Roger 165
Woody Herman Thundering Herd Big Band 39, 264
World Cup Final 1990, football 197
World Expo, Tsukuba, Japan 94
World Expo, Brisbane, QLD 131, 134
World Tour '90, recording 154
Wright, Darcy 68, 69, 284, 285

Y

Yanow, Scott 136
Yarrabah Band Festival, QLD 296
Young Northside Big Band, The 39, 40, 41, 43, 44, 45, 52, 69, 89, 136, 289
Young, Matthew 23

Z

Zavod, Allan 199, 205, 206
Zografakis, Peter 266
Zwartz, Jonathan 167, 173, 251, 271
Zuel, Bernard 185

The Author

Merv Collins is an experienced writer, educator and musician, who has been published in daily newspapers and a wide variety of magazines in Australia, New Zealand and the United Kingdom.

He has written on subjects as diverse as sport, aviation history, motherhood and music, and has won national awards for intergenerational journalism and for magazine feature articles.

Merv was a professional trumpeter, teacher, band conductor and adjudicator for more than thirty years. He writes extensively on musical topics, particularly profiles, histories and reviews. This, his first book, is a result of that undiminishing fascination.

He can be contacted at mervcollins@optusnet.com.au.

Top
Mona Vale Primary School Band 1972, with bandmaster Jack Akhurst (back row, left) James Morrison with mellophone (back row, right) and John Morrison with tuba (front row, right). Photo courtesy of John Morrison

Bottom
James on the Monterey tour in 1979, still trying out every instrument in the band room. Photo courtesy of Paul Pax Andrews

Top
James with the trombone at Monterey in 1979.
Photo courtesy of John Morrison

Middle
Young Northside Big Band at the Manly Jazz Festival in 1979, directed by John Speight, with Dale Barlow (left) and Paul Andrews (right) featuring on tenor saxes. James is in the centre with the trombone and, for once, not playing.
Photo courtesy of Paul Pax Andrews

Bottom
Count Basie receiving the Young Northside Big Band LP after the group's foyer performance preceding the Count Basie Orchestra concert at the Sydney Opera House in 1979. From left to right are band leader John Speight, band members Niki Mathews and Scott Kardash, Count Basie and Horst Liepolt.
Photo courtesy of Niki Mathews and Luke Bona

Top
The Morrison Brothers Big Bad Band aboard the 'rehearsal boat' *Tiki* on Pittwater in 1983. Back row is Steve Elphick, Peter Lothian, Peter Trotta, Dave Pudney, Warwick Alder, Glenn Henrich and John Morrison. Front row is Kevin Hunt, Tom Baker, Paul Pax Andrews, Jason Morphett and James Morrison.
Photo courtesy of John Morrison

Bottom
John Morrison concentrates intently at the Manly Jazz Festival in 1984.
Photo by Hardy Ahlhaus, Focal Point Photos, courtesy of Eric Myers

Top
Young James circa 1985.
Photo by Peter Sinclair, courtesy of Eric Myers

Middle
The prof and the protégé: Don Burrows and James at the Manly Jazz Festival 1986.
Photo courtesy of the Victorian Jazz Archive

Bottom
Dale Barlow and James front the band at the opening of the 11th Annual Music Awards 1986, with Cameron Undy (electric bass) and Carl Orr (guitar).
Photo courtesy of Eric Myers

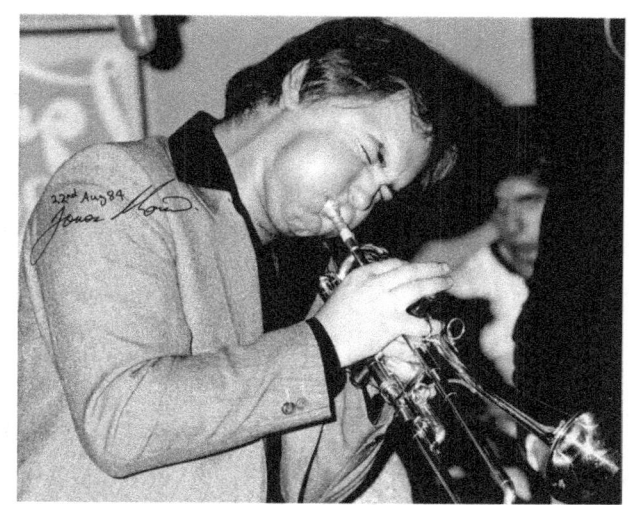

Top
James tearing it up at the Manly Jazz Festival in 1984.
Photo courtesy of Hardy Ahlhaus, Focal Point Photos

Middle
James and John at the 'Devonshire Arms', Felix Cappy's bar-room at home in Castlemaine in 1987.
Photo courtesy of Sue Cappy

Bottom
James with Sue and Felix Cappy, relaxing in Rio during the first South American trip in 1987.
Photo courtesy of Sue Cappy

Top
James and friends after his triumphant homecoming concert at the Sydney Town Hall in October 1987, following the first US tour. From left to right are Don Burrows, Andrew Firth, Craig Scott and John Morrison.
Photo courtesy of Eric Myers

Middle
Don Burrows performs with the Australian Jazz Orchestra on the steps of the Sydney Opera House in January 1988. With Bernie McGann (far left) and Dale Barlow (centre).
Photo courtesy of Eric Myers

Bottom
Something to celebrate: James and Judi getting married in October 1988.
Photo courtesy of Sue Cappy

Top

James with local musicians in La Paz, Bolivia during the second South American tour in 1989.

Photo courtesy of Sue Cappy

Bottom

James, Sue Cappy (far left) and friends ready to party at the Carnival in Rio in 1989.

Photo courtesy of Sue Cappy

Top
Publicity postcard promoting the album *Postcards from Down Under* with artist Ken Done in 1989.
Photo courtesy of Sue Cappy

Bottom
James' limerick for fellow 'petrolhead' Felix Cappy, on the reverse of the postcard.
Photo courtesy of Sue Cappy

Top
James in the trombone section of the Philip Morris Superband in 1989.
Photo courtesy of the Victorian Jazz Archive

Bottom
James with Ronnie Scott at Limerick Arms in South Melbourne in 1989, prior to his debut at Ronnie Scott's Jazz Club in London.
Photo courtesy of the Victorian Jazz Archive

Top

James in Felix Cappy's vintage car in Castlemaine in 1990.

Photo courtesy of Sue Cappy

Bottom

A good night's work! James after the Mo Awards in 1990, holding his trophies for Australian Performer of the Year, Ricky May Jazz Performer of the Year and Male Jazz Performer of the Year.

Photo courtesy of Eric Myers

Top
'This is Your Life, James Morrison'. With Judi, Sam and William Morrison (baby Harry was in hospital) and compere Mike Munro on the Nine Network in 1997.
Photo courtesy of the Victorian Jazz Archive

Bottom
The Morrison family circa 1999. With James, Sam, Harry, William and Judi.
Photo courtesy of Sue Cappy

Top
James loves to fly, even in a trike powered hang-glider.
Photo courtesy of John Morrison

Middle
James, John and Felix Cappy clowning around at Felix's fortieth birthday celebrations in 2002.
Photo courtesy of Sue Cappy

Bottom
Lalo Schifrin conducts James in a Jazz at the Symphony concert in Salzburg, Austria in 2007.
Photo courtesy of the author

Top
Student clarinettist Haydn Potter shares the spotlight with James at Penrith Anglican College concert in 2011.
Photo courtesy of Penrith Anglican College

Middle
James playing bass trumpet at the Penrith Anglican College concert in 2011.
Photo courtesy of Penrith Anglican College

Bottom
After the concert, the inevitable signing session. James autographs the instrument case of student Tyler Wilkinson at Penrith Anglican College in 2011.
Photo courtesy of Penrith Anglican College

Top
James brings a new dimension to brass band concerts. This one is with the Melbourne Staff Band of The Salvation Army in 2011.
Photo courtesy of the Melbourne Staff Band

Bottom
James being inducted into the Graeme Bell Hall of Fame at the Australian Jazz Bell Awards in May 2013. With Con Gallin, CEO of Allans Billy Hyde (left) and Michael Danby MP, Parliamentary Secretary for the Arts (right).
Photo courtesy of Albert Dadon, Australian Jazz Bell Awards

Top
James the alto saxophonist, in 2014.
Photo courtesy of Su O'Grady

Middle
James does his ever-popular duelling trumpet and trombone concert finale in 2014.
Photo courtesy of Su O'Grady

Bottom
James and John (on drums) doing the old routines at Jazz Up North at the Tanks Arts Centre in Cairns.
Photo courtesy of Su O'Grady

Top
The Big Top or, more correctly, the Morrison/Schagerl Pavilion at Generations in Jazz 2014, ready for an audience of 5000.
Photo courtesy of the author

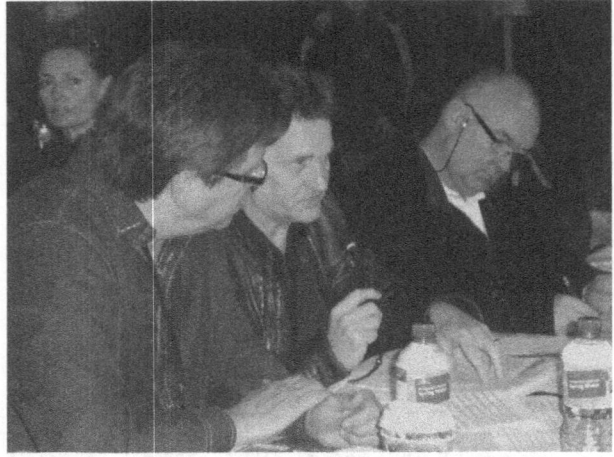

Middle
Adjudicators deliberating at the Division 1 Big Band section at Generations in Jazz 2014. From left to right are trumpet player Wayne Bergeron, Big Phat Band leader Gordon Goodwin and James Morrison.
Photo courtesy of the author

Bottom
James and Judi Morrison at Generations in Jazz 2014.
Photo courtesy of the author

www.ingramcontent.com/pod-product-compliance
Lightning Source LLC
Chambersburg PA
CBHW032033150426
43194CB00006B/256